SHORT RUNS IN BEAUTIFUL PLACES

SHORT RUNS
IN BEAUTIFUL
PLACES

JEN & SIM BENSON

National Trust

First published in the United Kingdom in 2020 by
National Trust Books
43 Great Ormond Street
London WC1N 3HZ
An imprint of Pavilion Books Company Ltd

ISBN: 9781911657040

A CIP catalogue record for this book is available
from the British Library.

25 24 23 22 21 20
10 9 8 7 6 5 4 3 2 1

Reproduction by Rival Colour Ltd, UK
Printed by 1010 Printing International Ltd, China

This book is available at National Trust shops and
online at www.nationaltrustbooks.co.uk, or try
the publisher (www.pavilionbooks.com) or your
local bookshop.

Previous page: View to Ibsley Common from Rockford
Common in Hampshire.

Right: Bath Skyline (see page 60).

Contents

South West England

South East England

Central England and East Anglia

Northern England

Wales, Northern Ireland and Scotland

Introduction

RUNNING IN BEAUTIFUL PLACES

The British Isles are home to an incredible variety of places to run. Across the length and breadth of the nation, an extensive network of footpaths and bridleways winds along spectacular stretches of coastline, through leafy woodland, over mountain ridges and down sheltered valleys. There are rivers and lakes to traverse, islands to circumnavigate, open areas of moorland, heathland, parkland and common to explore, and many excellent urban trails offering a great way to see some of the UK's most beautiful architecture.

The National Trust maintains many of Britain's trails and the surrounding areas, including almost 775 miles (1,247km) of coastline and more than 300 historic buildings across 613,000 acres (248,000ha) of land. The National Trust for Scotland has over 187,000 acres (over 75,000ha) of countryside, including 11,000 archaeological sites and 38 gardens and designed landscapes.

The National Trust works with many partners, from the National Trails to the National Parks; from English Heritage to Cadw; and from the John Muir Trust to the Landmark Trust, to maintain each mile of footpath and bridleway so that beautiful places are accessible. By buying this book and taking simple steps such as using local car parks and businesses, adhering to the Countryside Code and Scottish Outdoor Access Code and supporting conservation organisations through membership or donations, you are helping to look after the trails for future runners to enjoy.

RUNNING WITH THE NATIONAL TRUST

Research from England Athletics found that during 2018, 11.5 million people in England went for a run, with around 7 million doing so on a regular basis. Recent sport and physical participation data report that 17 per cent of people in Wales and 14 per cent in both Scotland and Northern Ireland participate in running or jogging. The National Trust works closely with Sport England to encourage running as well as other activities, including cycling and walking, at its places. The trust also links with England Athletics to promote its RunTogether initiative, a community of over 100,000 runners celebrating running and jogging as an activity for all.

An estimated 140,000 people take part in organised running events at National Trust places each year, from free, timed, weekly 5km (3-mile)

parkruns to free, monthly Trust10 runs for those wanting to hit that 10km (6 miles), as well as local groups offering training and motivation to help you reach your goals and have a great time along the way. Keep an eye out for organised night runs, dusk runs and, should you wish to give racing a go, the many competitive events that take place all across the country. If you prefer the peace and quiet of self-guided trails, a series of Ranger Runs takes in fascinating conservation stories, with routes chosen by the Trust's team of expert Rangers to showcase their local areas. Full details on all the National Trust's running activities can be found at www.nationaltrust.org.uk/running.

This book shares 100 of the very best trails, either wholly or partly maintained by the National Trust and the National Trust for Scotland, while at the same time celebrating these special places for their history, wildlife and people.

Above: Runners at Ashridge estate, Hertfordshire.

Above: Country lane on Bignor Hill in spring at Slindon estate, West Sussex.

A RUN AROUND THE BRITISH ISLES

Starting in the south west of England, you'll discover dramatic stretches of Cornwall's coastal paths, the tor-studded wilds of Dartmoor and Exmoor, the romantic ruins of Corfe Castle and the rolling ranges of the Quantock, Blackdown and Mendip Hills.

Heading east you can run in the footsteps of Tennyson on the Isle of Wight before relaxing with tea and scones overlooking The Needles. Follow the undulating trails that cross the North and South Downs or climb to the top of Box Hill and Leith Hill, both within easy reach of London.

The routes in central England and East Anglia take you from the rolling farmland of the borderland country of the Welsh Marches, across the gritstone edges of the Peak District to the Cambridgeshire Fens and the sandy beaches of the Norfolk coast, home to seals and seabirds.

Further north you'll find a higher, wilder kind of running. Trails cut through the Yorkshire Moors and Dales and along Hadrian's Wall to the big skies and castle-studded coast of Northumberland. Discover some of the area's most impressive buildings, including the remarkably beautiful Fountains Abbey and the eccentric genius of Cragside. In the Lake District, recently designated a UNESCO World Heritage Site, you'll follow waterside trails looping the lakes of Tarn Hows and Buttermere, pass the tumbling waterfalls at Aira Force, or trace the meanders of Great Langdale Beck to the National Trust's Sticklebarn pub.

Venturing into Wales you'll discover the contrasting coastlines of Gower and Pembrokeshire, rich in wildlife and ideal for combining running with sea swimming, surfing or family sandcastling. You'll conquer some mini mountains in the Brecon Beacons, taking in the breathtaking summit views from Skirrid and Sugar Loaf in the peaceful Black Mountain range. Heading north, past the castles and gold mines of central and eastern Wales, to the rugged peaks and ridges of Snowdonia, you'll explore some of the best lower-level trails, encircled by the jagged crags and ridges of the Carneddau and nearby Glyderau ranges.

Across to Northern Ireland and the Belfast Hills, trails pass through wildflower-rich grassland and overlook the city landscape. Nearby, the Castle Ward estate and the shores of Strangford Lough offer a network of waymarked trails through beautiful scenery.

Finally, to Scotland, where the dramatic headland and vast seabird colonies of St Abb's Head complement the peaceful wooded hills of the Balmacara estate, overlooking the serene expanse of Loch Alsh. And then there is Glencoe, which needs no introduction ...

BEST FOR ...

Running buggies and wheelchairs
- Plymbridge (see page 30)
- Tarn Hows (see page 176)
- Stowe (lakeside trail) (see page 108)
- The Lodes Way (see page 144)
- Cragside (see page 192)

Families
- Lacock (see page 62)
- Corfe Castle (see page 48)
- Osterley Park (see page 99)
- Formby (see page 154)
- Nostell (see page 162)

Beginner friendly
- Morden Hall Park (see page 95)
- Tarn Hows (see page 176)
- Dunwich Heath (see page 148)
- Souter Lighthouse (see page 188)

A real challenge
- Zennor (see page 20)
- Golden Cap (see page 42)
- Carding Mill Valley (see page 122)
- Roseberry Topping (see page 170)
- Craflwyn (see page 220)

THE COUNTRYSIDE CODE

Here's how to respect, protect and enjoy the countryside:

- Always park sensibly, making sure that your vehicle is not blocking access to drives, fields and farm tracks.

- Leave gates as you find them or follow instructions on signs. If running in a group, make sure the last person knows how to leave the gate.

- In fields where crops are growing, follow the paths wherever possible.

- Don't leave litter and leftover food – it spoils the beauty of the countryside and can be dangerous to wildlife and farm animals, too.

- Avoid damaging, destroying or removing flowers, trees or even rocks: they provide homes for wildlife and add to everyone's enjoyment of the countryside.

- Don't get too close to wild animals or farm animals – slow down or walk when passing livestock, as they can behave unpredictably.

- Be careful not to drop a match or smouldering cigarette at any time of the year, as this can cause fires.

- Keep dogs under control (see page 14).

Above right: More and more National Trust properties maintain tracks and trails suitable for running, including Kingston Lacy, Dorset, which has regular RunTogether events.

ABOUT THE ROUTES

The routes in this book are all circular, ranging from short and easy to longer and more challenging, with plenty in between. They vary widely in character – one of the many great joys of trail running – however, all have been carefully chosen to make the most of the location and terrain. Except for a few that follow surfaced, multi-user paths and quiet lanes, the running is predominantly off-road, so expect plenty of uneven ground, climbs and descents, twists and turns, roots, steps and – of course – mud, particularly if you're visiting during the Great British winter.

Useful info

Each route features a detailed introduction with helpful information such as accessibility for running buggies and wheelchairs, the types of terrain to expect, whether it gets particularly

wet or muddy, family and dog friendliness and if there's a café for post-run refuelling. Public transport options for getting to the start point are also included. Most of the routes start and finish at National Trust car parks, which are free for members.

Opening times

While some of the routes visit historic properties with fixed opening hours, others have no such restrictions. If you time your run carefully, before or after most visitors arrive, and you may find you have the place to yourself. Try a run on the coast path at dusk or dawn, as the sun's light sparkles gold across the sea and the only sounds are the chatter of birdsong, the soft wash of the waves and your feet tapping a happy rhythm along the trail. If you're lucky, you might spot seals in the water, birds of prey circling overhead, or wildflowers dotting the grass with colour.

Navigation

Many of the included routes are fully waymarked, using either dedicated running trails or existing walks that also work particularly well for running. Those without waymarkers you will need to navigate yourself, but there are clear, step-by-step directions for every route, including distances, and all runs follow good paths and trails. Where route-finding may be affected by poor visibility this is highlighted and it is strongly recommended that, unless you can navigate well, you avoid these except in favourable conditions.

Landscapes change with the seasons, and the experience of running through them changes, too. Routes in higher, colder or more exposed areas are likely to be considerably more challenging in winter than summer so take the location and conditions into account before you set off and always go prepared – see our recommended clothing and equipment on pages 15–16.

Above: Participants at the Night Run event in the park at Nostell, Yorkshire (see page 162).

RUNNING HINTS AND TIPS

With our long limbs, upright posture and ability to eat and drink on the go, human beings are perfectly evolved for distance running. While there are many creatures faster than us, the combination of our physiology, biomechanics and psychology means that, when it comes to running longer distances, we are amongst the best in the animal kingdom.

Once they've learned to do it, young children naturally spend a lot of their time running. They run to play, to interact and to experience that glorious feeling of speed and freedom. As adults, with our busy lives filled with desks, cars and comfy sofas, it's all too easy to forget that feeling. And yet, as awareness spreads of the countless benefits to our physical and mental well-being to be gained from spending time outdoors and being active, ever-increasing numbers of people are rediscovering the joys of running.

Getting started

If you're new to running or coming back after some time off, the most important thing to remember is to take it slowly. There are no expected times in this book, so you can spend as long as you wish running, exploring and stopping to take in the views. It's completely acceptable to walk the hills, or the second half, or everything

BRINGING YOUR DOG

Please help the National Trust keep the countryside a safe, healthy and enjoyable place for you and your dog, as well as other visitors, wildlife and livestock:

- Always keep your dog in sight and under control, using a lead if requested. (See 'About this run' feature on individual runs for specific information regarding the control of dogs.)

- Never let your dog chase wildlife or farm animals.

- Observe local notices when you're out and about. There may be restrictions in woodland or on farmland at sensitive times of year, like in spring, during the lambing season, and between the beginning of March and the end of July when ground-nesting birds such as sandpipers are on eggs or raising their young.

- Please always pick up after your dog. We ask that if your dog fouls, particularly in car parks, on paths and by picnic spots, you pick up and remove the mess. At some of our sites we've got dedicated dog-mess bins where you can dispose of it.

other than the first five minutes. Next time you might find you can run for ten minutes before you need to walk so don't ever be disheartened – stick with it and you'll be amazed how quickly it starts to feel easier.

Improvements in running come through doing it regularly; however, do too much too soon and you risk injury. If you can, running three times a week stimulates increases in strength and fitness while allowing plenty of time for recovery.

There are many theories about the 'best' way to run, but none of these is backed up by science and most are more likely to cause harm than good. In reality, starting slowly, running regularly and building up both pace and distance gradually – as you feel able to do so – will lead to the best way of running for you. The human body is much more complex than those selling techniques and high-tech gadgets give it credit for; if we simply allow it to adapt in its own time, given optimum conditions it will do so brilliantly. In essence: listen to your body.

Running with a group is great for motivation, meeting other runners and discovering new places to run. Many National Trust places have weekly, organised group runs that are inclusive, supportive and fun, with after-run cake and coffee all part of the experience (see pages 8–9).

Clothing

Running kit needs to be able to cope with heat, cold, wind and rain, as well as those days when you start out in bright sunshine and finish in hail.

It also needs to be comfortable and unrestrictive while you're running. Wearing several lighter layers rather than a single, heavier one allows you to vary your clothing throughout your run to stay comfortable.

Running generates a lot of heat so fabrics that are breathable, quick-drying and 'wicking' – i.e. move sweat away from the skin – work best. Particularly over the winter months you'll cool down quickly should you need to stop so it's always worth packing an extra layer if it's cold or you're going to be out for any length of time.

Accessories such as gloves and hats can also make cold weather running more enjoyable. A lightweight, packable waterproof jacket is an essential item for running in Britain.

Footwear

When you're running off-road, a good, well-fitting pair of shoes with enough grip for the conditions is essential. For very muddy conditions look for a sole with a deeper tread, while if you're running on hard-packed trails, a more cushioned model with a less aggressive tread will work better. If you're buying new shoes, try several before you commit – most running shops will let you take them for a run to test them out. Pay attention to your lacing as this will make all the difference to the fit of the shoe and invest in some good, lightweight, cushioned running socks.

Below: Runner on the South West Coast Path, Dorset. Coast paths are often strenuous, but the views make it all worthwhile.

Equipment

For most of the runs in this book you'll need little more than the kit described on page 15. When you're venturing further from civilisation, or embarking on a longer run, you may want to consider a pack for carrying food, water, spare kit and other essentials. Simple waist packs are great for everyday use; most will fit a phone, keys, snack and a lightweight waterproof jacket. If you need to carry more, a vest-style pack that distributes weight effectively around your body, while allowing easy access to pockets on the sides and straps is a great investment.

Food and drink

As a general rule, if you're running for less than an hour you probably won't need to take provisions. If you're out for longer, consider taking water – soft flasks, hand-held bottles or a reservoir that fits inside a pack work well and allow you to drink as you run – and snacks such as energy bars. Many of the routes in this book start and finish at a café.

Staying safe

Running is an incredibly safe sport, however, there are a few things you can do to make it even more so:

- Take a charged mobile phone
- Tell someone where you're going and what time you expect to be back, especially in areas where mobile-phone reception is poor
- Run with a group or a friend
- Consider not wearing headphones, or use a bone-conducting model that leaves the ear free
- Wear shoes with good grip on slippery or uneven ground
- Keep to the path and stay away from cliff edges.
- Take water, snacks and a packable jacket with you on longer or wilder runs
- Think about tying an In Case of Emergency (ICE) tag onto your shoe or kit. Visit www.icetags.co.uk/National-Trust10-ICEtags for further details.

Key to run symbols

1 Easy run

2 Moderate run

3 Challenging run

P Parking

Toilets

Café / refreshments

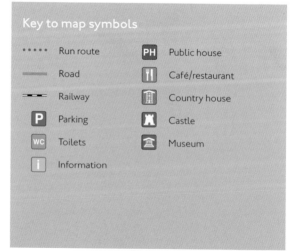

Key to map symbols

• • • • • Run route

——— Road

—▪—▪— Railway

P Parking

WC Toilets

i Information

PH Public house

Café/restaurant

Country house

Castle

Museum

South West England

South East England

Central England and
East Anglia

Northern England

Wales, Northern Ireland
and Scotland

South West
England

01. Zennor

Zennor village car park
Zennor, near St Ives
Cornwall
TR26 3BZ

ABOUT THIS RUN

Distance 5.2 miles (8.4km)
Ascent 1,053ft (321m)

Coastal
Well-maintained tracks
and trails, some uneven
sections
May be muddy
Unfenced drops and water
History/culture
Wildlife
Dogs welcome

Nestled on north-west Cornwall's Penwith heritage coast, the pretty village of Zennor has been a settlement for over 4,000 years. The grassy trail across Zennor Head winds its way through bright yellow gorse, and glorious views open out along this ruggedly beautiful stretch of coastline. The outward section of this run takes on a dramatic, rocky and undulating section of the South West Coast Path, towards St Ives. The West Penwith area has a long history of mining and farming, and the inland leg of this run crosses traditional Penwith field systems, enclosed by Cornish hedges and stiles hewn from local granite.

Above: Zennor Cliff view to Gurnard's Head in the distance.
Opposite: Running the South West Coast Path along Zennor Head.

THINGS TO SEE

Island visitors
The Carracks and Little Carracks (from the Cornish *kerrek*, meaning 'rocks') are two scattered groups of wave-washed islands lying just off the coast. These islands provide habitat for a variety of marine life, including dogfish, anglerfish and sea anemones. The wreck of the *Enrico Parodi*, a 3,800-ton steel ship that struck nearby Gurnard's Head in 1916, lies submerged 92ft (28m) below the waves and is popular with divers. The largest of the islands, sometimes called Seal Island, is a good place to spot Atlantic grey seals.

Ancient monuments
The windswept landscape of Penwith is peppered with thousands of prehistoric monuments, making this an internationally important area for archaeologists and a fascinating place to explore. On the high ground to the south and east of Zennor village are the Zennor and Sperris Quoits, two Neolithic chambered tombs topped by huge granite slabs. To the south-west are the remnants of hut circles, settlements and a chambered cairn.

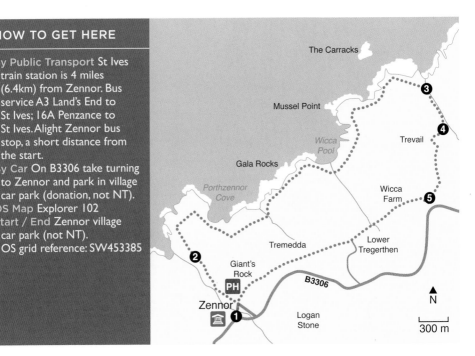

By Public Transport St Ives train station is 4 miles (6.4km) from Zennor. Bus service A3 Land's End to St Ives; 16A Penzance to St Ives. Alight Zennor bus stop, a short distance from the start.
By Car On B3306 take turning to Zennor and park in village car park (donation, not NT).
OS Map Explorer 102
Start / End Zennor village car park (not NT).
OS grid reference: SW453385

The Carracks

Mussel Point

Trevail

Wicca Pool

Gala Rocks

Porthzennor Cove

Wicca Farm

Tremedda

Lower Tregerthen

Giant's Rock

B3306

Zennor

Logan Stone

N

300 m

1. From the car park, turn left onto the road through the village, passing the Tinners Arms and the church. Just after the church turn left down a narrow track, signed to the coast path.

2. 0.5 miles/0.8km After the stile, continue straight ahead, following the South West Coast Path around Zennor Head in the direction of St Ives.

3. 3 miles/4.8km Once you have run past The Carracks – it's worth pausing here to look for seals, basking on the rocks or playing in the waves – turn right where the coast path continues straight on over a footbridge. Leaving the coast path, head inland up a small river valley to reach some buildings at Trevail Mill.

4. 3.2 miles/5.2km Turn right, following a track that bears left around buildings at Trevail and continuing due south to reach Boscubben.

5. 3.8 miles/6.1km Before you reach the B3306, turn right and follow a footpath through Wicca Farm, continuing through numerous small fields and the farms at Lower Tregerthen and Tremedda to return to Zennor village.

Other trails nearby
The South West Coast Path provides a wealth of excellent running in either direction; to the east it drops down to St Ives, with its stunning white sand beaches, numerous places to eat and drink, many art shops and the Tate St Ives gallery. Heading westwards takes you along a wild and rugged stretch of the Penwith Heritage Coast, around Gurnard's Head and to the impressive rocks and zawns (steep-sided sea inlets) at Bosigran.

02. Penrose

Penrose Hill car park
Penrose
Helston
Cornwall
TR13 0RD

ABOUT THIS RUN

Distance 5.8 miles (9.4km)
Ascent 643ft (196m)

Woodland and lakeside
  paths, surfaced trail,
  shingle beach
May be muddy
Be aware of tides, waves
  and seasonal flooding
History/culture
Wildlife
Dogs welcome on leads
Parkrun
NT café and toilets open
  daily (weekends only
  November–Easter)
No swimming, boating,
  watersports or fishing at
  Loe Pool and Loe Bar

The peaceful, wooded estate at Penrose, on the western coast of the Lizard Peninsula, surrounds Loe Pool, Cornwall's largest natural lake. Cut off from the sea by the wide, shingle bank of Loe Bar, the freshwater lake is a haven for wildlife and a fascinating place to explore. This run starts near the main parkland and follows the surfaced, multi-use trail towards Helston. The route takes you around the northern end of Loe Pool following winding, wooded trails with occasional glimpses across the pool, eventually tracing the shore around Carminowe Creek to reach Loe Bar. Running across the shingle is an incredible experience, with the sea to your left, the pool to your right and the beautiful Cornish coastline stretching away into the distance, edging the shingle bar with Porthleven Sands. The final miles climb up to the headland and follow a stony track back to the start, with plenty of great viewpoints out across the pool and estate.

Above: Loe Bar, separating Loe Pool from the Atlantic.
Opposite: Loe Pool and Bar from Lower Pentire.

THINGS TO SEE

Cornish wildlife

Penrose is a really exciting place to see wildlife. The rich variety of woods, farmland, cliffs, open water and reed beds combine to provide homes to common and rarer species of birds. Look out for barn owls, buzzards and kestrels, as well as herons, little egrets and kingfishers in the pool edges.

Work to improve water quality over the last 20 years has supported increasing numbers of otters – you may be lucky enough to spot one. In the evening, watch out for some of Penrose's resident bats: lesser and greater horseshoes, daubentons and soprano pipistrelles all thrive here, benefitting from the Trust's work over the last decade to provide more space for nature.

HOW TO GET HERE

By Public Transport Penzance train station 10 miles (16km) from Porthleven. Then bus First 2/2A or 7/8 towards Falmouth.

By Car Penrose estate is 2 miles (3.2km) south-west of Helston on the B3304. Turn left at signpost to Loe Bar and left into car park.

By Bicycle From Porthleven take the coast road to Penrose Hill; there are rides throughout the parkland and woodlands.

OS Map Explorer 103

Start / End: National Trust Penrose Hill car park.

OS grid reference: SW638258

Penrose Hill

Penrose

Degibna

Degibna Wood

Bar Walk Plantation

The Loe

Vellin-gluz Rocks

Pentire Wood

Carminowe Creek

Loe Bar

N

300 m

Other trails nearby

Explore many more trails around the estate, as well as the South West Coast Path, which runs north-west towards Land's End or south-east towards Kynance Cove and Lizard Point.

1. From Penrose Hill car park follow the route down the hill into the parkland. Continue through the parkland, keeping left where the routes split, and then follow the route to Helston, past Helston Lodge. Continue on this route until you reach a footpath sign opposite a bench directing you to the right.

2. 1.2 miles/2km Turn right, following the footpath over a footbridge to reach the bridleway on the other side. Turn right onto the bridleway and follow this back towards the pool. Run along the eastern shore of the lake, following the trail as it loops around Carminowe Creek, crossing a footbridge. After periods of heavy rain, some of these paths may be flooded, however diversions along higher paths are usually possible.

3. 4 miles/6.4km Bear right as you emerge onto Loe Bar, crossing the shingle with the lake on your right and the sea on your left. Climb the footpath up the headland opposite and turn right onto the main track, running along this with the lake on your right. After passing the Stables Café and walled gardens on your left, the route re-joins itself at the next parkland junction. Turn left here and return to the car park.

03. Pentire Point

Pentireglaze
New Polzeath
PL27 6QY

ABOUT THIS RUN

Distance **3.5 miles (5.7km)**
Ascent **827ft (252m)**

Coastal
Narrow, winding trails,
  bridleway and short
  section of quiet lane
May be muddy
History/culture
Wildlife
Dogs welcome

Pentire Point reaches out into the Atlantic from a remote and dramatic stretch of the North Cornwall coast between Polzeath and Port Isaac. At its northernmost point, the distinctively-shaped promontory of The Rumps, with its conical grassy hills, feels like somewhere far from south-west England. On a clear day, the views out along the coast in either direction are spectacular, taking in Stepper Point and the Camel estuary to the south and the castles of Doyden and Tintagel to the north. This is a great place to spot wildlife, too: look out for peregrine falcons hunting over the cliffs, Atlantic grey seals out on the wave-washed rocks and, over the summer months, dolphins and basking sharks. The 367-acre (148ha) headland has been looked after by the National Trust since 1936.

Above: Looking towards the Rumps at Pentire.
Opposite: Running across across the beach at Daymer Bay near to Pentire Head. There are beaches like this all around the South West, and you can have them pretty much to yourself early or late in the day.

THINGS TO SEE

The Rumps
Excavated in the 1960s, the distinctive conical headland of The Rumps lies across a narrow neck of land, known as an isthmus, from Pentire Point. Utilised as an Iron Age fort, the predominantly self-sufficient residents deepened the existing gullies and ditches and heightened the ramparts to protect access from the mainland. It is thought that the area was deserted following the Roman invasion of Britain in the 1st century. The small islands just off The Rumps are popular breeding grounds for seabirds including puffins, razorbills, guillemots, shags and herring gulls.

A mining history
The Pentireglaze silver-lead mine operated between 1580 and 1883, employing many generations of local people. Now overgrown and grazed by cattle, the disused mine makes a perfect roost for the rare greater horseshoe bat.

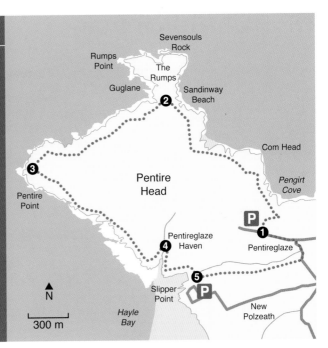

HOW TO GET HERE

By Public Transport The Western Greyhound 584/595 service passes through Polzeath; from here follow signs to the South West Coast Path.

By Car From the B3314 (between Wadebridge and the Port Isaac turn), follow the sign posts in the direction of Polzeath and then New Polzeath. The nearest postcode is PL27 6QY.

OS Map Explorer 106
Start / End National Trust Lead Mines car park.
OS grid reference: SW941800

N

300 m

1. Leave the car park heading north on a path that drops down to reach the South West Coast Path above Pengirt Cove. Turn left onto the coast path and continue to follow this as The Rumps come into view ahead.

2. 1 mile/1.6km Either continue along the South West Coast Path around the headland or detour out to explore The Rumps before returning to the coast path and continuing towards Pentire Point.

3. 1.7 miles/2.7km Round the sharp, rocky promontory at Pentire Point to be greeted by glorious views out across Padstow Bay to Stepper Point and Trevose Head.

4. 2.5 miles/4km Cross a small stream that runs down to a section of the beach at Pentire Haven. Avoid the footpath that heads left up the hill to Pentire Farm, but continue straight ahead, crossing a grassy headland and down to the main beach and buildings at Pentireglaze Haven.

5. 2.8 miles/4.5km Turn left after the first house, following a bridleway up a track and then alongside fields to reach a quiet lane. Turn left here and then left again to return to the car park.

Other trails nearby

The Camel Trail is an 18-mile (29km) level, surfaced trail for pedestrians, wheelchair users, horse riders and cyclists following a disused railway line through Wenfordbridge, Bodmin, Wadebridge and Padstow. From wide-open estuarine vistas to leafy wooded valleys, the trail is a great way to explore the area. Maps, bike hire, toilets and cafés are available at several locations along the route. Visit the Sustrans website for more information.

04. Lanhydrock

**Lanhydrock
Bodmin
Cornwall
PL30 5AD**

ABOUT THIS RUN

Distance 3.1 miles (5km)
Ascent 502ft (153m)

Waymarked route
Well-maintained tracks and
  trails, some uneven
  sections
Parkrun
History/culture
Wildlife
Family friendly
Dogs welcome – assistance
  dogs only in formal
  gardens

The Lanhydrock estate, near Bodmin in east Cornwall, is
a beautiful place to run, with a well-maintained network
of inviting trails. The grand Victorian country house is
set within 900 acres (364ha) of historic parkland, ancient
woodlands and an imposing beech-lined avenue, overlooking
the wide meanders of the River Fowey. This run follows the
course of Lanhydrock's weekly parkrun, held every Saturday
at 9am and fully signed with Run England waymarkers,
leaving you free to enjoy the experience of running in this
special place. Starting downhill past the house the route
takes in the picturesque views of South Park and winds
through leafy woodland, following peaceful trails alongside
the River Fowey. After a steady climb back through the
park there's a well-earned downhill to finish.

Above: Sunset over Beech Avenue
at Lanhydrock.
Opposite: The sight of Lanhydrock
gatehouse will get you excited about
what's to come.

THINGS TO SEE

Incredible trees
Lanhydrock is famous for its trees and has a
large collection of ancient and veteran trees.
Over the years, many new trees have been
planted, creating a rich mix that is a delight to
wander through. Rare lichens grow on many of
the older trees, flourishing in Cornwall's sunny
but damp climate and clean air, while several
species of bat make their homes on the estate.

Cycle trails
Lanhydrock is also great for exploring on two
wheels. Bike hire is available on site and exciting,
purpose-built mountain-bike trails include a short,
green-graded easy trail, suitable for beginners and
families; four blue-graded moderate trails; the
red-graded Saw Pit trails, packed with technical
features; and a skills area. Pick up a map of the
trails at the main visitor reception.

By Public Transport From Bodmin Parkway station, 1.75 miles (2.8km) on foot via original carriage drive, 3 miles (4.8km) by road.
By Car 2.5 miles (4km) south-east of Bodmin. Follow signposts from either A30 or A38 Bodmin to Liskeard, or take B3268 off A390 at Lostwithiel. Parking in National Trust main car park or at Respryn car park.
OS Map Landranger 200
Start / End National Trust Lanhydrock car park.
OS grid reference: SX088636

Cutmadoc

Lower Park

❶
Ⓟ WC ⑪

🏛

Lanhydrock House

South Park

Newton

❹

❷

Great Wood

❸

▲ N

⊢—— ——⊣
100 m

1. From the start follow the path downhill past the house and into Great Wood, looking out for the Run England waymarkers.

2. 0.5 miles/0.8km Bear left and run through the woodland, following waymarkers in a wide loop around the woods, before bearing right on Newton Lane and following the waymarkers down to the River Fowey, following this for a short distance before bearing left away from the river to reach Newton Lane.

3. 1.9 miles/3km Turn right onto Newton Lane and continue on, passing some cottages. At Newton Lodge turn left onto Beech Avenue running along the line of beech trees back towards the house.

Other trails nearby

Follow the lane from the southern edge of Lanhydrock to Restormel Castle, a 13th-century circular keep set on an earlier Norman mound (not NT). To the north-east, the wilds of Bodmin Moor await exploration, with many running opportunities.

4. 2.2 miles/3.6km Turn right, running uphill across Lower Park to reach a path. Turn left here and follow the path, bearing left at the path junctions to return to your outbound route past the house. In front of the house, turn left down Beech Avenue to finish.

05. East Soar

East Soar car park
Near Malborough
Devon
TQ7 3DR

ABOUT THIS RUN

Distance 4.2 miles (6.8km)
Ascent 587ft (179m)

Coastal
History/culture
Wildlife
Dogs welcome
Walkers Hut cafe

The South West Coast Path dips and climbs along the rugged cliffs of Devon's South Hams, a land of contrasts where rolling verdant grassland meets a sea that glows blue in the sun. Cattle graze the fields, while buzzards circle overhead and rare cirl buntings – relatives of the yellowhammer found only in the southern reaches of Devon and Cornwall – flutter between the hedgerows. This run takes in a glorious stretch of the coast path south of Overbeck's, with its exotic clifftop garden overlooking Salcombe and the Kingsbridge estuary, and rounds the peaceful yet dramatic headland at Bolt Head, a former RAF runway.

Above: Runner on the South West Coast Path at East Soar. Opposite: Soar Mill Cove, East Soar, is a little way further west but well worth a visit at low tide.

THINGS TO SEE

Hidden beaches
This stunning stretch of South Hams coastline is dotted with small coves and beaches, perfect for exploring, picnics or a post-run dip. Starehole Cove can be found around the halfway point of the run, while Soar Mill Cove lies 1 mile (1.6km) west of the start. The infamous Salcombe Bar stretches across the mouth of the estuary to Leek Cove. At an ebb tide this sand bar, inspiration for Tennyson's poem 'Crossing the Bar', lies just 2ft (60cm) below the surface of the water, ready to catch out unsuspecting vessels.

East Soar Outdoor Experience
Situated on a National Trust farm, the Walkers' Hut at East Soar Outdoor Experience is a lovely, quirky honesty café with a good range of refreshments – check the website for seasonal opening times and bring plenty of small change to pay for your cakes and scones. The farm also offers organised events, particularly for children and school groups, as well as glamping and holiday cottages.

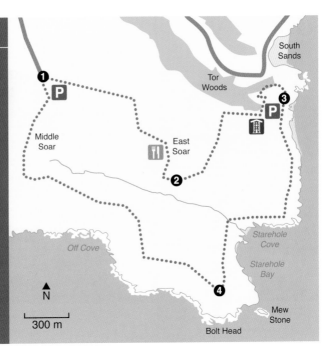

HOW TO GET HERE

By Public Transport Totnes train station 20 miles (32km); Plymouth train station 25 miles (40km). Regular bus services from Totnes train station and Plymouth city centre to Kingsbridge. From Kingsbridge there are buses to Salcombe.

By Car A379 from Plymouth and A381 from Totnes both meet at Kingsbridge. A381 continues south to Salcombe where you can follow signs to Soar.

OS Map Explorer OL20
Start / End National Trust East Soar car park.
OS grid reference: SX713375

1. Leave the car park through the gate furthest from the road, signed to the coast path, and follow this track past East Soar Farm, continuing as it becomes a footpath.

2. 0.9 miles/1.4km Bear left, staying on the headland rather than dropping down to Starehole Bottom, and follow the footpath across fields to Tor Woods. Bear right and follow the zig-zag path down through the woods until it reaches the South West Coast Path above Splatcove Point.

3. 1.7 miles/2.7km Turn right onto the South West Coast Path and follow this south, rounding Sharp Tor, dropping down to Starehole Cove and climbing back up the other side, continuing until you reach the rugged and remote promontory of Bolt Head.

4. 2.7 miles/4.3km From Bolt Head continue for 1.1 miles (1.7km) until you can take a footpath to the right to Middle Soar. Stay right to join a track past some buildings to the left and continue along this path to return to the car park.

Other trails nearby

Following the South West Coast Path to the west takes you over Bolberry Down to beautiful Bolt Tail, the pretty twin villages of Inner and Outer Hope and the beach at Hope Cove. Or catch a ferry across to East Portlemouth and explore the coast path around Prawle Point, a coastguard station and lookout.

06. Plymbridge

**Plymbridge Woods
Near Plympton
Devon
PL7 4SR**

ABOUT THIS RUN

Distance **4.7 miles (7.6km)**
Ascent **656ft (200m)**

Multi-user surfaced path,
woodland trails
Can be made suitable
for bikes and buggies
Family friendly
Parkrun
Woodland wildlife
Dogs welcome

The Plym Valley, on the south-western edge of Dartmoor, is a wonderfully varied landscape of ancient woodlands, meadows, moorland, wild river valleys and rugged granite crags. This run explores the area, predominantly using the excellent, traffic-free, multi-user surfaced path that was once the Great Western Railway track, and is now also the West Devon Way, as far as Bickleigh Bridge. For a longer run, or if you're exploring by bike, this path continues to the wooded valley below the imposing crag of the Dewerstone, a place shrouded in local legend and a favourite haunt of rock climbers. There's also a winding section alongside the River Plym, a perfect place to spot kingfishers, sea trout, dippers, peregrine falcons, deer and other wildlife.

Above: The River Plym.
Opposite: The West Devon Way through Plymbridge Woods. This easy-walking trail passes near Lydford Gorge, a National Trust property that is well worth a visit if you are in the area.

THINGS TO SEE

Plymbridge peregrines

The woodland at Plymbridge is buzzing with wildlife, including rare birds. Peregrine falcons have been nesting at Cann Quarry in Plymbridge Woods for more than 50 years and, in 2001, the Plym Peregrine Project was set up by the local rangers and volunteers to monitor and protect these fascinating birds. Since then, 34 chicks have fledged, which usually happens around the last week in June, some of which have gone on to raise their own broods.

The fastest animal on the planet, peregrines can reach speeds of over 320km/h (200mph)

and perform spectacular flying displays. As well as protecting the birds, the project works to educate and inspire visitors, school groups and local clubs to discover the local wildlife and those who want to can get involved as volunteers.

As well as the peregrines the local rangers look after nearby wildflower meadows for the benefit of bees and other insects, and manage the woodland carefully for nature conservation.

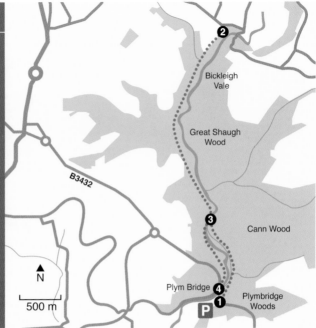

HOW TO GET HERE

By Public Transport Trains to Plymouth, 6 miles (9.7km) away. Regular buses to Plympton.

By Car From A38 Marsh Mills exit, head towards Plympton and follow signs to Plymbridge Woods, 5 miles (8km) north-east of Plymouth.

By Bicycle NCN27, the Plym Valley Trail, starts in Plymouth, in the grounds of Saltram House. Visit the Sustrans website for more information.

OS Map Explorer OL20

Start / End National Trust Plymbridge Woods car park.

OS grid reference: SX523585

1. Leave the main National Trust car park at Plymbridge Woods and run up the slope onto the old Great Western Railway line, now National Cycle Network route 27. Turn right, away from the city of Plymouth, and follow the trail north. The Cann Viaduct after about 0.5 miles (0.8km) is home to the peregrine viewing platform.

2. **2.4 miles/3.8km** On reaching Bickleigh Bridge, turn around and follow the trail back south.

3. **4 miles/6.4km** Take the right-hand turn off route 27, just before the Cann Viaduct and follow down the slope into the valley. Then follow the path alongside the river to reach the road.

4. **4.6 miles/7.4km** Turn left and go under the bridge to return to the start.

Other trails nearby

Nearby Cann Woods, which is worked by the Forestry Commission, is a nature reserve and contains several miles of cycling and walking trails.

07. Parke

Bovey Tracey
Devon
TQ13 9JQ

ABOUT THIS RUN

Distance 4 miles (6.4km)
Ascent 617ft (188m)

Multi-user surfaced path,
  woodland trails
Family friendly
Parkrun
Woodland wildlife
Dogs welcome

Nestled on the south-eastern fringes of Dartmoor, just outside the small market town of Bovey Tracey, the National Trust's Parke really does have something for everyone. An excellent network of trails weaves through deciduous woodland, alongside the fast-flowing River Bovey, across open fields and includes a section of the multi-user path and former Moretonhampstead and South Devon Railway. Wide, shingle beaches and intriguing boardwalks are ideal for kids to play on and it's a great place to take the dog for a walk, too. After your run there's plenty of opportunity for a relaxing stroll, including the vegetable garden, orchards and formal gardens – or sit in the sunshine with a Devon cream tea at Home Farm café. This run follows a slightly extended version of Parke's weekly parkrun, taking in a bit of everything around the estate.

Above and opposite: Running trails weave through woodland alongside the River Bovey.

Other trails nearby

The West Devon Way runs for 37 miles (60km) between Okehampton in the north and Plymouth in the south passing Lydford, Tavistock, Yelverton along the way, meaning it's well-serviced with public transport and refreshment stops.

THINGS TO SEE

Dartmoor

Covering 368 sq. miles (953 sq. km) of wild and windswept moorland, ancient woods, clear streams and grassland grazed by native ponies, Dartmoor National Park is rich in wildlife and human history. Rocky granite tors dot the moorland, laid bare by millennia of weathering of the overlying earth. Some of these tors are stacked with huge boulders, hundreds of feet high, and two – High Willhays and Yes Tor – are officially classified as mountains, both rising to over 2,000ft (610m) above sea level. Haytor

rises just a few miles from Parke, and a walk – or run – up one of the clear paths to the top is greeted by glorious views of the surrounding moorland to the sparkling sea beyond. The ancient sessile oak woodlands that stand in pockets around the moor are some of the highest oakwoods in Britain. It's a fascinating experience to wander amidst the twisted, moss- and lichen-clad boughs, walking through a lush carpet of bilberry – known locally as whortleberry – wood anemone and bramble.

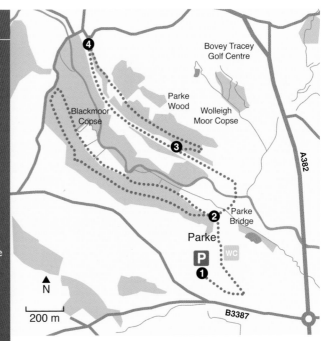

HOW TO GET HERE

By Public Transport Newton Abbot train station, 6 miles (9.7km) and Exeter St David's train station, 17 miles (27.3km). Bus 39 to Bovey Tracey, 1 mile (1.6km) by footpath from Parke.
By Car 3 miles (4.8km) from A38 Devon Expressway, connecting Plymouth to Exeter. Follow signs to Bovey Tracey, then brown signs to Parke.
By Bicycle The Newton Abbot to Bovey Tracey cycleway is a moderate 9-mile (14.5km) cycle route along fairly quiet roads, with some traffic-free sections, waymarked with blue cycleway signs.
OS Map Explorer OL191
Start / End National Trust Parke car park.
OS grid reference: SX805786

1. Leave the car park at Parke and head back down the drive, turning left towards the main house. Follow this path downhill across fields, passing the house on your left.

2. 0.4 miles/0.7km At the gate and path junction, keep straight past the building with the barn on your left (don't turn left up the main path). After the barn, follow the left-hand trail uphill through woodland. Just as the trail reaches the boundary of the estate, turn sharp right and follow the lower parallel path back down the hill to emerge to the left of the building. Turn left here, cross two bridges and carry straight on to reach the surfaced cycle path. Turn left here and follow it until you can turn right onto a footpath.

3. 2 miles/3.2km Turn right and climb up through the woods to reach a footpath junction. Turn left here and follow the footpath through woodland until it brings you back out onto the surfaced cycle path.

4. 2.7 miles/4.3km Turn left and follow the cycle path until reaching your outward path. Turn right, recrossing the two bridges. At the gate at the bottom of the hill, bear left and run back up the footpath through fields and past the house to return to the start.

08. Killerton

Killerton
Broadclyst
Exeter
EX5 3LE

ABOUT THIS RUN

Distance 3.7 miles (6km)
Ascent 403ft (123m)

Woodland
History/culture
Parkrun
Wildlife
Dogs welcome (not in
  house or formal gardens)
Family friendly

Having been in the Acland family since the 1600s, Killerton House and its surrounding 6,400-acre (2,590ha) estate was gifted to the National Trust by Sir Richard Acland in 1944. Today, Killerton's rolling farmland, wildlife-rich woodland, parks, orchards and even an Iron Age hill fort and an extinct volcano are open for the public to enjoy.

Above: View across Killerton parkland.
Opposite: Runner at Killerton.

This run follows the waymarked 5km (3-mile) parkrun route along a series of gravel, grass and field paths and trails right around the edge of the main estate. Varied in terrain and landscape, it takes in a bit of everything from leafy woodland north of the house to open farmland at Columbjohn to the west, the Acland family's original place of residence that was demolished around 1700; only the chapel and gatehouse remain.

THINGS TO SEE

The butterfly forest

Also part of the Killerton estate, Ashclyst Forest, on the opposite side of the M5 motorway from the house, is a magical woodland, networked with trails, some of which are waymarked, and home to many different species of butterfly. Look out for peacocks, green-veined whites and orange tips in spring; gatekeepers and speckled woods later in the year; pearl bordered, silver washed and dark green fritillaries; skippers and ringlets; and, if you're lucky, rare purple emperors, purple hairstreaks and white admirals.

Killerton's orchards

Once an important apple-growing county, 90 per cent of Devon's traditional orchards have been lost since the 1950s. The Killerton estate has over 50 acres (20.2ha) of orchard with over 100 varieties of apple tree, habitat that supports over 1,800 different species of wildlife. Sparrow Park orchard is a great place to explore; you can also get involved in harvesting apples in the annual Big Pick Up, followed a week later by Killerton's Apple Festival, celebrating national Apple Day with cider-making, story-telling and local crafts.

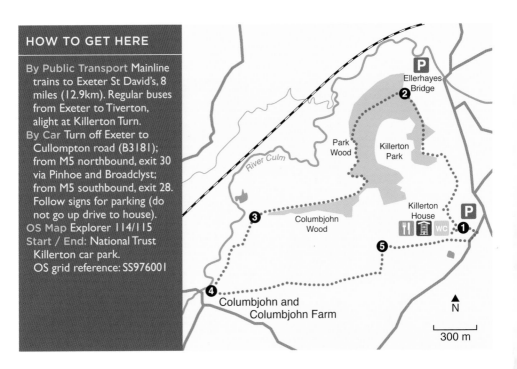

HOW TO GET HERE

By Public Transport Mainline trains to Exeter St David's, 8 miles (12.9km). Regular buses from Exeter to Tiverton, alight at Killerton Turn.
By Car Turn off Exeter to Cullompton road (B3181); from M5 northbound, exit 30 via Pinhoe and Broadclyst; from M5 southbound, exit 28. Follow signs for parking (do not go up drive to house).
OS Map Explorer 114/115
Start / End: National Trust Killerton car park.
OS grid reference: SS976001

1. Pick up the waymarked parkrun course a short distance into the estate from the car park. From the Stable Block arch, turn right into the parkland and follow the path up the hill towards the metal gate into the Deer Park. From here, follow waymarkers north across the parkland and into the woods.

2. 0.9 miles/1.4km Follow the path as it curves around the hill to the left, then as it descends through Columbjohn Wood to reach the edge of the woodland, shortly before the River Culm.

3. 2 miles/3.2km Turn left and follow the footpath alongside the river to Columbjohn Farm.

4. 2.4 miles/3.8km Turn left and follow the track past the farm and alongside fields, bearing left where the track splits.

5. 3.2 miles/5.2km Turn right and run across the parkland back to the car park.

Other trails nearby
Numerous trails wind around nearby Ashclyst Forest, perfect for exploring on foot or by bike. A few miles south, the Exe Estuary Trail follows the wide sweep of the estuary for 26 miles (42km) between the coastal towns of Exmouth and Dawlish, both connected by train to Exeter.

09. Arlington Court

Arlington Court
Arlington
Near Barnstaple
Devon
EX31 4LP

ABOUT THIS RUN

Distance 3.9 miles (6.3km)
Ascent 866ft (264m)

Steep steps in places
Woodland
History/culture
Wildlife
Family friendly
Dogs welcome but must be
 on leads at all times
Admission charges apply

Set within the verdant Yeo Valley on the western edge of Exmoor, the Arlington estate covers 2,700 acres (1,093ha) of lush Devon countryside. Over 20 miles (32.2km) of well-maintained trails wind through woodland, wildflower meadows, pasture and deer park, alongside the river and around the lake, making this a perfect place for on-foot exploring. Expect a few good hills but there are plenty of downs as well as ups.

This run combines two existing waymarked routes to create one longer one: the deer park walk, marked with green arrows, and the centenary walk, marked with orange arrows, making navigating straightforward and leaving you free simply to enjoy running through this special landscape. This route isn't suitable for larger groups and some paths are used by horses, buggies, walkers and cyclists. Woodland trails may be closed occasionally for management.

Above: Arlington Court in Devon overlooks acres of countryside, which includes miles of well-maintained running trails.

THINGS TO SEE

Wonderful wildlife

Arlington is home to one of the largest colonies of lesser horseshoe bats in Devon, with between 90–150 in number. These tiny creatures tend to hunt at dusk so you may see them on an evening run when they'll be busy catching some 3,000 bugs each.

Arlington's last owner, Rosalie Chichester, who donated the estate to the National Trust in 1949, was a passionate conservationist and many of her legacies remain. A heronry and bird hide can be found at the lake while Tucker's Bridge, crossed shortly after the halfway point of this run, is an important wildlife area where a mixture of wet woodland and boggy grassland provides habitat for bats, butterflies and lichen.

Herds of wild red deer also visit the estate, possibly seeking shelter from the windswept wilds of neighbouring Exmoor. It's thought around 70 deer are in the park at any one time, although they can be quite wary of people and often hard to spot. You may also meet some of the less-wild creatures that live on the estate, including Jacob sheep and Ruby Red Devon cattle.

HOW TO GET HERE

By Public Transport
Barnstaple, 10 miles (16km)
from Arlington. TW Coaches
309, Barnstaple–Lynton,
infrequent.
By Car 9 miles (14.5km)
north-east of Barnstaple,
off the A39 to the National
Trust Arlington car park.
Sat Nav EX31 4LP.
By Bicycle National Cycle
Network Regional route 56
passes near property.
OS Map Explorer OL9
Start / End National Trust
Old Kitchen Tea Room.
OS grid reference: SS611405

1. From the start, run along the surfaced path, following orange signs to the lake and wider estate, continuing through the gates and along Monkey Puzzle Avenue until you reach the lake.

2. 0.9 miles/1.5km Cross the dam over the lake and run along the bank and, continuing to follow orange signs, head into Woolley Wood, climbing up through the trees and over a stile to emerge into fields on the opposite side. Turn left and run across the fields to re-enter the woods over a stile and a narrow footbridge, and then a second stile.

3. 1.7 miles/2.8km Turn left onto the path through the woods, bearing right at the junction to follow orange waymarkers downhill. Bear right onto a smaller path and descend some steps to reach a main track at the edge of the wood.

4. 2.2 miles/3.5km Leave the orange route here; do not cross the footbridge, instead turn right onto the main track, joining the green waymarked Deer Park route and following it all the way to the finish. Follow this as it

curves to the right around the edge of the woods and crosses a stream at Tucker's Bridge. Turn left after the bridge into Deer Park Wood, following the main track around to the right to join a bridleway.

5. 2.9 miles/4.7km Follow the bridleway downhill, emerging from the wood and following the main track straight up the hill to reach the Sawmill building. Bear left through a small patch of woodland to reach the Carriage Museum, continuing straight on here to return to the tea room where refreshment awaits.

Other trails nearby

Exmoor is home to outstanding running opportunities, from the windswept reaches of the high moors to the steep-sided wooded valleys through which its rivers drain to the sea. Start with our Heddon Valley run, route 10, on Exmoor's beautiful north coast.

10. Heddon Valley

Hunter's Inn
Near Parracombe
Barnstaple
Devon
EX31 4PY

ABOUT THIS RUN

Distance 6 miles (9.5km)
Ascent 2,778ft (847m)

Coastal
Woodland
History/culture
Wildlife
Dogs welcome
Family friendly

Heddon Valley lies on the north coast of Exmoor, a steep-sided, wooded cleft that runs to the sea at Heddon's Mouth. At the heart of the valley, the National Trust-owned Hunter's Inn is a perfect base from which to explore this stunning part of North Devon. This run follows an historic 19th-century carriageway up and out of the valley, taking you through peaceful Hollow Brook Combe, flanked with sessile oaks and rare whitebeams, and past Martinhoe Beacon Roman Fortlet, abandoned in 75AD. The return trip takes you along a dramatic section of the South West Coast Path, rising and falling along the high cliffs, home to a wide variety of seabirds.

Above: Trail above Heddon Valley.
Below: Blue tit at Heddon Valley.
Opposite: Beach at Heddon's Mouth. The fairly flat walk from Hunter's Inn to Heddon's Mouth is under 1 mile (1.6km) for those not wishing to face the steep cliff paths.

THINGS TO SEE

Woody Bay
If you want to escape the hustle and bustle, Woody Bay is the perfect location. Walk down the steep track to this secluded pebble beach, towered over by looming cliffs, and listen to the sounds of seabirds.

Originally known as 'Wooda Bay', the estate came under the care of the National Trust in 1965, after almost being turned into a holiday resort by Victorian entrepreneur, Colonel Benjamin Greene Lake. The sea swimming pool and remains of the pier can still be seen at Woody Bay Beach.

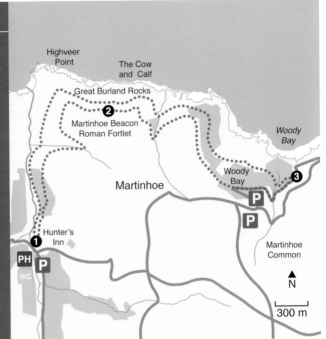

By Public Transport
Barnstaple, 16.5 miles
(26.5km) from Heddon
Valley. Regular service from
Barnstaple to Lynton (passing
Barnstaple train station),
alight just north of
Parracombe, 2 miles (3.2km)
from the Hunter's Inn.
By Car Halfway along A39
between Combe Martin
and Lynmouth, turn off for
Hunter's Inn. Postcode for
SatNav EX31 4PY.
By Bicycle National Cycle
Network Regional Route 51
passes nearby.
OS Map Explorer OL9
Start / End National Trust
Heddon Valley car park,
opposite National Trust shop.
OS grid reference: SS655480

1. From the start, run down the road towards the Hunter's Inn, passing the inn on a bridleway on its right. Where the path forks, bear right on to The Carriageway through Road Wood, signed to Woody Bay. Keep on this path heading up hill and eventually emerging onto open hillside with great coastal and moorland views.

2. 1.4 miles/2.3km Detour up to Martinhoe Beacon Roman Fortlet, signed to your right, returning to The Carriageway and continuing on towards West Woody Bay through Hollow Brook Combe and West Woody Bay Wood. Where the footpath meets a road, bear left and follow it down some steep hairpin bends.

3. 3 miles/4.9km At a sharp right-hand bend turn left onto the South West Coast Path signed to Hunter's Inn. Follow this (also a section of the Tarka Trail) all the way along the clifftop path until it descends back into Heddon Valley. Retrace your steps past Hunter's Inn to return to the start.

Other trails nearby
The Two Moors Way runs through the Teign Valley on its 102-mile (164km) route from Ivybridge in the south of Dartmoor National Park to Lynmouth on the North Devon Coast of Exmoor National Park. The Tarka Trail is a 180-mile (290km), walking and cycling trail traversing North Devon and Exmoor. It includes the longest traffic-free cycle route in the UK.

11. Branscombe

Margells Bridge
Branscombe
Devon
EX12 3DB

ABOUT THIS RUN

Distance 5 miles (8.1km)
Ascent 1,037ft (316m)

Coastal
Some steep terrain, may be
 muddy/slippery
History/culture
Wildlife
Dogs welcome
NT toilets and café operate
seasonal opening hours.

Starting in the pretty seaside village of Branscombe, this run takes you through rolling Devon countryside and across the wave-washed pebbles of Branscombe beach where the anchor of the MSC Napoli has lain since it grounded here in 2007.

The steep climb up the long, grassy slope of East Cliff is handsomely rewarded with outstanding views along the Jurassic Coast followed by a long, easy descent into the village of Beer. It's well worth stopping for a breather to explore the bustling village centre and the beach with its colourful fleet of fishing boats.

The run back to Branscombe follows an adventurous section of the South West Coast Path through the Hooken Undercliff, an area of landslips rich in flora and fauna. Keep an eye out for dolphins playing in the waves below and the peregrines that make their nests in the cliffs above.

Above: Branscombe is a sheltered destination with a long shingle beach. From East Cliff you can enjoy spectacular panoramic views over the bay.

THINGS TO SEE

Historic Branscombe

Nestled in a steep-sided valley between Seaton and Sidmouth, where lanes lined with thatched cottages and wildflowers lead down to the sea, the picturesque village of Branscombe – thought to be the longest village in the country – is an intriguing and enjoyable place to explore. The Forge, the oldest working thatched forge of its kind in England; the Old Bakery, with its cosy tea room and pretty garden; and fascinating Manor Mill, that still draws water from the neighbouring leat to power its huge wheel, are all National Trust-owned and free for members to visit.

A run through time

The Jurassic Coast UNESCO World Heritage Site runs for approximately 96 miles (154km) between Exmouth in East Devon and Studland Bay in Dorset. The exposed cliffs along this section of the south coast tell the story of 185 million years of Earth's geological history, though an almost continuous sequence of rock formation covering the Triassic, Jurassic and Cretaceous periods. The fossilised records of the creatures that have lived here, through times of desert, shallow tropical sea and marsh, remain preserved in the rocks.

By Public Transport The Axe Valley 899 bus from Sidmouth to Seaton (connections from Axminster railway station or Honiton railway station) stops at the bus stop next to the Village Hall and National Trust car park at the starting point of this walk.

By Car Branscombe village is signposted from the A3052. The National Trust car park is located next to the Forge at Margells Bridge, Branscombe, Devon, EX12 3DB.

By Bicycle National Cycle Network route 2 linking Dover in Kent with St. Austell in Cornwall passes through Branscombe.

OS Map Explorer OL9

Start / End National Trust car park, Margells Bridge, Branscombe.

OS grid reference: SY196886

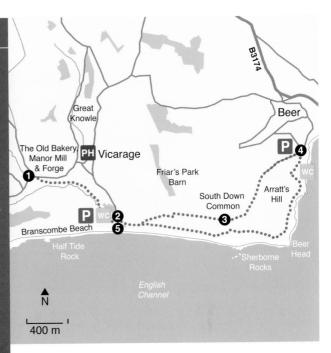

Other trails nearby

The South West Coast Path continues east past Lyme Regis to Golden Cap, home to incredible coastal and woodland trails. To the west, the Exe Estuary Trail is a 26-mile (42km) multi-user trail between Exmouth and Dawlish.

1. Leave the car park and turn left, following the road as it curves to the right and then bearing right down the narrower Mill Lane, signed to Branscombe Mouth and the coast path. The lane becomes a track at National Trust Manor Mill; continue straight on here, following signs to the coast path.

2. 0.75 miles/1.2km On reaching Branscombe Mouth, bear left and cross the beach, passing the Sea Shanty Beach Café (not NT) on your left. Straight ahead, the grassy stretch of East Cliff rises above you, a path clearly visible to its summit. Follow this, leaving the South West Coast Path where it forks right to take a lower path, and continuing up and over South Down Common.

3. 1.5 miles/2.5km As you begin to descend towards Beer, stay left and continue until the footpath becomes a lane at Common Hill. Follow this into Beer village, well worth a detour to explore.

4. 2.4 miles/3.8km At the bottom of Common Hill, just before the beach, a sharp right joins the South West Coast Path along Little Lane. Follow this back towards Branscombe, staying on the signed coast path around Beer Head and along the lower path through the Hooken Undercliff. This path may be slippery after rain.

5. 4.2 miles/6.8km The coast path winds through a caravan park and emerges onto the beach. Cross the beach and bear right after the café, rejoining your outward route to the finish.

12. Golden Cap

Langdon Hill car park Morcombelake Dorset DT6 6EP
ABOUT THIS RUN
Distance **2.8 miles (4.5km)** Ascent **741ft (226m)**
Coastal Summit Family friendly History/culture Wildlife

Golden Cap, the summit of which, at 626ft (191m), is the highest point on the south coast of England, rises like a mini Matterhorn from the rugged Jurassic Coast. Best viewed from the sea, or further along the coast, the triangular golden summit that gives the hill its name is formed from local greensand rock. This run starts with a section that takes you around leafy Langdon Wood, carpeted with bluebells in spring, and where regular breaks in the trees offer surprise views over the rolling west Dorset countryside. With your warm-up done there's a steep ascent to the summit of Golden Cap to tackle, handsomely rewarded with outstanding coastal views from the wide, flat summit plateau. A fun hairpin descent takes you around the base of the hill, past St Gabriel's Wood and the remains of St Gabriel's Church, before diving back into the shady woodland to finish.

Above: South West Coast Path below Golden Cap.
Opposite: View across the Golden Cap estate.
Following page: South West Coast Path below Golden Cap.

THINGS TO SEE

Explore the estate

The National Trust-owned Golden Cap estate covers a sizeable swathe of the west Dorset coast. An intriguing landscape shaped by centuries of farming, the estate is rich in wildlife, with wildflowers, birds, insects and small mammals thriving in the meadows and hedges, and frogs, newts and dragonflies to be found in the streams.

This is a fantastic area for running, and Golden Cap itself is also an enjoyable walk or a perfect mini mountain for a family adventure – there's a

play area near to Langdon car park and the 1-mile (1.6km) circuit around Langdon Wood is suitable for multi-terrain buggies. Settlements at St Gabriel's (point 4 on the map) date back to Saxon times; today there's a ruined medieval chapel to explore and four National Trust holiday cottages – a great base for the superb running in and around the estate. Thorncombe Beacon, on the coast to the east of Golden Cap, has been a signal station since the 16th century, built to warn of invasion from the sea.

1. From the car park go through the gate signposted Golden Cap, turning right on the main path. Follow this path as it curves around Langdon Hill, running through beautiful mixed woodland.

2. 0.9 miles/1.5km Turn right off the main path and leave the woodland, signed to Golden Cap. Stay left and follow the most direct path to the summit, with several stepped sections along the way. Take a moment at the top to catch your breath and admire the outstanding coastal views.

3. 1.2 miles/2km Leave the summit of Golden Cap at the opposite end to where you arrived, following the South West Coast Path as it zigzags down the hillside. Crossing the field boundary at the bottom of the main slope, bear right and head across the field to St Gabriel's.

4. 1.7 miles/2.7km Join the path at St Gabriel's and turn right, running back around the base of Golden Cap to rejoin your outward path emerging from Langdon Wood.

5. 2.2 miles/3.6km Turn right onto the main circular path around Langdon Hill and follow this back to the car park.

Other trails nearby
Running right over the top of Golden Cap, the South West Coast Path starts in Poole, to the east, and follows the edge of the south-west peninsular 630 miles (1,014km) around to Minehead on the Exmoor coast. There are 25 miles (40.2km) of footpaths to explore within Golden Cap estate.

HOW TO GET HERE

By Public Transport Nearest station is Axminster, 7 miles (11.3km). Coastline X53 and First 31 services run through Morcombelake; alight next to Moores' biscuit factory and walk along the footpath behind the factory following signs to Langdon Hill.

By Car From Bridport and the east, drive through Chideock village on the A35 and at the top of the steep hill, take the next left into the narrow, unmarked lane. From the west, go through Morecombelake and after passing Felicity's Farm Shop, take the first turn right into the unmarked, easily missed lane. Take the first left and follow the signposted track into the National Trust car park.

OS Map Explorer 116
Start / End: National Trust Langdon Hill car park.
OS grid reference: SY412930

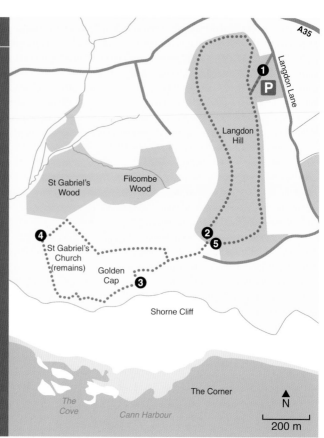

13. Brownsea Island

Poole Harbour
Poole
Dorset
BH13 7EE

ABOUT THIS RUN

Distance **5.3 miles (8.6km)**
Ascent **243ft (74m)**

Family friendly
History/culture
Wildlife
Admission charges apply
Seasonal opening hours,
  check website for details

Brownsea is the largest island in Poole Harbour, with fine views across to the Isle of Purbeck. There are no public cars or bikes allowed on the island, so running here is incredibly peaceful, but provides an exciting island adventure at the same time. This run takes in the main loop around Brownsea, starting and finishing at the pier; however, there are countless opportunities to detour off into the woods or down to the shoreline to explore further – South Shore beach is one of the best places for this. The northern half of the island, including the lakes, is managed by Dorset Wildlife Trust.

Above: Brownsea Island offers the opportunity to run in a peaceful, virtually traffic-free environment.

THINGS TO SEE

Island life
A peaceful, virtually traffic-free environment and a surprising diversity of habitats, including mixed woodland with over 100 different species of tree, open heathland and a lagoon, mean wildlife thrives on Brownsea Island. It's a birdwatcher's paradise, with woodland birds including coal, blue, great and long-tailed tits, great spotted woodpeckers, nuthatches and jays. There are 11 species of bat, including the noctule bat that roosts in hollow trees. Visit the lagoon to spot grey herons and little egrets, as well as the flocks of avocets that congregate in winter. Brownsea is one of the few places in southern England where wild native red squirrels survive and they are

often easy to spot; you may also encounter some imported residents, including shy sika deer grazing among the trees, and peacocks strutting across the grass.

Remnants of history
The field near to point 4 on the map still bears the long, straight furrows of the daffodil plantation that was established in the early 20th century by the Van Raalte family, owners of Brownsea Island at the time. The Outdoor Centre and campsite at point 3 marks the location of the first experimental Scout Camp held by Lord Baden Powell over 100 years ago.

HOW TO GET HERE

By Public Transport Poole station to Poole Quay, 0.5 miles (0.8km); Branksome or Parkstone stations to Sandbanks Jetty, 3.5 miles (5.6km).

By Car There are no cars permitted on Brownsea – you will need to park your car and catch a ferry across to the island (see below). To reach the ferry car park, follow signs to Poole Quay or Sandbanks. To access Poole Harbour from the west take the A35/A350 Dorchester–Poole road. From the east take the A31 Ringwood–Poole road. From the north take the A3081/A350 Shaftesbury–Poole road.

Parking Poole: follow signs to visitor quayside car park, where you can use pedestrian signage to locate the quay. Sandbanks: there is metered road parking available on the peninsular leading up to the ferry and a large car park within a 10-minute walk from the Sandbanks jetty from where the boats depart. Phone and Pay code is 3262 for the main Sandbanks car park, http://www.phoneandpay.co.uk/howitworks

SatNav Sandbanks Jetty, BH13 7QJ; Poole Quay, BH15 1HP.

Ferries Poole Quay Greenslades Pleasure Boats and Brownsea Island Ferries run ferries from 10am, then every half hour throughout the day. Ferries depart Brownsea back to Poole at 20 mins past and 10 mins to each hour. Sandbanks Jetty: Brownsea Island Ferries run from 10am then every half hour throughout the day. Ferries depart Brownsea at 15 mins past and 15 mins to each hour. Please note there is no 1pm or 1.15pm service. All visitors, including National Trust members, need to purchase tickets. Last boats leave the island at 5pm. For service information please see: Greenslade Pleasure Boats: 01202 669955 www.greensladepleasureboats.co.uk and Brownsea Island Ferries 01929 462383 www.brownseaislandferries.com

OS Map Explorer OL15

Start / End Brownsea Island Quay. OS grid reference: SZ031877

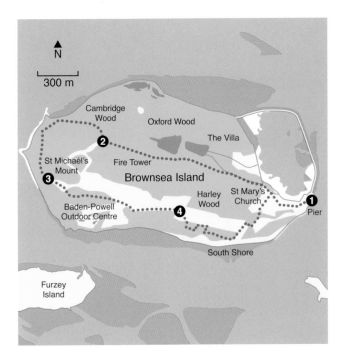

Other trails nearby
The Poole Harbour Trails are six linear and 13 circular trails, taking in some of the best sights of this vast natural harbour – see www.pooleharbourtrails.org.uk for full details.

1. From the pier head along the main path, with the church on your left. Continue along this path in the same direction, passing the Vinery and the East and West Lakes to your right.

2. 1.1 miles/1.8km Just after the children's play area, a wide track heads off to the left, a short-cut across to the south of the island. Carry straight on here towards the sea. Follow the path as it curves around to the left just before the shore, passing the bare ruins of Maryland village and the small shingle beach at Pottery Pier.

3. 1.7 miles/2.7km Pass the other end of the shortcut path on your left; continue straight ahead, passing the Baden Powell Outdoor Centre on your right.

4. 2.4 miles/3.8km Turn right at the track junction and head for the coast, taking in the viewpoints from the South Shore – a good place to explore the sandy beach, too. From here, bear left alongside the castle, running past the visitor centre and turning right on reaching the main path to return to the pier.

Opposite: Buggy running on Brownsea Island.
Below: Exploring Brownsea Island.

14. Corfe Castle

Castle View
Corfe Castle
Dorset
BH20 5DR

ABOUT THIS RUN

Distance 5.3 miles (8.6km)
Ascent 722ft (220m)

Family friendly
History/culture
Wildlife
Dogs welcome

Above:
Corfe Castle
overlooks the
Purbeck Hills.

Dorset's Purbeck Hills rise and fall along a ridge of chalk downland between Lulworth Cove in the west and Old Harry Rocks in the east. This sculpted landscape is exciting to explore, with trails that trace the tops of the long, grassy ridgelines and plenty of leg-sapping ascents and exhilarating descents should you choose to take them on. The fairy-tale ruins of Corfe Castle stand on the top of a hill guarding the principal route through the Purbeck Hills.

This run begins at the castle and links the Purbeck Way and the Hardy Way, combining excellent running on well-maintained trails with straightforward, waymarked navigation. The early section takes you through wildlife-rich chalk downland and woodland and past the Furzebrook Blue Pool (paid entry), before a steady climb up to the ridge joins the Purbeck Way, following this back to the castle with glorious views in all directions.

THINGS TO SEE

Corfe Castle

Corfe Castle was built in the early 12th century for King Henry I, son of William the Conqueror, on the site of an earlier castle. Standing guard over the main through-route to the Purbeck Hills, it withstood the English Civil War as a Royalist stronghold, besieged twice, in 1643 and again in 1646, only to be destroyed on the orders of Parliament. The castle was given to the National Trust in 1982, along with neighbouring estate Kingston Lacy.

Old Harry Rocks

Less than 6 miles (9.7km) along the Purbeck Ridge to the east, Old Harry Rocks overlook the wide, sandy arc of Studland Bay. This triplet of chalk formations, just off the mainland at Handfast Point, marks the easternmost end of the Jurassic Coast World Heritage Site, 95 miles (153km) from its western extremity in the town of Exmouth, East Devon.

By Public Transport Train
station at Wareham, 4.5 miles
(7.2km). The bus service
Wiltshire and Dorset 40,
Poole to Swanage (passing
Wareham station). Corfe
Castle station (Swanage
Steam Railway) is a few
minutes walk away.

By Car The A351, Wareham to
Swanage, runs through Corfe
Castle village to National
Trust Castle View car park,
postcode BH20 5DR, 800
yards walk uphill.

OS Map Explorer OL15
Start / End National Trust
Castle View car park.
OS grid reference: SY959825

(Map showing: PH, Furzebrook, A351, Norden, B3351, Blue Pool, Norden Station, West Hill, Knowle Hill, Cocknowle, Corfe Castle, Church Knowle, PH, 500 m, N; numbered points 1, 2, 3, 4)

1. From the car park cross the A351 with care. Head to the right of the castle, following the Purbeck Way west along the base of the chalk ridge.

2. **0.9 miles/1.5km** Follow the Purbeck Way as it turns right and runs along the edge of a campsite, then turns left alongside woodland. Continue as the trail winds through the woods, crossing a footbridge and curving to the left around the north of the Blue Pool, eventually coming to a track junction with the Hardy Way.

3. **2.4 miles/3.9km** Turn left onto the Hardy Way, joining a lane and passing another campsite.

4. **3.2 miles/5.1km** Turn left off the road and onto a footpath, still following the Hardy Way as it climbs steeply to the top of the ridge. Turn left onto the main ridge path and follow this eastwards all the way back to Corfe Castle, descending steeply off the ridge and heading to the left of the castle to return to the car park.

Right: **Exploring the ruins of Corfe Castle.**

Other trails nearby

The Purbeck Way runs for 15.5 miles (25km) from Wareham Quay to Corfe Castle, passing Stoborough and Creech Heaths. At Corfe Castle either walk south to Chapman's Pool or east to Ballard Down – both finish at the Jurassic Coast where the South West Coast Path runs east to Poole or west all the way around the south-west peninsula to Minehead on the north Somerset coast. For a (much) longer adventure, the Hardy Way covers 220 miles (354km) of glorious and diverse Dorset and Wiltshire countryside.

15. Wellington Monument

Wellington Monument
Wellington
Near Taunton
Somerset
TA21 9PB

ABOUT THIS RUN

Distance 1.7 miles/2.8km
Ascent 236ft (72m)

Woodland
Steep steps
May be muddy
History/culture
Wildlife
Dogs welcome
Family friendly

This shorter run still packs plenty of interest – and a good hill – into its distance and is perfect for those getting started in off-road running, as a challenging hill for any runner, or as an enjoyable walk that's suitable for families. It lies within easy reach of the pretty town of Wellington and, being on the edge of the Blackdown Hills Area of Outstanding natural Beauty, there's plenty to explore further afield. This run begins along a majestic beech avenue, ascending to the monument across wildlife-rich grassland, peppered with field scabious, bird's-foot trefoil and lousewort. Listen out for green woodpeckers, with their distinctive yaffling calls, flying between the trees. The enjoyable loop from the monument includes a set of steep steps, and the section alongside the woods can get muddy, so a grippy pair of shoes is recommended.

Above: Beech woodland near the Wellington Monument.
Opposite: Wellington Monument.

THINGS TO SEE

The monument

Wellington Monument was constructed as a tribute to Arthur Wellesley, 1st Duke of Wellington, after the Battle of Waterloo. Standing at 175ft (53m), it is, today, the tallest three-sided obelisk in Britain; but it hasn't always been so. The result of an architectural competition, the original design was completed in the 1820s at 140ft (43m). Due to a lack of funds, the statue that was intended to stand on the top was never made, classifying it as an obelisk rather than a plinth. Lightning strikes caused severe damage in 1846 and the early 1850s, coinciding with the Duke's death, and several periods of repair and neglect followed. The National Trust took over ownership in 1934 and has been gradually restoring the monument; further restoration is likely to be undertaken in the future.

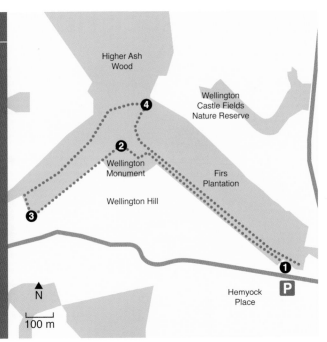

Higher Ash Wood

Wellington Castle Fields Nature Reserve

Wellington Monument

Firs Plantation

Wellington Hill

Hemyock Place

N

100 m

1. From the car park run along the beech-lined avenue until you emerge onto an area of grassland. Head straight across to the monument.

2. 0.5 miles/0.8km From the monument turn left into woodland, following National Trust waymarkers along the edge of a field, down some steps and through an earth bank.

3. 0.8 miles/1.2km Turn right and then right again, following the path through woodland back towards the monument. Go around the hill with the monument on your right.

4. 1.2 miles/1.9km Rejoin your outward path and follow this across grassland and back down the beech avenue to the car park.

Other trails nearby

The Blackdown Hills Area of Outstanding Natural Beauty covers 140 sq. miles (363 sq. km) along the Devon/Somerset border. An excellent network of footpaths and bridleways covers the area, perfect for further exploration.

16. Quantock Hills

Crowcombe Park Gate
car park
Holford
Taunton
TA4 4AR

ABOUT THIS RUN

Distance 5.7 miles (9.2km)
Ascent 1,105ft (337m)

Woodland
Summit
History/culture
Wildlife
Dogs welcome

The Quantock Hills run for about 15 miles (24km) between the Vale of Taunton Dean, north-west to Kilve and West Quantoxhead on the coast of the Bristol Channel. England's first Area of Outstanding Natural Beauty, designated in 1956, the Quantock Hills are a haven for a rich diversity of flora and fauna, from the many trees that cloak the sloping sides of the hills to Atlantic heathland. It is a special place to spot birds: look out for buzzards, skylarks, meadow pipits, redpolls, jays and yellowhammers.

This run follows the medieval Drove Road along the great ridge, climbing to the highest point of the hills, Wills Neck at 1,260ft (384m). On a clear day the views are superb, reaching to Glastonbury Tor and the Mendips in the east, the Gower Peninsula to the north, the Brendon Hills and Exmoor to the west, and the Blackdown Hills to the south. Dropping down to the valley at Triscombe there's a good climb up the flanks of the National Trust-owned Great Hill to finish.

Above, right and following page:
Running on the Quantock Hills.

THINGS TO SEE

The Drove Road
The medieval Drove Road that runs along the summit ridge of the Quantocks is part of King Alfred's Way – the route taken by Alfred the Great during the resistance to Viking invasion from Athelney, south-east of the Quantocks – and the Macmillan Way West, a long-distance footpath that runs for 102 miles (164km) from Castle Cary in Somerset to Barnstaple in Devon. Lined with beech trees on either side, the path is peppered with cairns and barrows dating back to the Bronze Age.

Literary inspiration
The Quantock Hills have inspired many great writers, including Samuel Taylor Coleridge, who wrote *The Rime of the Ancient Mariner* while he lived there, and Edward Thomas' *In Pursuit of Spring*, about a bicycle ride to the hills. John le Carré's novel *Tinker, Tailor, Soldier, Spy* opens in the Quantocks, while Wordsworth and his sister Dorothy lived at Alfoxton House in Holford in 1797 and 1798.

HOW TO GET HERE

By Public Transport Mainline trains to Taunton. First Bus 28 and Webber Bus 18, Taunton to Minehead; alight main road adjacent to Crowcombe village. Walk into village. From centre of Crowcombe (road junction between church and school) take road up Crowcombe Combe, signposted Over Stowey. A steep climb on a metalled road to cattle grid, then West Hill entrance stile.

By Car From north take junction 23/24 on M5. At Bridgwater take A39 towards Minehead, follow signs for Over Stowey then Crowcombe. West Hill entrance is on left just prior to descending the hill into Crowcombe. From south take junction 26/25 on M5. At Taunton take A358 to Crowcombe then drive up Crowcombe Combe. From centre of Crowcombe (road junction between church and school) take road up Crowcombe Combe, signposted Over Stowey. A steep climb on a metalled road to cattle grid, then West Hill entrance stile. From Minehead take A39/A358 to Crowcombe, then as before.

OS Map Explorer 140

Start / End National Trust Crowcombe Park Gate car park.

OS grid reference: ST150375

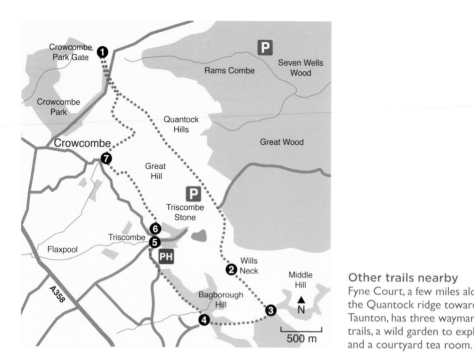

Crowcombe
Park Gate ❶

Crowcombe
Park

Rams Combe

Seven Wells
Wood

P

Quantock
Hills

Crowcombe

Great Wood

❼

Great
Hill

P

Triscombe
Stone

❻
Triscombe ❺
Flaxpool
PH

Wills
❷ Neck

Bagborough
Hill
❹

Middle
Hill

❸

▲
N

500 m

Other trails nearby
Fyne Court, a few miles along
the Quantock ridge towards
Taunton, has three waymarked
trails, a wild garden to explore
and a courtyard tea room.

1. From the car park run south along the
main Drove Road, also the Macmillan Way
West, following signs to Triscombe Stone. At the
Triscombe Stone parking area, continue straight
on through a gate, staying right where the path
forks and following the Macmillan Way West to
the summit of Wills Neck.

2. 2 miles/3.2km Continue following the
Macmillan Way West down the sloping ridge

of Wills Neck to reach a path junction with
a byway just before some trees.

3. 2.5 miles/4km Turn right onto the byway and
follow this downhill through trees, descending
Bagborough Hill.

4. 3 miles/4.8km As you emerge into open fields
just before Smokeham Farm, turn right at the track
junction and contour the base of the hill at the
edge of woodland. Eventually the path reaches a
narrow, wooded lane; turn right onto this and
follow it to a T-junction. Turn right and then take
the first lane on the right, signed with a blue
arrow, opposite the Blue Ball pub.

5. 3.9 miles/6.2km Where the lane bends to
the left, turn right through a gate and up a track.

6. 4 miles/6.4km Where the track forks, stay
left, contouring around the base of Great Hill.

7. 4.7 miles/7.5km At the track junction turn
right, following Little Quantock Combe back
to the Drove Road along the top of the ridge,
turning left to return along your outward route
to the car park.

17. Crook Peak

Parking area off
Webbington Road
Compton Bishop
Axbridge
Somerset
Nearest postcode
BS26 2HF

ABOUT THIS RUN

Distance 6 miles (9.7km)
Ascent 1,082ft (330m)

Summits
History/culture
Wildlife
Dogs under close control
  welcome

A summer run on the Mendip Hills is a joyful experience, with short-cropped, springy grass traced with clear ridge-top paths, and valleys either side carpeted in flowers. Over the wetter months, the hills can become very muddy, but pop on a pair of studded fell-running shoes and it only adds to the fun. This run takes in Crook Peak and Wavering Down, the westernmost tops of the Mendips, a range of grassy hills that stretch across Somerset to Frome in the east of the county. Starting through the villages and farmland at the foot of the hills, a winding woodland trail brings you out on a long, grassy ridge with a trail leading along its length. A final descent through limestone outcrops returns you to the start.

Above: Crook Peak, where skylarks soar and meadow pipits shoot up suddenly from the vegetation.

THINGS TO SEE

Crook Peak

From the M5 motorway – the closest many people get to experiencing it – Crook Peak's distinctive conical shape makes it look like a mini mountain, rising invitingly from the Somerset Levels. In fact, 'Crook' derives from an old English word cruc, meaning 'peak'. Despite its proximity to the motorway, the long ridgeline that curves in a horseshoe shape around to Wavering Down feels empty and wild, with extensive views of the Mendips, the Somerset Levels and across the Bristol Channel to Wales. The National Trust looks after just over 716 acres (290ha) of common land at this western end of the Mendip Hills, rebuilding drystone walls and managing woodland and scrub. This is also a place rich in wildlife and a designated Site of Special Scientific Interest – look out for dark green and small pearl-bordered fritillary butterflies and, if you're there in the evening, greater and lesser horseshoe bats that roost in the area's many caves.

1. From the car park, cross the road and follow the footpath bearing right alongside trees to the ridge of the hill. (Don't follow the path that goes straight ahead through the gate – this is your return route). Cross straight over the ridge path and bear left, downhill and through woodland. The path joins into the top of Vicarage Lane – follow this downhill to reach a T-junction.

2. 0.4 miles/0.7km Turn left and run uphill, bearing right down Church Lane where the road forks. Just after the church, where the road curves to the right, go straight ahead up a track with a footpath sign. Follow this track, continuing straight ahead at junctions, until it brings you out onto the road at Cross. Turn left and run through the village, taking care of any traffic.

3. 2.2 miles/3.5km After the White Hart pub and some houses on your left take a bridleway left and uphill. Follow this as it skirts around the hills through woodland to reach a path junction just before the road at Winscombe Hill – there is an alternative car park here, ideal for a fantastic out-and-back run along the ridge.

4. 3.1 miles/5km Turn left onto the West Mendip Way and follow this along the ridgeline and over the tops of first Wavering Down and then Crook Peak.

5. 5.4 miles/8.7km From the summit of Crook Peak, turn left and head south-east down the long ridgeline trail. Keep an eye out for the parking area coming into view on your right, dropping off the ridge to the right to reach the gate and crossing the road to finish.

Other trails nearby
There's a fantastic network of trails to explore along the length of the Mendip Hills, including Cheddar Gorge, the largest gorge in England, where the northern half is owned by the National Trust.

HOW TO GET HERE

By Public Transport Trains to Weston-super-Mare, 9 miles (14.4km). First bus 126, Weston-Super-Mare (passing close to train station) to Wells, alight at Winscombe.

By Car The Mendip Hills are located between M5 junctions 21 and 22. Crook Peak and Wavering Down are 2 miles (3.2km) west of Axbridge.

By Bicycle Strawberry Line (National Cycle Network route 26) is an 8-mile (12.9km) trail linking Cheddar to King's Wood, leading to Wavering Down and Crook Peak.

OS Map Explorer 141

Start / End Parking area on Webbington Road south of Compton Bishop (not NT). OS grid reference: ST392550

Opposite and left: Exploring Crook Peak.

18. Tyntesfield

Wraxall
Bristol
North Somerset
BS48 1NX

ABOUT THIS RUN

Distance 3.1 miles (5km)
Ascent 426ft (130m)

Good trails and paths,
  some grassy sections
Waymarked route
Urban escape
Wildlife
History/culture
Family friendly
Dog friendly

The Grade I-listed Victorian Gothic revival mansion at Tyntesfield stands grandly amidst over 540 acres (219ha) of green rolling parkland. Just a few miles from Bristol, this is a perfect place to escape the pavements and experience the joys of running on woodland trails and over springy open grassland. A free Trust10 event is held around two laps of this route every month apart from May and August or, alternatively, you can follow the waymarked 5K course at any time during opening hours, free to enjoy the surroundings without worrying about map reading. Starting and finishing at Home Farm, this route takes in a varied loop of the grounds with plenty of hills. Accessing the route does require payment or NT membership so please check in at reception before heading out for your run.

Above: Sunset over the parkland at Tyntesfield.
Opposite: Running at Tyntesfield.

THINGS TO SEE

The estate

There's a wonderful variety of things grazing and growing at Tyntesfield, including sheep and cattle (their milk makes cheese for the excellent cheese scones on sale in the Cow Barn restaurant and Pavilion café on the estate). These grazers help keep the grass under control and their trampling and dung promote wildlife such as beetles, bats and wildflowers. Fruit and vegetables, picked by volunteers from the kitchen garden, are used for the restaurant and are also available to buy. Work is also underway to restore orchards to the estate, and the first new trees were planted in 2014 following the lines of 19th-century hedgerows. Future planting will bring a range of native trees to the orchard, including apples, pears, mulberries, damsons, quince and walnuts.

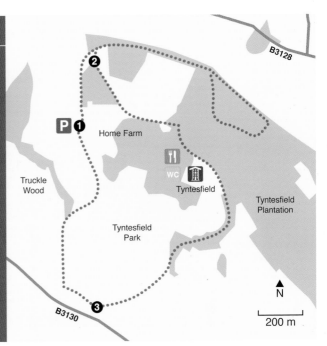

B3128

Home Farm

Truckle Wood

Tyntesfield

Tyntesfield Plantation

Tyntesfield Park

B3130

▲ N

200 m

Other trails nearby
Ashton Court (not NT) has an excellent network of running trails, including a 5k (3-mile) parkrun and it also has several mountain-bike trails.

1. From the start at Home Farm, follow Trust10 signs north with trees on your right. Turn right and cross the main drive, running up the pathway signposted to Summerhouse Cottage.

2. 1.4 miles/2.3km On rejoining the main drive, turn left and follow this towards the mansion, bearing left at the grass triangle. Run to the left of the mansion and follow the path as it curves to the right, passing the kitchen garden on your left.

3. 2.5 miles/4.1km Just before you reach the road, turn right and follow the footpath across grassland to meet a track. Turn right here and follow the track as it runs steadily uphill, weaving through areas of woodland to return to Home Farm.

19. Bath Skyline

| Claverton Down |
| Bath |
| BA2 7BR |

ABOUT THIS RUN

Distance **3.1 miles (5km)**
Ascent 180ft (55m)

Gravel, grass and surfaced
    paths. One flight of steps
Urban escape
History/culture
Wildlife
Dogs welcome

Starting less than 1 mile (1.6km) from the city centre, take in the grassy meadows, ancient woodlands and secluded valleys that rise high above the city to form the Bath Skyline. Escape the crowds that flock to Bath and instead immerse yourself in soothing birdsong, leafy woodland and glorious views out across the city and beyond. There are plenty of surprises along the way too, including gentle herds of cattle, part of a conservation grazing project, Prior Park Landscape Garden, and the almost two-dimensional Sham Castle, a short detour off the main route, built for local entrepreneur and philanthropist Ralph Allen in 1762. This run takes in a shorter section of the Bath Skyline, on a course used for the weekly parkrun.

Above: Running on the Bath Skyline.

THINGS TO SEE

Beautiful Bath

A combination of grand Georgian architecture and honey-coloured stone brings a rare beauty to Bath, particularly on summer evenings when the buildings seem to glow gold in the sun. An easy stroll along Great Pulteney Street followed by a coffee overlooking the much-photographed weir below Pulteney Bridge is a fitting way to relax after a run around Bath's famously steep hills. Or head to the Thermae Bath Spa, the only place in Britain where you can still bathe in water from natural hot springs. As a UNESCO World Heritage Site, the city draws millions of visitors each year, yet the winding side streets are alive with chic cafés and interesting shops and never see the crowds that flock to the popular tourist spots. The National Trust's Prior Park Landscape Garden with its rare Palladian bridge, waymarked walks and sweeping grassy valley lies on the southern edge of the city, just five minutes from the Skyline route.

HOW TO GET HERE

By Public Transport Bath Spa station is 0.8 miles (1.3km) from the start (point 1 on the map). From the city centre bus station take the 2 bus to Hadley Arms. Then walk along Claverton Down Road until the zebra crossing, then take a left onto the cycle path.

By Car Directions are for drop-off only as there is no on-site parking. From the M4 motorway, exit at J18 and take A46 towards Bath. At the A46/A4 junction, follow signs for A4 West towards Bath. After 1 mile (1.6km), turn left at traffic lights onto A36 towards the city centre. Follow A36 signs to Bristol and turn left at the first roundabout onto Bathwick Hill. Continue onto Claverton Down Road, passing Bath University on your left. The site entrance can be accessed from North Road / Claverton Down Road, opposite Shaft Road.

By Bicycle National Cycle Network route 4 passes through Bath. Follow route 4 until you reach Bathwick Hill. Go up Bathwick Hill, take a right at Copseland, go straight across to Quarry Farm Road and follow the cycle path until it goes past a playing field on the right. The route starts in the next field on the right.

OS Map Explorer 155

Start / End Free Fields.
OS grid reference: ST765629

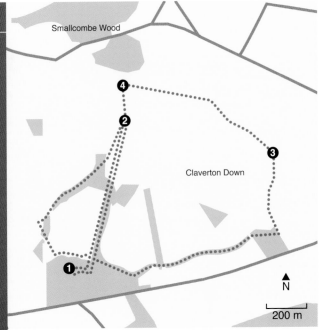

Smallcombe Wood

Claverton Down

N

200 m

1. The course consists of a small loop followed by a long anti-clockwise loop around Claverton Down. From the start at Free Fields, turn left and follow the path around the playing field. Go down a rocky slope and follow the path, keeping the views of Bath on your left. Go up the wooden steps and take the path straight through the field.

2. 0.7 miles/1.2km When you reach the gravel cycle path take a right and follow it down until you reach a wooden gate into the woods on your left. Follow the path through the woods, past the woodland play area and take a left at the junction.

3. 2 miles/3.2km Follow the footpath until you reach another wooden gate on your left. Go across the field, with the farm on your right. Go through the wooden gate. Follow the path, through another three gates. Go diagonally across the large open field until you reach the cycle path.

4. 2.5 miles/4km Turn left onto the cycle path and follow it straight ahead to return to the start.

Other trails nearby
Walk to the View is a 3-mile (4.8km) route from the city centre out to the countryside and back, or there's a 2-mile (3.2km) route around the Family Discovery Trail that is accessible for pushchairs and wheelchairs.

20. Lacock

Hither Way
Lacock
Chippenham
SN15 2LG

ABOUT THIS RUN

Distance 1.9 miles (3km)
Ascent 89ft (27m)

Riverside trails, grass,
  quiet road
May be muddy
History/culture
Family friendly
Wildlife
Dogs welcome on leads
  on this route and in
  the abbey grounds
  1 November–31 March
  only.

The pretty medieval village of Lacock, with its timber-frame cottages and stunning abbey, almost all of which is looked after by the National Trust, is set amidst rolling Wiltshire countryside and near to the River Avon. Walking up the main street it feels as though you've been transported back 800 years, making Lacock a fascinating place to visit and one much treasured by film-makers. This run takes you on an easy yet enjoyable loop around the abbey, starting and finishing in the village and heading out to explore the fields and farmland, including a delightful stretch alongside the River Avon, as it flows through the valley of Snaylesmeade. Please take care on road crossings and be aware of livestock on the route, particularly if you're running with a dog.

Above: Lacock Abbey, founded in the early 13th century.
Opposite: The Mechlin Pot of 1500 was said to have been used as a cooking pot for the nuns of the abbey.

THINGS TO SEE

Magical Lacock

If you're a Harry Potter fan there's lots to see at Lacock. Wander around the village spotting scenes from the films including the 15th-century former wool merchant's house, now a pub, that stood in for the Babberton Arms in *Harry Potter and the Half-Blood Prince*, and Harry's house from the *Harry Potter and the Philosopher's Stone*. Head for the abbey, once a medieval nunnery, and its ornate cloisters that has formed part of Hogwarts and also featured in the acclaimed television production of *Wolf Hall*, as well as *Fantastic Beasts: The Crimes of Grindelwald*. In one of the adjoining rooms a giant cauldron could easily be straight from Harry Potter, but it was made in Antwerp in 1500.

HOW TO GET HERE

By Public Transport
Chippenham train station is 4.8 miles (7.7km) away. Then bus service X34/First 234 Chippenham to Frome.
By Car 4.8 miles (7.7km) south of Chippenham. M4, exit junction 17, signposted to Chippenham (A350). Follow A350 (signposted Poole/Warminster) until you reach Lacock, then follow signs for main car park.
By Bicycle National Cycle Network 403 runs along a short section of the route.
OS Map Explorer 156
Start / End National Trust Lacock car park.
OS grid reference: ST917682

Reybridge

N

100 m

R. Avon

A350

St Cyriac's Church

Lacock

Lacock Abbey

WC

PH

Fox Talbot Museum

P

1. From the car park, cross the road and follow the brown tourist signs into the village, where you'll emerge in front of the Fox Talbot Museum and entrance to Lacock Abbey. Run along the High Street then turn right onto East Street, passing the Tithe Barn and then the Village Hall.

2. 0.3 miles/0.5km Turn left just before the church and follow the lane, passing houses and allotments. At the end of the houses, bear right on a footpath straight across a field, heading between the two buildings in the far-right corner to reach a road. Turn right onto the road and then right again over the bridge.

3. 0.7 miles/1.2km Just after the bridge take the footpath on the right, running across fields following the course of the River Avon, with the river to your right. Continue to follow the riverside path until you reach a road.

4. 1.6 miles/2.5km Turn right onto the road and follow it, with care, back to the car park.

Other trails nearby
There's an extensive network of footpaths exploring the area, including the longer-distance routes of the Kennet and Avon Canal (95 miles/152km), the White Horse Trail (94 miles/151km) and the Mid-Wilts Way (68 miles/109km).

21. Avebury

Avebury
Marlborough
Wiltshire
SN8 1RD

ABOUT THIS RUN

Distance 6.2 miles (10km)
Ascent 344ft (105m)

Family friendly
History/culture
Wildlife
Dogs welcome (apart from
    in Avebury Manor and
    garden and café)

This run takes you on a journey through the ancient open landscape around Avebury, recognised as a World Heritage Site for its wealth of Neolithic and Bronze Age remnants. This circular route follows the popular Trust10 run, held on the fourth Sunday of every month, beginning outside Avebury chapel, along the Ridgeway, and finishing back at Avebury. Take in sweeping views over the surrounding landscape, with some challenging climbs to get to them. The terrain is a mix of tarmacked roads, grassy tracks and footpaths; some of which are rutted and can get muddy. There are pink Trust10 makers along the way to guide you.

Other trails nearby
There's huge potential for many more routes taking in the vast network of excellent trails in the area surrounding Avebury. Explore further afield on the sweeping chalk grasslands of the Marlborough Downs, creating links between the White Horse Trail, Wessex Ridgeway and Ridgeway National Trail.

THINGS TO SEE

The Stones and henge
Dating back to 2850–2200BC, Avebury's vast henge – a Neolithic circular earthwork consisting of a bank and a ditch – runs for over 0.7 miles (1.2km) around the village. Set within this, a large outer stone circle, that once would have consisted of around 100 stones, contains two smaller inner circles, all made from local sarsen stone. A square-shaped stone monument has also recently been discovered on the site that may be one of the very earliest structures here. The West Kennet Avenue, down which this run finishes, was once a ceremonial route, linking the henge to a timber and stone circle known as the Sanctuary.

Silbury Hill
Part of the Avebury World Heritage Site, and a Site of Special Scientific Interest, Silbury Hill is the largest artificial mound in Europe. This mysterious conical hill compares in height and volume to the roughly contemporary Egyptian pyramids, dating to around 2400BC. While it is not thought to have been a burial mound, its purpose and significance remain unknown.

Above: The stones at Avebury.
Opposite: Running on the Ridgeway at Avebury.

HOW TO GET HERE

By Public Transport Swindon train station is 11 miles (17.7km) away. Bus service 49 operates an hourly service from Swindon to Avebury and stops at The Red Lion pub.

By Car 6 miles (9.7km) west of Marlborough on the A4361. Main car park is a short distance from the stone circle and facilities in the Old Farmyard. Parking pay and display; National Trust and English Heritage members free. Overnight parking prohibited. Please respect the community and do not park on the village streets; SatNav use SN8 1RD to find the main visitor car park.

By Bicycle National Cycle Network routes 4 and 45.

OS Map Explorer 157

Start / End National Trust Avebury car park.

OS grid reference: SU099696

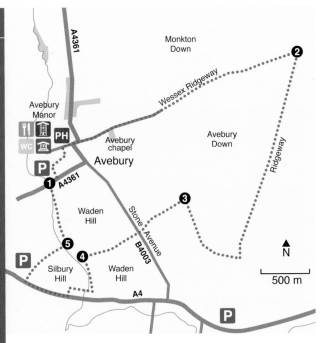

1. From the car park, walk to Avebury chapel, taking care when crossing the main road at The Red Lion pub. Here the 6.2-mile (10km) run begins. Head straight on along the tarmac road and up the chalk track that ascends to the Ridgeway.

2. Turn right, signposted 'Ridgeway' with a Trust10 marker. After 1.2 miles (2km), as the path slopes down, turn right down a grassy footpath, signposted 'Byway', past a gate on the left.

3. Turn left at an unsigned grass track and follow this downhill until you reach the road (B4003). Take care when crossing the road and enter the field opposite through the left of two wooden gates. Continue straight on, heading up to the top of Waden Hill and straight down the other side, until you reach the footpath at the bottom.

4. At the junction, turn left and follow the footpath along the fence. Just before the road, turn sharp right and go through two pedestrian gates. Turn left through a gate and onto a tarmacked pavement along the A4. At Silbury Hill car park, follow the footpath off to the right through a metal gate, signposted 'Avebury 1 mile', until you reach a bridge.

5. Straight after the bridge turn left through a wooden gate with a Trust10 marker, and follow the path back towards Avebury, until it reaches the road. Cross the road with extreme caution and you are back at the National Trust car park.

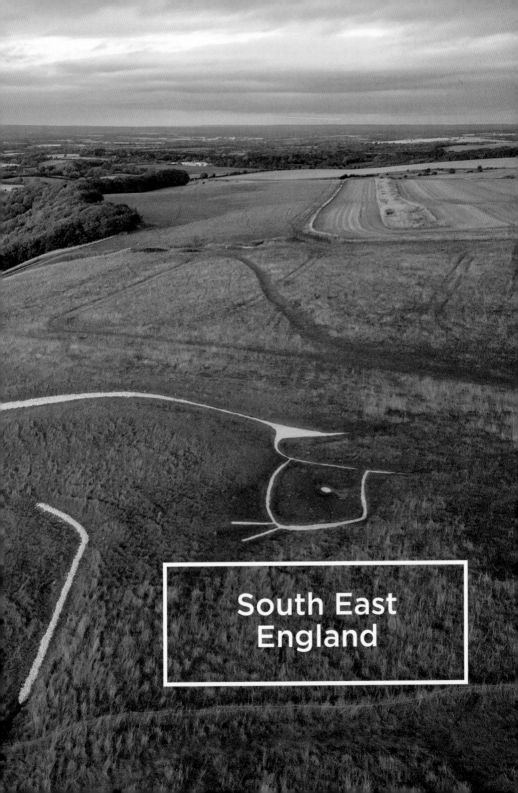

South East
England

22. The Needles, Isle of Wight

High Down Chalk
 Pit car park
Isle of Wight
Nearest postcode
PO39 0HY

ABOUT THIS RUN

Distance 5.9 miles (9.4km)
Ascent 745ft (227m)

Coastal
Woodland
History/culture
Family friendly
Dogs welcome
Wildlife
Take care on cliff edges

Lying just 2 miles (3.2km) off the coast of Hampshire at its closest point, the Isle of Wight is a county in its own right and Britain's second most populous island. This run explores the island's western reaches, taking in the iconic Needles and the open, grass- and gorse-covered downland at Tennyson Down. Visit its prominent monument to Alfred, Lord Tennyson, who moved to West Wight in the 1870s and wrote some of his best-known pieces here. Heading out through fields and farmland to reach the end of Tennyson Down, the route then turns towards the coast, with a long, breathtaking section along the high chalk cliffs all the way to the Needles, passing the Tennyson Monument, the highest point on the cliffs at 482ft (147m). The final miles return inland, through peaceful woodland and fields.

Above: The Needles, Isle of Wight.
Opposite: Running on the Isle of Wight.

THINGS TO SEE

Sporting heritage
The Isle of Wight has a strong sporting and outdoors heritage. The Isle of Wight Challenge is a long distance walking/running event with distances up to 66 miles (106km) (www.isleofwightchallenge.com).

There's also a walking festival, held each spring; over 200 miles (322km) of cycleways and an annual cycling festival; Cowes Week – the oldest and largest annual sailing regatta in the world; and the Isle of Wight Marathon – the UK's oldest continuously held marathon, which has been run every year since 1957.

The Needles and the Batteries
One of Britain's best-known landmarks, the Needles are the visible remains of a chalk ridge that it is thought once connected the Isle of Wight to Old Harry Rocks on the Dorset coast, 20 miles (32.2km) away, until the Solent River breached the ridge, creating the Isle of Wight. Originally four rocks, the fourth – the tallest and most needle-shaped – collapsed during fierce storms in 1764.

HOW TO GET HERE

By Ferry Wightlink from Yarmouth, 4 miles (6.4km); Fishbourne, 18 miles (30km); Red Funnel from East Cowes, 18 miles (30km).
By Public Transport Bus service 7, Newport to Alum Bay, half-hourly.
By Car B3322 from Yarmouth/ Totland or Alum Bay road from Freshwater Bay. Nearest postcode is PO39 0HY. By Bicycle The 'Round the Island' National Cycle Network Regional Route 67 passes through Freshwater Bay.
OS Map Explorer OL29
Start / End National Trust High Down Chalk Pit car park.
OS grid reference: SZ324855

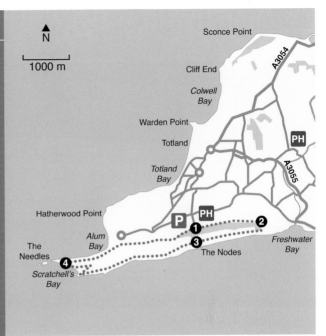

Perched high above the Needles, the Old Battery is a Victorian fort, built in 1862 and used during both World Wars. The world's first radio station was set up by Marconi in 1897 at the Battery and, in 1898, the first paid wireless telegram (called a Marconigram) was sent from here. Today you can enjoy a cup of tea at the Old Battery, accompanied by some of the best views around.

1. From the start, head east, following a footpath that runs between the wooded slopes of Tennyson Down and the fields below.

2. 0.9 miles/1.5km Turn right where the woods end, before reaching the buildings and road at Freshwater Bay. At the coast path, turn right again and follow this with the sea on your left, until you reach Tennyson's Monument.

3. 2 miles/3.2km From the monument you can turn right and cut across to the finish, however, to complete the full run, continue along the coast path all the way to the Old Battery on the headland, overlooking the Needles.

4. 4 miles/6.5km From the Old Battery, continue following the coast path up the opposite coast. At the Needles car park, leave the coast path and continue straight ahead, running along the base of Tennyson Down to return to the car park.

Other trails nearby

The Isle of Wight is a joy to explore on foot, with trails through fields, forests and an incredible 64 miles (103km) of coastal paths.

23. Birling Gap

**Birling Gap Road
Wealden
BN20 0AB**

ABOUT THIS RUN

Distance **4.8 miles (7.7km)**
Ascent **856ft (261m)**

Coastal
History/culture
Family friendly
Dogs welcome
Wildlife
Take care on cliff edges

Birling Gap, east of the Seven Sisters chalk cliffs on the East Sussex coast, is a small, National Trust-owned hamlet that's ideally placed for exploring this fascinating area. Seen from the South Downs Way, running along the clifftops, the undulating land seems to rise and fall like the waves. Inland, a green swathe of ancient downland, rich in wild flora and fauna, gives way in all directions to wide views of Friston Forest, the rolling Sussex countryside and out across the sparkling sea. This run takes in a wonderfully varied landscape, starting along the South Downs Way at Birling Gap and then heading over the chalk downland to the hamlet of Crowlink, finishing along the coast above the Seven Sisters.

Other trails nearby
The South Downs Way National Trail runs for nearly 100 miles (160km) between Winchester and Eastbourne, right across the South Downs National Park. Friston Forest, just to the north of this route, has an excellent network of trails for exploring on foot or bike.

THINGS TO SEE

More about Birling Gap
Nestled between the better-known Beachy Head and Seven Sisters, the hamlet of Birling Gap houses a National Trust café, shop and visitor centre along with a row of former coastguard cottages. Some of the buildings have already been claimed by coastal erosion, which is reducing this stretch of coastline at a rate of up to 3.3ft (1m) a year, while others remain inhabited. The beach at Birling Gap, also a marine nature reserve, is excellent for exploring, with rock pools and areas of pebbles and sand.

Disappearing history
This dramatic section of East Sussex coastline has been inhabited by humans for millennia, a story that archaeologists are piecing together from the area's many ancient monuments and intriguing finds.

The hilltop enclosure of Belle Tout, sited above Birling Gap, is thought to have been the largest prehistoric enclosure in Britain some 5,000 years ago, while the prominent ridge at Baileys Hill features several Bronze Age burial mounds, along with evidence of settlement and farming.

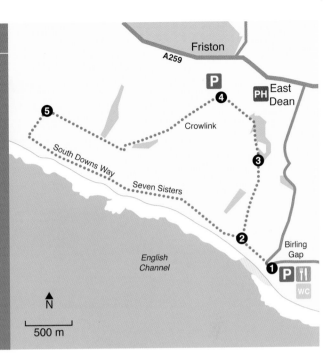

HOW TO GET HERE

By Public Transport
Eastbourne station 5.5 miles
(8.9km); Seaford station 8
miles (12.9km). Bus 13X runs
Eastbourne Terminus Road to
Brighton via Birling Gap –
seasonal timetable variations.
By Car 5 miles (8km) west of
Eastbourne and 6 miles east
of Seaford. Birling Gap car
park is signposted from A259
at East Dean, between
Seaford and Eastbourne.
Parking at Birling Gap (pay
and display).
OS Map Explorer 123
Start / End: Car park at
eastern end of Birling
Gap (not NT).
OS grid reference: TV566954

N

500 m

1. From the start, follow the South Downs Way west through Birling Gap.

2. 1.2 miles/1.9km After the last house in Birling Gap, turn right, leaving the South Downs Way and heading inland across the downs.

3. 1.8 miles/2.9km Where the track forks, bear left and run north-west across the downs to the car park at Crowlink.

4. 2.3 miles/3.7km Turn left onto a bridleway and follow this through the hamlet of Crowlink and down Gap Bottom. About 220 yards (200m)

from the coast, bear right and follow a trail across the grassland parallel to the coast.

5. 2.7 miles/4.4km Turn left to reach the coast path, turning left again onto the South Downs Way and following this along the coast all the way back to Birling Gap.

Opposite: Birling Gap and the Seven Sisters.
Below: Belle Tout lighthouse can be spotted in the distance along the route.

24. Ditchling Beacon ①Ⓟ

Ditchling Beacon
West Sussex
BN1 9QD

ABOUT THIS RUN

Distance **4.3 miles (7km)**
Ascent **610ft (186m)**

Well-maintained tracks and
trails, some uneven
sections
History/culture
Wildlife
Family friendly
Dogs welcome

Nestled in a haven of green just a few miles north of bustling
Brighton, Ditchling Beacon is the highest point in East
Sussex. This run starts and finishes at the beacon – make
sure you detour to the summit for outstanding 360-degree
views to the sea in the south, north to the Weald and across
the Downs to either side. Heading out along the South
Downs Way, the run crosses wildlife-rich Ditchling Down,
following a grassy ridge (take care – the ridge drops away
exhilaratingly to your right). The route then traces the
Sussex Border Path south, finally winding through farmland
and grassy valleys to return to the Beacon.

Above: View to Ditchling Beacon.
There are fine views from the top.

THINGS TO SEE

South Downs National Park
England's newest national park, designated
in 2011, the South Downs cover an area of
628 sq. miles (1,627 sq. km) across the counties
of Hampshire, West Sussex and East Sussex. The
Park encompasses the chalk hills of the South
Downs, including the white coastal cliffs of the
Seven Sisters and Beachy Head, as well as the
western Weald, with its heavily wooded
sandstone and clay hills.
   The South Downs Way, running 100 miles
(161km) between Winchester in the west and
Eastbourne in the east, passes close to Ditchling
Beacon and is the only National Trail that lies
wholly within a national park.

Downland wildlife
Ditchling Beacon Nature Reserve is managed by
the Sussex Wildlife Trust, using conservation
grazing to control scrub on the chalk downland.
The resulting pockets of grassland are rich in
wildflowers, including many common and rare
orchids. The old grass-covered chalk pits and
scrubland at Ditchling Down, with its small copse
of whitebeam trees – a rare sight in the wild in
southern England – provides an ideal habitat for
green hairstreak and marbled white butterflies.
Look out for vast numbers of farmland birds
during the warmer months and flocks of linnet
and red-brown kestrels hovering overhead
throughout the year.

By Public Transport Mainline trains to Brighton; Falmer 4 miles (6.4km), Hassocks station 5 miles (8km). Bus service 79 from Brighton to Ditchling Beacon. Weekends and public holidays in the winter – please check before travelling.

By Car From central Brighton, follow Ditchling Road from St Peter's Church (just off London Road). Continue straight, crossing A27, for 5 miles (8km) to Ditchling Beacon car park. A27 (from Brighton), turn off A27 at Hollingbury, go straight at roundabout, then sharp left onto Ditchling Road (signposted Ditchling). Continue north along Ditchling Road to Ditchling Beacon car park.

On Foot or Bicycle Ditchling Beacon is on the South Downs Way National Trail and bridleway.

OS Map Explorer OL11

Start / End: National Trust Ditchling Beacon car park.

OS grid reference: TQ333129

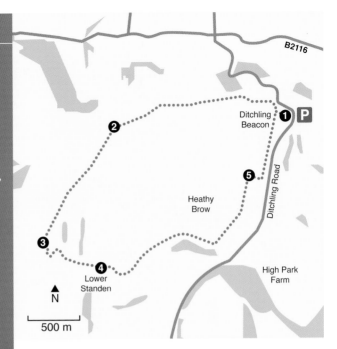

Other trails nearby
The South Downs Way passes Ditchling Beacon along its 100-mile (161km) route between Winchester in Hampshire and Eastbourne on the East Sussex coast. The Sussex Border Path, which this run joins briefly, is a linear walking trail of 137 miles (220km) following the old inland border of Sussex (now divided into East Sussex and West Sussex) between Thorney Island and Rye.

1. Take the chalk and flint path leading out of the back of the car park in a westerly direction and continue along the chalk ridge, passing a trig point on the left.

2. 1.1 miles/1.8km At the path junction, turn left onto the Sussex Border Path and follow this south, with fine views across to the sea.

3. 2 miles/3.2km Turn right, leaving the Sussex Border Path and following a bridleway past Lower Standen farm.

4. 2.5 miles/4km Continue following the bridleway into the tree-lined valley at North Bottom, then as it heads north, parallel to Ditchling Road.

5. 3.7 miles/5.9km Turn right off the bridleway and cross to the parallel path nearer to the road, continuing north to return to Ditchling Beacon.

25. Harting Down

Harting Down
Near South Harting
South Downs
West Sussex
Nearest postcode
GU31 5PN

ABOUT THIS RUN

Distance **3.7 miles (6km)**
Ascent **735ft (224m)**

Good paths and trails
National Trail
History/culture
Wildlife
Dogs welcome

This route takes in the pristine chalk downland surrounding Harting Down in West Sussex, a haven for wildlife that's also dotted with fascinating remnants of human history. The run heads out along the South Downs Way, tracing the crest of the downs from where there are far-reaching views out across the Weald towards the North Downs to the north and across the Solent to the Isle of Wight in the south. A long, snaking descent takes you through rolling fields and farmland before the final miles link up long, hidden valleys and follow winding trails through leafy woodland and across open scrub, climbing back up to finish on the main ridge of the downs.

Above and opposite: Snow on Harting Down. Even if the conditions are not right for a run, a brisk walk here is still exhilarating.

THINGS TO SEE

Dramatic downs

One of the largest areas of chalk downland looked after by the National Trust, Harting Down boasts a beautiful mixture of sheep-cropped grassy hilltops, secluded valleys, scrub and woodland – a diverse range of habitats that nurtures a rich variety of wildlife.

Skylarks chatter overhead; songbirds flit between the trees and shrubs, including the native common juniper; red kites, sparrowhawks and buzzards hunt in the vast, open skies; and mice and voles rustle in the undergrowth. The

area is also buzzing with insect life, and many butterflies, including the grizzled skipper and the rare Duke of Burgundy fritillary, as well as the blue carpenter bee and cheese snail can be seen. On a summer evening you might even spot glow-worms lighting the brambled edges of Round Down.

Intriguing evidence of human activity includes an Iron Age hill fort and cross-ridge dykes, as well as the remains of a telegraph station from the Napoleonic Wars located on Beacon Hill, the highest point on Harting Down.

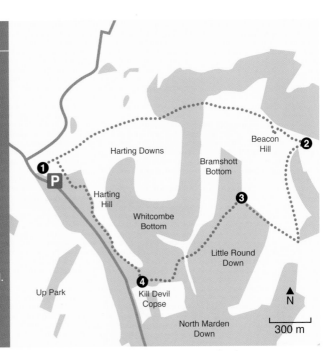

By Public Transport
Petersfield train station is 5.5 miles (8.9km) away. Bus stop in South Harting, 1 mile (1.6km) away. Bus service 54, Petersfield to Chichester; 91, Petersfield to Midhurst; X72, Alton to Midhurst.

On Foot Public footpaths from South Harting. Harting Down is on the South Downs Way National Trail.

By Car 5.5 miles (8.9km) miles south-east of Petersfield; 1 mile (1.6km) south of South Harting off the B2141. Nearest postcode GU31 5PN.

OS Map Explorer 120

Start / End National Trust Harting Down car park.

OS grid reference: SU791180

1. From the car park, follow signs to Harting Down, running along the South Downs Way in an easterly direction. Continue along the South Downs Way as it rises and falls, eventually climbing over Beacon Hill, with its trig point-topped summit, and descending the other side.

2. **1.4 miles/2.3km** Turn right and follow the footpath south, with trees and a valley to your left, descending gently to reach a path junction just above Telegraph House. Turn right here, following the South Downs Way with trees on your left.

3. **2.3 miles/3.7km** Take the first path left, running downhill through trees to reach a path junction just before the road.

4. **2.9 miles/4.7km** Turn right and run north, parallel to the road, back to the car park.

Other trails nearby

The South Downs Way runs for 100 miles (161km) between Winchester and Eastbourne, right across the South Downs National Park. To the north of Harting Down, the Sussex Border Path runs along the old county boundary between Thorney Island and Rye, a distance of 137 miles (220km).

26. Sissinghurst

Sissinghurst Castle
Biddenden Road
Near Cranbrook
Kent
TN17 2AB

ABOUT THIS RUN

Distance 3 miles (4.8km)
Ascent 236ft (72m)

Grassy footpaths, quiet
  lane, surfaced tracks
May be muddy/slippery
  in parts
History/culture
Wildlife
Dogs welcome in estate
  – not garden

Set in the High Weald of Kent, Sissinghurst Castle was the 1930s home of poet and writer, Vita Sackville-West, and her diplomat and author husband, Harold Nicolson. Together they worked to transform the former manor house and its garden into a celebration of their combined creative vision.

Today, Sissinghurst's famous gardens are a delight to walk around and the surrounding 450-acre (182ha) estate offers plenty of opportunity for running, too. This route begins at the castle, heading straight into open fields and farmland and along the edge of Saw Lodge Wood. After half a mile (0.8km) of easy running along the peaceful, and brilliantly-named, Digdog Lane, there's an enjoyable run through fields back to the castle. The final loop takes you through Roundshill Park Wood and up through gently sloping grassland to return to the start.

Other trails nearby

Roundshill Park Wood, to the south of the castle and also part of the Sissinghurst estate, has a network of trails to explore, winding through deciduous trees. Further south, across the A262, Hemsted Forest, managed by Forestry England, is also great to explore on foot. The High Weald Landscape Trail is a 90-mile (145km) route between Horsham, West Sussex and Rye, East Sussex, passing through the main landscape types of the High Weald Area of Outstanding Natural Beauty.

Above: The Rose Garden at Sissinghurst.
Opposite: The White Garden at Sissinghurst.
Following page: Blackberry Lane on the Sissinghurst estate.

THINGS TO SEE

The garden

'The heavy golden sunshine enriched the old brick with a kind of patina, and made the tower cast a long shadow across the grass, like the finger of a gigantic sundial veering slowly with the sun. Everything was hushed and drowsy and silent but for the coo of the white pigeons', wrote Vita Sackville-West of her garden at Sissinghurst. And, even though it attracts over 200,000 visitors each year, wandering around the garden on a warm summer afternoon, this could easily have been written today.

Overlooked by the 16th-century castle tower, one of the few remnants of the former manor house, the garden is divided into areas, each filled with informal arrangements of plants around a variety of themes: the White Garden, the Purple Border, the Rose Garden, the Herb Garden, the Lime Walk and the Cottage Garden. The orchard is another echo of the estate's past, kept by Sackville-West and Nicolson for its disordered planting, in contrast to the rest of the garden.

HOW TO GET HERE

By Public Transport Regular train service to Staplehurst from London Charing Cross. From here take bus service 5 to Sissinghurst.
By Car 2 miles (3.2km) north east of Cranbrook, 1 mile (1.6km) east of Sissinghurst village on A262.
OS Map Explorer 136
Start / End: National Trust Sissinghurst car park.
OS grid reference: TQ807384

N

200 m

Saw Lodge Wood

Sissinghurst Castle and Gardens

Roundshill Park Wood

A262

1. Turn left out of the car park and follow the track north-west to reach a bridleway at the edge of Saw Lodge Wood. Turn right onto the bridleway and follow this until it reaches the road at Digdog Lane.

2. 0.8 miles/1.3km Turn right onto the lane and follow it for about half a mile (0.8km), crossing a bridge at the halfway point, until you can turn right onto a public bridleway across fields. Follow this until you reach the corner of the castle gardens.

3. 1.7 miles/2.7km Turn left and follow the track past the gardens and straight on between the ponds and into the woods. Turn right after the ponds and follow the main path along the edge of the woods until you reach their western boundary.

4. 2.3 miles/3.7km Turn right, leaving the woods and crossing the main track. Continue trending north to reach the bridleway just west of where you joined it in point 1. Turn right here and then right again to return to the car park.

27. Scotney Castle

Lamberhurst
Tunbridge Wells
Kent
TN3 8JN

ABOUT THIS RUN

Distance **2 miles (3.2km)**
Ascent **203ft (62m)**

Grassy paths and quiet
    lane, steps
Waymarked route
History/culture
Family friendly
Wildlife
Dogs welcome on leads

Nestled within the Bewl Valley in Kent, Scotney Castle estate boasts the romantic partial ruins of a 14th-century moated castle and a grand Victorian country mansion with a fascinating history. Surrounding the castle are 780 acres (316ha) of ancient, Grade I-listed parkland including 300 acres (121ha) of Wealden woodlands, crisscrossed by waymarked trails and perfect for exploring at a run. This route follows the enjoyable Parkland Trail, taking in the gently undulating terrain around the park and the many viewpoints offering picturesque scenes of the estate. Starting at the house it traces the perimeter of the garden with views of the old castle and moat before heading out across open grassland. After the River Bewl the final stretch winds its way pleasantly back along quiet lanes and through fields to return to the house.

THINGS TO SEE

The estate

The Scotney Castle estate has a long and varied history, associated with an important dwelling in the area for over 1,000 years. The park and woodlands, characteristic of the Wealden landscape, have long been a part of a wildlife-rich wood-pasture system, with a past that features charcoal and hop production – the tenant farmer at Little Scotney Farm still grows, picks and dries hops. Grazing by Sussex cattle is an important part of looking after the grassland, and these gentle creatures with their dark red colouring, have been a feature of the landscape since Victorian times. Particularly on a warm day, the leafy woodland offers a perfect haven of dappled shade – explore on the 1.5-mile (2.4km) Woodland Trail, which can be added to the Parkland Trail for a slightly longer run.

Above: Scotney Castle.
Following page: Exploring the Scotney Castle estate.

HOW TO GET HERE

By Public Transport
Wadhurst train station 5.5 miles (8.8km), then bus service 256 or 258 to Lamberhurst.
By Car Signposted from A21.
By Bicycle National Cycle Network Route 18 passes through nearby Kilndown.
OS Map Explorer 136
Start / End National Trust Scotney Castle car park.
OS grid reference: TQ688353

A21

River Bewl

WC

Scotney
Castle

Scotney
Castle
(remains)

Kildown
Wood

A21

Bewl
Bridge

N

200 m

---

1. This run follows the blue waymarked Parkland Trail throughout. From the bottom of the car park follow the road to the right, heading towards the large white Salvin Gate. Please be careful as there may be traffic on this section. Go through the gate and follow the carriageway, crossing the Sweet Bourne stream and then the River Bewl, continuing up the hill until you reach a path junction.

2. **0.4 miles/0.6km** Turn left and follow the blue markers across the fields, crossing a footbridge and carrying on until you reach a road, turning left on the road and following it for a short distance – approximately 110 yards (100m).

3. **1.3 miles/2.1km** Turn right into a field and follow waymarkers, passing some bomb craters on your right.

4. **1.8 miles/2.9km** Turn left onto a lane, then right onto a road and right again through the old barn to return to the car park.

Other trails nearby

Explore the other waymarked trails around the Scotney estate, or head to nearby Bewl Water (not NT) for some peaceful waterside and forest running.

28. Petts Wood & Hawkwood

Chislehurst
Kent
BR5 1NZ

ABOUT THIS RUN

Distance **3.1 miles (5km)**
Ascent **253ft (77m)**

Good paths and trails
Woodland
Urban escape
History/culture
Wildlife
Dogs welcome

A green jewel set in the busy suburbs south-east of London, the National Trust owned Petts Wood and neighbouring Hawkwood cover more than 300 acres (121ha) of parkland and mixed woodland.

This run sets out along the Jubilee Park Nature Trail (not NT), taking the footbridges over the railway to reach Petts Wood. Following the London Outer Orbital Path — more usually the 'London LOOP' – waymarked path through the trees, it passes the Willett Memorial and the Edlmann Monument before heading for the Hawkwood estate. Once you've wound your way around Flushers Pond, the final stretch follows Botany Bay Lane back across Kyd Brook and the railway line to return to Jubilee Park. Starting from within the park, an alternative route of about the same distance can be run by linking up the two waymarked walks – the green woodland walk and the yellow farm walk.

Above: Petts Wood on a frosty morning.
Following page: Willett Memorial Sundial in Petts Wood.

THINGS TO SEE

The Willett Memorial

William Willett was an Edwardian builder who lived locally to Petts Wood. As a keen sportsman, he strongly believed the British were wasting the light summer mornings sleeping when they should be enjoying the great outdoors. His original idea was for four separate time changes throughout the year. Daylight saving time was eventually adopted in 1916, to increase productivity in factories and save fuel used for lighting, a year after Willett's death. The Willett Memorial Sundial, set permanently to British Summer Time, stands in a leafy north-eastern corner of the wood.

Woodland life

The estates are alive with birds, butterflies, amphibians, plants and fungi, while in the woods you'll find oak, birch, rowan, alder, ash, hornbeam and sweet chestnut. As well as managing the woodland habitat for the many species that live there, the Rangers on the estate continue the ancient tradition of charcoal burning – using ring kilns to make barbeque charcoal from local, sustainably-harvested, seasoned wood. The charcoal is available to buy on the estate.

By Public Transport Nearest station Petts Wood. Buses 208, R3 or R7.
By Car Turn on to Crown Lane Spur, off the main A21 at Bromley Common. Continue east onto Southbrough Lane and continue until junction with Crest View Drive. Continue until junction with Tent Peg Lane. Nearest postcode BR5 1BY.
OS Map Explorer 162
Start / End: Tent Peg Lane car park (not NT).
OS grid reference: TQ440679

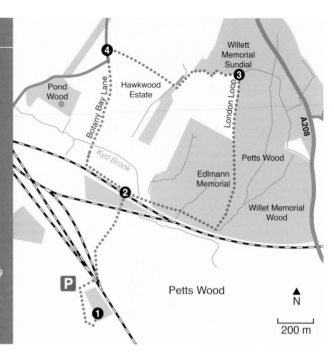

1. Leave the car park following the Jubilee Park Nature Trail signs and run along the footpath until you reach a path junction. Turn right here, following the London LOOP, and cross three railway footbridges, a road and the bridge over Kyd Brook to reach Petts Wood.

2. 0.6 miles/0.9km Turn right, following the main bridleway as it bends to the left and heads through Petts Wood.

3. 1.4 miles/2.3km Emerging from the woodland, turn left, leaving the bridleway and following a footpath downhill, past Flushers Pond, to reach Botany Bay Lane.

4. 1.9 miles/3.1km Turn left onto the lane, following it past Tongs Farm and over Kyd Brook to reach the railway. Turn left here, following the footpath until you rejoin your outward path over the railway bridges to return to Jubilee Park.

Other trails nearby
There's a network of signed footpaths and bridleways around the estates, including the waymarked woodland and farm loops. The London LOOP — is a 150 mile (241km) waymarked walk along public footpaths and through parks, woods and fields around outer London. Bromley Circular Walks are a series of interlinking waymarked walks – full details and downloadable directions at www.bromley.gov.uk.

29. Frensham Common

Priory Lane
Frensham
Surrey
GU10 3BT

ABOUT THIS RUN

Distance **5 miles (8km)**
Ascent **256ft (78m)**

Good paths and trails
Urban escape
Buggy friendly
Family friendly
Wildlife
Dogs must be on leads
  during ground-nesting
  bird season (March–
  September)
No swimming at Little
  Pond (NT)

Frensham ponds are set amidst 900 acres (364ha) of wildlife-rich heath and woodland on the western edge of the Surrey Hills Area of Outstanding Natural Beauty. The commons and Little Pond are now owned by the National Trust. Crisscrossed by inviting trails, perfect for exploring at a run, this is a tranquil haven in the busy South East and a perfect car-free escape from London by train to Farnham. This route sets out from Little Pond, taking in a fantastic clockwise loop of the common, skirting Great Pond before returning through woodland to Little Pond, with its beach-side café.

THINGS TO SEE

Swim wild

Frensham Great Pond and Little Pond were originally created in the 13th century to supply fish for the Bishop of Winchester on his visits to Farnham Castle. Today, they provide a habitat for a wide variety of water flora and fauna and the Great Pond (not NT) is a perfect place to cool off with a post-run dip or relax on the sandy beach. There are two marked areas where swimming is permitted and, particularly at quiet times of day, this is a wonderful way to experience the peaceful surroundings of Frensham. Blue-green algae is sometimes present in the pond, in which case clear warning signs will be out and the swimming area will be closed. Swimming is not permitted in Little Pond.

Above: View across Frensham Little Pond.

Wonderful wildlife

Frensham Common is a designated Site of Special Scientific Interest, as well as an AONB. The diverse and internationally rare range of habitats includes dry heath, wet heath, open water, reedbeds, alder carr and mixed woodland, together supporting a wealth of wildlife that includes sand lizards, Dartford warblers and unusual plants like the insectivorous sundew. Listen out for resident woodlarks and, at dusk, the 'churring' call of the nightjar.

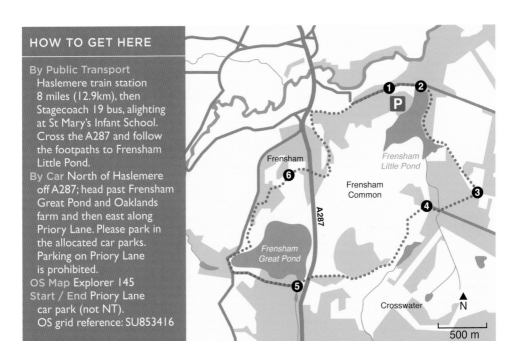

1. From the car park follow the footpath north-east, alongside the lane and around the northern tip of Frensham Little Pond.

2. **0.4 miles/0.7km** Take a moment to enjoy the view across Little Pond before continuing. Then turn right, following the footpath running down the eastern shore of Little Pond, continuing along this path through areas of woodland and grassland to reach houses and a road at Rushmoor.

3. **1.3 miles/2.1km** Turn right onto a bridleway and follow this through woodland, emerging onto a lane and bearing right.

4. **1.7 miles/2.8km** At Gray Walls house, bear left, following a bridleway through trees and past a pond on your left. Continue until you reach the A287 main road at the south-eastern corner of Frensham Great Pond.

5. **2.7 miles/4.4km** Cross the road with care and follow Pond Lane around the southern end of the Great Pond, then bear right off the lane and the follow footpath up the western side of the pond.

6. **4 miles/6.5km** Bear right, following a bridleway straight across the A287 (cross with care), taking the first left onto another bridleway and following this north to a footpath just before Priory Lane. Turn right here, following the footpath to return to the car park.

Other trails nearby
There's a great network of trails around Frensham Common and neighbouring Tilford and Hankley Commons. The Greensand Way runs to the east of Frensham, while Hindhead Common and the Devil's Punchbowl (run 30) are also nearby.

Left: **Running through woodland on Frensham Common.**

85

30. Devil's Punch Bowl

London Road
Hindhead
Surrey
GU26 6AB

ABOUT THIS RUN

Distance **4.5 miles** (7.3km)
Ascent **522ft** (159m)

Good paths and trails
Urban escape
Wildlife
Dogs must be on leads
during ground-nesting
bird season (March–
September)
NT toilets open during café
opening hours

The Devil's Punch Bowl is a deep hollow in the heaths and commons of the Surrey Hills, forming a steep-sided nature reserve; a microcosm of flora and fauna. This run traces the rim of the bowl, following clear, inviting trails with glorious views out across the surrounding countryside and exploring the intriguing landscape of this fascinating natural amphitheatre.

The first section along the western edge is followed by a fun descent into the heart of the valley, crossing the brook that runs along its central line, before a zig-zag ascent up to the eastern ridge is rewarded with further fine views. The return trip takes you alongside the former A3, its route still clearly visible though what is now a gently-winding track, passing the outstanding viewpoint at Gibbet Hill.

Above: Running around the Devil's Punch Bowl.

THINGS TO SEE

The Devil's Punch Bowl

The Devil's Punch Bowl has long drawn people to its precipitous edges and over the centuries many different stories have emerged to explain its creation. One claims the bowl was created by the Devil scooping up handfuls of earth to throw at Thor, god of thunder, in order to vex him, hence the name of the local village of Thursley. Another suggests it was the result of two arguing giants: one scooped up a huge handful of earth to throw at the other, creating the Punch Bowl, and the earth, missing its target, became the Isle of Wight. The real reason most probably lies in the layered bedrock beneath this part of the Surrey Hills, where an upper layer of sandstone overlies clay. The bowl is thought to have been caused by underground springs eroding the sandstone and causing it to collapse.

By Public Transport
Haslemere train station is
3 miles (5km) away, then take
Stagecoach 18A, 18 or 19 bus,
alighting at Hindhead
crossroads.
By Car From the north:
continue south along A3
through tunnel then first exit
(A333) signposted Hindhead
(Devil's Punch Bowl). At
traffic lights carry straight on
– car park on left-hand side.
From the south: continue
along A3 north of Liphook
and take exit signposted
'PROHIBITED VEHICLES'
(A333) towards Hindhead
(Devil's Punch Bowl). At
traffic lights carry straight
on – car park is on your
left-hand side.
OS Map Explorer 133
Start / End National Trust
Devil's Punch Bowl car park.
OS grid reference: SU890357

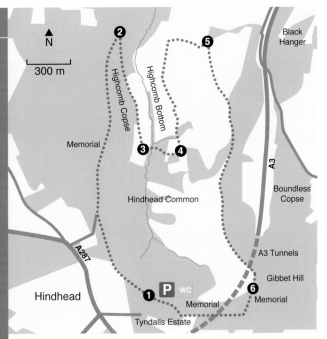

Other trails nearby

The waymarked Greensand Way runs for
108 miles (174km) across Surrey and Kent,
starting in the nearby town of Haslemere
and around the Devil's Punchbowl. Frensham
Common (see page 83) has a fantastic network
of running trails and is only a few miles away.

Rewilding

The Devil's Punch Bowl has been a designated
Site of Special Scientific Interest for over 20 years.
Extensive work has been undertaken to restore
the fragile heathland habitat and, as a result, it has
seen the return of an abundance of wildlife,
including rare breeding birds such as woodlarks
and nightjars.

1. From the car park head for the viewpoint and
turn right, following the obvious bridleway north
along the main ridge on the western side of the
Devil's Punch Bowl.

2. 1.3 miles/2.1km Turn right onto a bridleway
and follow this down to the bottom of the valley.

3. 1.9 miles/3km Turn left, leaving the
bridleway and crossing the footbridge over
the stream, running straight ahead through
woodland.

4. 2 miles/3.3km As the path begins to climb,
bear left and follow the track first contouring the
hillside and then curving to the right to climb
towards the top of the bowl.

5. 2.7 miles/4.4km At the track junction turn
right, making the final ascent to the ridge and
following the path along it, reaching the course
of the old A3.

6. 4 miles/6.4km Bear right after the viewpoint,
following the curve of the bowl around to the
right until you rejoin your outward path to return
to the car park.

31. Leith Hill

Near Coldharbour village
Dorking
Surrey
RH5 6LU

ABOUT THIS RUN

Distance **4.3 miles** (7km)
Ascent **692ft** (211m)

Woodland and heathland
    trails, surfaced paths
Family friendly
History/culture
Wildlife
Dogs welcome on leads

Leith Hill rises from within the Surrey Hills Area of Outstanding Natural Beauty, a place with a real feel of escape within easy reach of central London. The gothic tower that stands on the hill's rounded summit reaches to the highest point in south-east England at 965ft (294m), with views to match. This run follows an enjoyable, varied loop, taking in the steep but eminently worthwhile climb up to Leith Hill Tower twice – once near the beginning and once near the end. It explores a winding trail through pine and birch woodland carpeted with bilberry and ventures into the high, sandy open heath of Duke's Warren where heather, bracken and gorse cloak the landscape. The varied habitat is home to a great diversity of wildlife, particularly woodland birds such as coal tits, blue tits, great tits, long-tailed tits, nuthatches, treecreepers and goldcrests. On a summer evening you might even hear rare woodcock 'roding' and nightjars 'churring' on Duke's Warren.

THINGS TO SEE

Leith Hill Tower

The top of the fortified folly that stands on Leith Hill's summit marks the highest point in south-east England. Built in 1765 by Richard Hull of Leith Hill Place as 'a place for people to enjoy the glory of the English countryside', the tower commands 360-degree views, including north to London and south the English Channel. It is said that, on a clear day, 14 counties can be seen from the top. Climbing the 78 steps – decide carefully whether to do so before, after or even during your run – affords you both a fantastic viewpoint and a telescope. You might be able to spot ships out at sea, the arch of Wembley Stadium, the vast wheel of the London Eye or even the clock face at Big Ben. The tower has a long and chequered history and an information room halfway up is home to a wealth of intriguing facts and figures. Or simply relax and refuel after your run at The Servery, run by Tanhouse Farm Shop.

Above: You'll feel a sense of achievement when you reach Leith Hill tower for the second time after a steep climb.

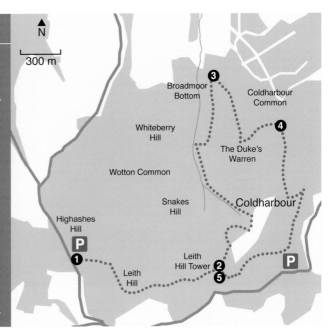

By Public Transport Nearest train stations are Holmwood (not Sunday), 2.5 miles (4km) or Dorking 5.5 miles (8.9km). Then bus services Arriva 21, Guildford to Dorking. Alight Holmbury St Mary, 2.5 miles (4km), not Sunday or Public Holidays.

By Car Leith Hill is signposted from the A25 at Wotton and from the A29 at Ockley. 1 mile (1.6km) south-west of Coldharbour A29/B2126. Follow signs for Starveall Corner car park.

OS Map Explorer 146

Start / End National Trust Starveall Corner car park.

OS grid reference: TQ130432

Other trails nearby

A comprehensive network of footpaths and bridleways crosses the Surrey Hills, including the Greensand Way, which runs 108 miles (174km) between Haslemere in Surrey and Hamstreet in Kent.

1. Leaving the car park at the rear, follow the waymarked route up through the woodland to Leith Hill Tower. Passing the tower, descend a steep slope (watch out for tree roots) to a path junction at the bottom.

2. 0.7 miles/1.2km Continue straight ahead through the gateway. After 150m (164 yards), turn left and follow the green trail around a loop with views of the valley on your left. Turn left onto the main track again, then after 100m (110 yards) turn sharp left down a steep and stony path along the bottom of the heathland. Follow this for 500m (550 yards) and then turn up to the right and then left to continue.

3. 1.9 miles/3.1km Follow the sharp right bend back through the heathland, passing a string of ponds on the right. Go straight across the crossroads and, after 100m (110 yards), turn left on the green trail passing through a metal kissing gate.

4. 2.5 miles/4km Turn right onto a track taking you past a small pond and behind a cricket pavilion. Bear left through the single-bar gate and then right, following the green trail through the barrier and back into the woodland. Follow the green trail through the woodland where it rejoins the main track and down to the major junction at the bottom of the steep climb.

5. 3.6 miles/5.8km Take the steep climb on the left back up to the tower and follow the main track straight down, following signs back to Starveall Corner car park.

32. Box Hill

Box Hill Road
Tadworth
Surrey
KT20 7LB

ABOUT THIS RUN

Distance **5.7 miles (9.2km)**
Ascent **935ft (285m)**

Good trails and paths
Woodland
Wildlife
Family friendly
Dogs welcome

Starting at the top of Box Hill gives you views of both the North and South Downs on this lovely run, heading out along a section of the Pilgrims' Way, a 119-mile (192km) historical route from Winchester to the shrine of Thomas Becket at Canterbury in Kent. A wide loop takes you through Box Hill village and around to the northern end of the hill, climbing back up to the top via the beautiful valley of Juniper Bottom, also known as Happy Valley, finishing back along the Pilgrims' Way. The terrain is as varied as the scenery, following winding trails and broad tracks through leafy woodland, airy hilltops and peaceful valleys. There are some steep climbs but these are well-rewarded with glorious views – and plenty of fun, fast descents, too.

Above: Viewpoint at Box Hill. This is a popular destination, especially in summer, so try to avoid peak times.

THINGS TO SEE

Fantastic flora
Stick to the trails to avoid damage to the local flora – in late spring and early summer the woods at Box Hill are carpeted in native wild bluebells. Other wildflowers that grow here include *Mercurialis perennis*, or dog's mercury; blue violet; and lords and ladies. Look out for a great range of different trees, too, such as holly, juniper, hazel, oak, beech and the box trees that give Box Hill its name.

Weypole Stepping Stones
The Weypole is a 5.9-acre (2.4ha) semi-circular area between the foot of Box Hill and the River Mole. A ford across the river is thought to have existed at this point since prehistoric times, and the weypole was a notched post secured in the riverbed, indicating the depth of the water. Stepping stones at this site are first recorded in 1841, while the current stones were installed in 1946, replacing those destroyed during the Second World War as an anti-invasion measure. Today, the stones are an enjoyable way to cross the river, and the 2-mile (3.2km) Stepping Stones Walk is a great trail for younger walkers to follow and also passes the Fort, one of Box Hill's oldest buildings.

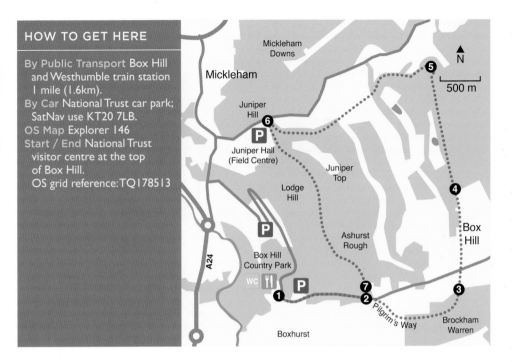

HOW TO GET HERE

By Public Transport Box Hill and Westhumble train station 1 mile (1.6km).
By Car National Trust car park; SatNav use KT20 7LB.
OS Map Explorer 146
Start / End National Trust visitor centre at the top of Box Hill.
OS grid reference: TQ178513

1. Begin at the visitor centre and head to the viewpoint, turning left here and running downhill towards the woods, following the purple waymarked Juniper Top trail and the Pilgrims' Way.

2. 0.6 miles/1km Where the Juniper Top trail turns off left across the road, keep straight on, following the Pilgrims' Way through Oak Wood.

3. 1.3 miles/2.1km Just before the caravan park, where the Pilgrims' Way bears right, turn left onto a bridleway, heading up the left-hand side of the caravan park and crossing Boxhill Road. Continue north, following the bridleway along the edge of Box Hill village.

4. 1.9 miles/3.1km After the village, continue straight ahead through woodland and past High Ashurst Outdoor Education Centre.

5. 2.7 miles/4.3km Leave the bridleway and turn left onto a footpath, following this through trees in a south-westerly direction, parallel to Headley Lane, continuing until you reach a T-junction with a bridleway.

6. 3.9 miles/6.2km Turn left onto the bridleway and follow this all the way up Juniper Bottom/Happy Valley, taking in the great views from the top. Run along the right-hand side of the caravan park to reach Boxhill Road.

7. 5.1 miles/8.2km Turn right onto the Pilgrims' Way, rejoining your outward route to return to the viewpoint and café.

Other trails nearby
2-mile (3.2km) waymarked family play trail. Mole Valley parkrun takes place every Saturday morning at Denbies Wine estate in Westhumble, just west of Box Hill. The Pilgrims' Way runs for 119 miles (192km) between Winchester and Canterbury, passing Box Hill along the way.

33. Polesden Lacey

Great Bookham
Near Dorking
Surrey
RH5 6BD

ABOUT THIS RUN

Distance 6.1 miles (9.8km)
Ascent 1,075ft (328m)

Waymarked trail
Woodland
May be muddy
Wildlife
History/culture
Trust10
Dogs welcome

Set within the rolling North Downs, the open spaces and varied terrain of the 1400-acre (567ha) Polesden Lacey estate offer a wonderful escape from the bustle of the nearby towns and cities. Yet nearby Bookham station is less than an hour by train from Central London. This enjoyable run follows the waymarked Trust10 route around the estate, leaving you free to enjoy flying across Grade II-listed parkland and zig-zagging along trails through ancient mixed woodland. Don't forget to stop now and then to take in the glorious views out across the surrounding Surrey Hills countryside. This is a fantastic run at any time of the year, although some trails may be muddy in winter. If you'd prefer not to run it alone, Polesden Lacey's free, non-competitive Trust10 event takes place on the fourth Sunday of every month.

THINGS TO SEE

Grassland restoration

Polesden Lacey estate includes two working farms, ancient woodlands, former farmsteads and downland, providing a diverse range of habitats. Lying on the chalk escarpment of the North Downs, there's huge potential for wildlife here, with chalk grassland being one of the most species-rich habitats in the world, supporting wildflowers like orchids, and insects such as the chalkhill blue butterfly.

A large area of neglected chalk downland in Polesden Valley is currently undergoing restoration, using carefully managed conservation grazing to return it to its former glory.

Outdoor culture

Over the summer months there's music and theatre to enjoy in the gardens. From relaxed jazz sessions to pop-up plays, there's something to suit everyone. Some events require payment and pre-booking, while others are free to National Trust members/with admission.

Above: Polesden Lacey.
Opposite: Enjoying the daffodils at Polesden Lacey.

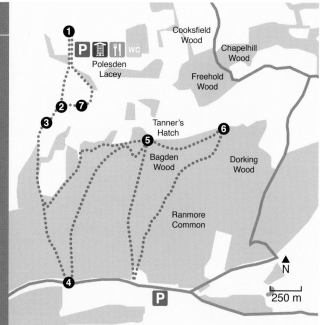

HOW TO GET HERE

By Public Transport Train stations at Box Hill and Westhumble 2.5 miles (4km); Bookham 2 miles (3.2km), Dorking 3.6 miles (5.8km), Leatherhead 3.3 miles (5.3km). Buses to Great Bookham.

By Car SatNav: Please use postcode KT23 4PZ. From Junction 9 of the M25: follow the A243 (signed A24 Epsom, Dorking and Leatherhead), before picking up the A24 and then the A246 (following the brown signs, but taking care not to take a hard right onto the B2033 Reigate Road). Don't miss the brown sign as you enter Great Bookham, indicating the left turn up to Polesden. From Guildford: Follow the A246, past East Clandon and East Horsley. Don't miss the brown sign as you enter Great Bookham, indicating the right turn up to Polesden.

OS Map Explorer 146
Start / End: National Trust Polesden Lacey car park.
OS grid reference: TQ133524

1. Head out of the south-west corner of the car park and turn left. Continue down the causeway under two bridges and onto the track enclosed by yew trees.

2. 0.4 miles/0.6km Turn right at the junction at the end of the track and continue towards Yew Tree Farm.

3. 0.5 miles/0.8km Pass the farm and continue on the track, following the track that forks left at the edge of the woodland, until you reach Ranmore Common Road.

4. 1.3 miles/2.1km Don't cross the road but turn sharp left and follow the bridleway down the valley to the northern edge of the woods, curving to the right to reach a path junction close to Tanner's Hatch Youth Hostel.

Other trails nearby
Box Hill (run 32), Black Down and Leith Hill (run 31), all National Trust, are nearby and great for running. The North Downs Way covers 153 miles (246km) between Farnham and Dover and passes by the estate, as does the Greensand Way.

93

5. 2.2 miles/3.6km Turn sharp right and head back up the hill to the road. Then take a sharp left and follow this track to a track junction at the north-eastern corner of the woodland.

6. 3.9 miles/6.2km Pass close to point 5 and continue along the edge of the woodland to the track, turning left at Prospect Lodge, which will bring you back to the junction at the edge of the woodland. Turn right, back onto the track that leads to Yew Tree Farm.

7. 5.7 miles/9.1km Shortly after the farm, leave the outbound track and turn right through some woods towards Polesden Farm. Turn left onto a path passing the farm and then right at the next junction, back under the two bridges and to the gate to the car park.

Below: Autumn colour at Polesden Lacey.

34. Morden Hall Park

Morden Hall Road
Morden
London
SM4 5JD

ABOUT THIS RUN

Distance 1.9 miles (3km)
Acent 26ft (8m)

Surfaced paths and
  grassy trails
Urban escape
Family friendly
Buggy and wheelchair
  friendly
History/culture
Wildlife
Dogs welcome in
  most areas
Limited parking in National
  Trust car park

One of the few remaining estates that once lined the River Wandle, Morden Hall Park is a secret garden in the heart of busy South London. Passing under the archway, through the gates in the high wall that encircles the park, is an escape into a different world where a meandering river, mature trees, grassy meadows, parkland and a sublimely scented rose garden await discovery. There's a friendly, community feel, centred around the renovated Stable Yard with its bookshop, exhibition space and a selection of cafés making it a popular place for sociable meetings or peaceful reflection. Local craftspeople use some of the former estate buildings as workshops, while the western mill is used as a classroom. This run takes in a figure-of-eight around the park, a short, easy but thoroughly enjoyable run in a truly special place. Entry to the park is free for all.

Above: Runner at Morden Hall
Park, where London seems a
million miles away.

THINGS TO SEE

Urban wild

Surrounded by meadows, trees and wetlands, and with the River Wandle flowing through its centre, Morden Hall Park is a haven for wildlife in the city as well as for the people that visit. Donated to the Trust in 1941 by Mr Hatfeild to prevent its rapidly shrinking open spaces from further urban encroachment, and in an area where there are few remaining snippets of natural habitat, the park is vitally important for wildlife. The wetlands, pitted with sedge beds, are home to a rich variety of species, including one of the closest heronries to central London. You might spot a kingfisher or a little egret if you're lucky, as well as the resident mallard ducks and Egyptian geese, while the 1,600 roses in the rose garden are popular with pollinators. The park is equally important for those for whom this represents a regular dose of nature, within a friendly, inclusive setting.

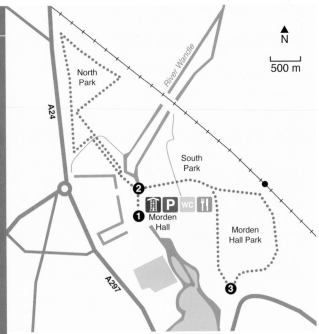

Underground to Morden
(Northern Line), then a
500 yard (460m) walk
along Aberconway Road;
Wimbledon (District Line)
then tram to Phipps Bridge
or bus to Kenley Road. The
following bus services stop
on the boundary of the park:
80, 118, 157, 164, 201, 470, 93;
the K5 terminates at
Morden station.
By Car Off A24, and A297
south of Wimbledon, north of
Sutton. Very limited parking
available on site, please
consider other ways to travel.
By Bicycle National Cycle
Network Route 20 passes
through the park.
On Foot Start your run
along the Wandle Trail from
Croydon or Carshalton to
Wandsworth.
OS Map Explorer 308
Start / End The Riverside
Café, next to National
Trust Morden Hall garden
centre car park.
OS grid reference: TQ262686

Below: The footbridge at Morden
Hall Park.

1. From the start, run straight ahead with the Stable Yard
on your left and the river on your right. Don't turn right over
the first footbridge but carry on straight ahead, crossing the
double footbridge, then straight on again over a third wooden
bridge into North Park. Take a sharp left and then turn right.
The main road will now be on your left. Keep on straight,
leaving the main surface for a wide grassed path. Carry on
clockwise around North Park, taking a right turn when you
meet the main surfaced path again, follow this path over the
three footbridges, crossing these in reverse.

2. 0.9 miles/1.5km This time, turn left and cross the
footbridge, heading straight ahead into South Park. Follow
the main surfaced trail clockwise around the park boundary.

3. 1.4 miles/2.3km Turn right, following the main path rather
than taking the smaller path through the rose garden. Turn left
at the path T-junction and recross the footbridge over the
River Wandle for a final time to return to the start.

Other trails nearby
The 12-mile (19.3km) Wandle Trail passes through the park,
following the route of the River Wandle between Croydon
and Wandsworth. There are both walking and cycling routes
which allow you to enjoy the heritage, flora and fauna of this
typical chalk stream.

35. Ham House & Garden from Richmond

Ham Street
Ham
Richmond-upon-Thames
Surrey
TW10 7RS

ABOUT THIS RUN

Distance 4.5 miles (7.2km)
Ascent 279ft (85m)

Good trails and paths;
  the Thames Path is
  occasionally affected
  by flooding
Urban escape
Wildlife
History/culture
Not suitable for dogs

Set on the banks of the River Thames in Richmond, just a short hop by train south-west of central London, Ham House and Garden stands surrounded by its own formal and kitchen gardens and a patchwork of green fields edged with mature trees and crisscrossed with footpaths and bridleways. A perfect escape from the hubbub of the city, this run is easiest by far done by public transport. Starting along Richmond's elegant high street, it takes you along the western edge of Richmond Park, a perfect point at which to extend your run around the many paths and trails that lead invitingly from here. Entering Pembroke Lodge Gardens you'll make an ascent of King Henry's Mound before heading for Ham House and Garden itself. The final miles trace the course of the River Thames back to Richmond.

Above: Ham House and Garden, said to be haunted by at least 15 ghosts and home to an amazing collection of cabinets.

THINGS TO SEE

King Henry's Mound
At 184ft (56m), the steep-sided prominence of King Henry's Mound in Pembroke Lodge Gardens is one of the highest points in London. The view on a clear day from here to St Paul's Cathedral, some 10 miles (16km) away, is protected by law from being obscured by development, one of eight such sites around the capital. A story has it that King Henry VIII stood on the mound on 19 May 1536 to see a rocket fired from the Tower of London, the signal that his wife Anne Boleyn had been executed for treason, and he was free to marry Lady Jane Seymour. The hill was originally a Bronze Age burial chamber and was later used as a viewpoint for hunting and falconry.

Ham House and Garden
The grand Stuart house, with its internationally important collection of paintings, furniture and textiles, offers a fascinating insight into the life of the wealthy some 400 years ago. Outside, wander around the formal and kitchen gardens or have a picnic in the Wilderness.

By Public Transport The run begins at Richmond train station with London Overground and Underground services.

By Car Ham House and Garden is located on the south bank of the River Thames, west of A307, between Richmond and Kingston. Ham is readily accessible from the M3, M4 and M25 and the Richmond Park Ham Gate exit. The Ham Street turning, where Ham House and Garden is located, is opposite the Hand and Flower Pub along the A307. Free parking, 400 yards (360m) from Ham House and Garden in riverside car park at end of Ham Street (not NT).

On Foot The Thames Path passes the main entrance to Ham House and Garden.

OS Map Explorer 161

Start / End Richmond station.

OS grid reference: TQ180751

Other trails nearby

The Thames Path runs for 184 miles (296km) from the Cotswolds to the sea at the Thames Barrier. Richmond Park is networked with many excellent paths and tracks, including the Tasmin Trail, ideal for exploring further.

1. Leave Richmond station via the main exit, turn left and run along the High Street, carrying straight on over the mini roundabout and up to the top of Richmond Hill. Go through Richmond Gate and bear right at the mini roundabout to reach the entrance to Pembroke Lodge Gardens.

2. 1.2 miles/1.9km Go through the entrance into Pembroke Lodge Gardens and continue straight ahead to reach King Henry's Mound. Stop here to take in the views to St Paul's Cathedral, 10 miles (16km) away.

3. 1.6 miles/2.6km Head straight down the hill towards the river, going through two gates and then a kissing gate to reach Petersham Road. Cross the road with care and turn left, following the road around to the left. Once

around the corner, take the first left into Ham Avenues. Follow this until you can turn right after the polo club to reach the entrance to Ham House and Garden.

4. 2.5 miles/4.1km With the gates on your right, continue straight ahead across a meadow and wooden bridge to reach the Thames Path. Turn right onto the path and run along here for approximately 1.3 miles (2.1km), passing Petersham Meadows, Buccleuch Gardens and under Richmond Bridge to reach Friars Lane.

5. 4 miles/6.4km Turn right onto Friars Lane and follow this up to Richmond Green. Cross the green to reach the road at Little Green, following this over the bridge and then turning right down Old Station Passage to return to Richmond station where you started.

36. Osterley Park

**Osterley Park
Jersey Road
Isleworth
TW7 4RB**

ABOUT THIS RUN

Distance 1.6 miles (2.6km)
Ascent 33ft (10m)

Well-maintained tracks
  and trails
History/culture
Wildlife
Family friendly
Dogs in park only, on leads
Parkrun and junior parkrun
Waymarked

Just a short train ride from Central London, Osterley Park is one of the few remaining country estates in London. The impressive 18th-century mansion stands within 364 acres (147.3ha) of gardens, parkland, lakes, open fields and tenanted farmland grazed by Charolais cattle – a green jewel set within busy West London. This run follows an easy loop of the part of the estate nearest the house, mostly following the new multi-user trail, but with an enjoyable detour out around the open grasslands of Wyke Green. Visit the ancient oaks in the parkland and, in spring, run on trails lined by cherry blossom and bluebells.

Above: Osterley Park, described by Horace Walpole as 'the palace of palaces'.

THINGS TO SEE

A changing landscape
The striking Neo-classical mansion at Osterley Park was built in the second half of the 18th century on the site of a former Tudor manor house. Acquired by the Childs, a wealthy banking family, it was extensively and lavishly remodelled by sought-after Scottish architect, Robert Adam. At the time, the estate was surrounded by open countryside; today it retains a feeling of open space and escape from the busy hubbub of the capital.

Take to your wheels
In conjunction with Sport England and the London Marathon Charitable Trust, Osterley Park has recently upgraded much of its path network, creating a 1.5-mile (2.4km) multi-user trail around the estate. Suitable for buggies, wheelchairs and balance bikes, as well as for runners, walkers, dog walkers and leisure cyclists, this is a perfect way to enjoy the park at any time of the year. There's a popular bike skills area, too.

By Public Transport Isleworth train station 1.7 miles (2.7km). Nearest step-free access station: Hounslow 2.7 miles (4.3km). London Underground: Osterley (Piccadilly Line), 1 mile (1.6km); nearest step-free access station Hounslow East (Piccadilly Line), 2 miles (3.2km).

By Car On A4 between Hammersmith and Hounslow. Follow brown tourist signs on A4 between Gillette Corner and Osterley underground station; from west M4, exit 3 then follow A312/A4 towards Central London. Main gates at junction with Thornbury and Jersey Roads. Parking 400 yards (365m) up the main driveway. SatNav enter Jersey Road and TW7 4RB.

OS Map Explorer 161

Start / End National Trust Osterley Park main car park. OS grid reference: TQ148773

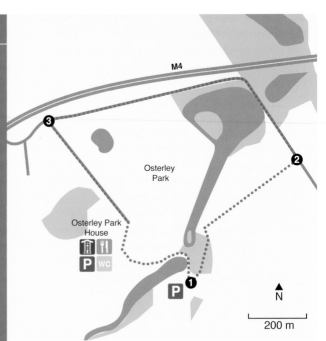

1. Head out of the north side of the car park, following the path along the grassland.

2. 0.4 miles/0.6km At the fork, turn left and continue to follow the waymarker points through the gap between the lakes and around a left-hand corner.

3. 1 mile/1.6km Continue following the main path around to the left, past the house and back to the car park.

Above: Running at Osterley Park.

Other trails nearby
The Thames Path National Trail follows the River Thames for 184 miles (296km) from its source near Kemble in the Cotswolds to the Thames Barrier in south-east London, and can be accessed to the south of Osterley. To its north, the Grand Union Canal path runs 138 miles (222km) from Birmingham to London, joining the Thames Path at Brentford. Nearby Richmond Park (not NT) has a fine network of trails to explore.

37. White Horse Hill

Near Woolstone
Faringdon
0.6 miles (1km) south
of SN7 7QN

ABOUT THIS RUN

Distance 7.3 miles
(11.8km)
Ascent 495ft (151m)

Surfaced, gravel and grassy
  trails, some quiet road
Partly waymarked
Wildlife
History/culture
Dogs welcome on leads
Toilets at Ashdown House
  (subject to opening times)

This enjoyable and varied route on inviting trails across chalk downland is a perfect way to explore this fascinating area and its long human history, including Uffington Castle and White Horse and a delightful stretch of the Ridgeway National Trail, one of England's oldest routes. From the start it follows the Lambourn Valley Way past Uffington Castle, joining the Ridgeway and visiting the Neolithic long barrow at Wayland's Smithy. A run through woodland brings you out at Ashdown, with its unusual Dutch-style house. Climbing steeply back up to the escarpment, the final miles cross open downland with spectacular views of the surrounding countryside before rejoining the Ridgeway to the finish.

Above: White Horse Hill, where the iconic white horse was cut up to 3ft (1m) deep into the landscape.

THINGS TO SEE

The White Horse and Uffington Castle
Three incredible prehistoric sites lie beside this stretch of the Ridgeway, the ancient route that once ran from Dorset to the Wash and still crosses the chalk ridges of the Berkshire, Oxfordshire and Wiltshire Downs. At the summit of White Horse Hill, Oxfordshire's highest point, from where you can see over six counties on a clear day, the well-preserved earthworks of Uffington Castle are an outstanding example of a large Iron Age hillfort, dating back around 2,500 years. While the White Horse itself, measuring

360ft (110m) from nose to tail and carved deeply into the hillside, is the oldest chalk-cut hill figure in Britain, thought to be over 3,000 years old.

White Horse wildlife
The open chalk grasslands around White Horse Hill are a great place for bird-watching. Look for buzzards, kestrels or red kites hunting voles and field mice from the skies. In spring and summer listen for the babble of skylarks, or see if you can spot meadow pipits, corn buntings and partridges, which come here to breed.

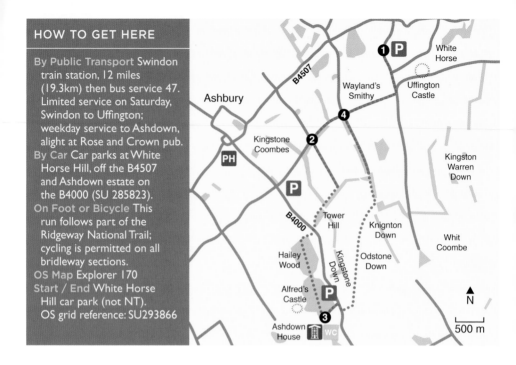

HOW TO GET HERE

By Public Transport Swindon train station, 12 miles (19.3km) then bus service 47. Limited service on Saturday, Swindon to Uffington; weekday service to Ashdown, alight at Rose and Crown pub.
By Car Car parks at White Horse Hill, off the B4507 and Ashdown estate on the B4000 (SU 285823).
On Foot or Bicycle This run follows part of the Ridgeway National Trail; cycling is permitted on all bridleway sections.
OS Map Explorer 170
Start / End White Horse Hill car park (not NT).
OS grid reference: SU293866

1. Turn left out of the car park and follow the track to reach a four-way junction. Turn right here onto the Ridgeway. Follow this, passing Wayland's Smithy on your right, until you reach a junction with the D'Arcy Dalton Way.

2. 1.5 miles/2.4km Turn left and follow the path through a large field, passing a barn on your right. At the edge of the field, turn right, following the path along the line of trees until you reach the B4000. Cross the road with care and enter the woodland. Take the path on your left until you come out onto a wide grassy avenue leading to the tenanted Ashdown House.

3. 3.7 miles/5.9km Before you reach the house, turn left where signposted to the carpark and recross the B4000. Carry straight on, climbing steeply up Kingstone Down to reach a footpath

junction at the top. Turn left and follow the footpath trending north-east across the downs until you reach a line of trees and a bridleway. Turn left onto the bridleway and follow this along the line of trees until you rejoin the Ridgeway.

4. 6.2 miles/10km Turn right onto the Ridgeway and follow it for about 0.6 miles (1km) until you can turn left back to the car park. To explore Uffington Castle and White Horse, carry straight up and turn left through a gate at the top of the hill. Then take the grassy footpath from White Horse downhill to the car park.

Other trails nearby
The Ridgeway National Trail runs for 86 miles (138km) between Ivinghoe Beacon in the Chilterns and Avebury in Wiltshire.

38. Cookham Commons

**Cookham
Berkshire
SL6 9SG**

ABOUT THIS RUN

Distance **3.9 miles (6.3km)**
Ascent **203ft (62m)**

Woodland and field paths
Waymarked route
May be muddy
History/culture
Wildlife
Dogs welcome on leads
Cafe and toilets at Red
   Lion Tearoom (not NT)

Covering an area of over 840 acres (340ha) of the Thames Valley, within easy reach of London and yet offering a great feeling of wildness and escape, the Cookham commons are a series of commons that include Cookham and Widbrook in the east, Cock Marsh and Winter Hill in the north and Cookham Dean in the west. This wonderfully diverse landscape of open grassland, lush wildflower meadows, riverside trails and ancient woodland and wood pasture inspired Kenneth Grahame, who lived in nearby Cookham Dean as a child, to write his much-loved book, *The Wind in the Willows*. Crisscrossing the area are many miles of footpaths and bridleways, giving easy access to the countryside. This run follows a picturesque, waymarked circuit, taking in many of the best bits of Cookham, including a steep (but short) climb up Winter Hill – well rewarded with fine views across the Thames Valley.

Above: Cookham Commons.

THINGS TO SEE

Cookham wildlife
With its mixture of ancient wood pasture, secondary woodland, open chalk grassland and meandering river, Cookham is a fantastic place for wildlife. Look out for butterflies, including silver-washed fritillaries, speckled woods, commas, ringlets, meadow browns, skippers and whites; insects and small mammals; wild flowers such as orchids and rock rose; and birds from the great crested grebes that sail by on the river to the fork-tailed red kites circling overhead.

Winter Hill
Created long ago through erosion by the River Thames, the steep chalk escarpment of Winter Hill is well worth the climb to discover stunning views out across the Thames Valley. One of the highest Thames terraces, Winter Hill is believed to have been used as winter pasture for livestock during times of flooding, giving it its name. These terraces have seen human habitation dating back 350,000 years when they were first colonised by the nomadic hunter-gatherers of the Old Stone Age. Bronze Age burial mounds and Roman pottery have also been discovered here.

By Public Transport Bourne
End train station 1.5 miles
(2.4km) and Cookham 0.5
miles (0.8km).
By Car From the A4094, take
the B4447 into the High
Street. Go through the village
centre to the Cookham
Village Memorial and
Cookham Moor. The National
Trust car park is 220 yards
(200m) on the right.
By Bicycle Cookham is easily
accessible by bicycle from
Maidenhead on National
Cycle Network Route 52.
Please note that no cycling is
allowed on the trail including
the Thames Path.
OS Map Explorer 172
Start / End National Trust
Cookham Moor car park.
OS grid reference: SU892853

River Thames

N

200 m

Cock
Marsh

Bourne
End

PH

Winter Hill
Golf Club

A4094

A4094

P

B4447

1. This run follows the waymarked Cookham and Cock Marsh route throughout. From the car park, cross the B4447 and head up to the bridge, turning left and running along the causeway. Continue along Cookham High Street, turning left at the T-junction.

2. **0.4 miles/0.6km** Bear left off the main road, running past the church on your right to reach the river. Turn left and follow the riverside path, with the river on your right. The path passes under a railway bridge and then past some houses on your left.

3. **1.8 miles/2.9km** At the end of the houses, turn left and cross Cock Marsh to reach the path running around the bottom of the terrace at Winter Hill. Turn right onto the path and then left to zigzag to the top of the hill. Emerging onto the edge of a golf course, turn right and then left around the corner of the golf course. Run along the edge of the course on the Chiltern Way to reach the house at Greythatch. Continue to follow the Chiltern Way, turning left and running along the southern boundary of the golf course to reach the railway.

4. **3.4 miles/5.5km** Cross the footbridge over the railway and then turn right, leaving the Chiltern Way and following a footpath across grassland and past some houses and gardens on your right until you reach a road. Turn left here, following another footpath straight ahead, bearing right just before the pond to return to the car park.

Other trails nearby
There are many excellent trails in the surrounding area and further afield in the Chilterns, perfect for exploring at a run. A great place to start is the waymarked Wind in the Willows routes at Cookham.

39. Bradenham

Bradenham village
Wycombe
Buckinghamshire
Nearest postcode
HP14 4HF

ABOUT THIS RUN

Distance 5.6 miles (9.1km)
Ascent 636ft (194m)

Woodland and field paths,
   some quiet roads
Wildlife
Dogs welcome – on leads
   around horses/livestock
History/culture

The pretty National Trust village of Bradenham, with its 17th-century manor house (not open to the public) and 18th-century brick and flint cottages arranged around the village green, nestles within a sweeping estate of farmland, woodland and classic Chilterns chalk countryside. This run begins in the village, heading out across open grassland, before winding through the trees of Park Wood. A steady climb along a quiet lane brings you out at the highest point of the run at Darvillshill, from where there are fine views out across the Chilterns. From here there's an enjoyable descent through a typical chalk dry valley to North Dean, finishing with a stretch through the beautiful beechwoods of Naphill Common.

Above: Woodland at Bradenham. A woodland run is a good choice on a hot day.

THINGS TO SEE

Palaeogene puddingstones
Along the northern edge of Bradenham village green are lumps of Palaeogene (66–23 million-year-old) puddingstone, a fascinating and intensely hard rock. Found only in parts of Hertfordshire, Buckinghamshire and Essex, its knobbly exterior is quite distinctive and in cross-section it resembles an old-fashioned pudding.

The village
Most of the buildings in Bradenham village date from the 18th century, with the area around the village green boasting 18 listed buildings. Bradenham Cricket Club has a long history here, having held matches on the green since the 1860s.

Park Wood
Grim's Ditch, thought to be an Iron Age boundary marking, appears sporadically across a stretch of the Chiltern Hills over 11 miles (18km) long. Two sections can be seen in Park Wood and Beamangreen Wood, just a short detour from the route.

1. From the car park head north along the top edge of the village green and past the front of Bradenham Manor. Cross Bradenham Wood Lane with care and take the footpath opposite, following this across open grassland with woodland to your right. Continue following the footpath across the fields, approaching Park Wood on your right.

2. 0.9 miles/1.4km Where the path turns left and downhill, bear right through a gate into Park Woods. After about 110 yards (100m) bear left onto a wide footpath which joins from the right and follow this downhill. Continue, heading up a short, steep hill to reach Smalldean Lane. The next section is along a narrow country lane, however it is unusually quiet and part of the Chilterns Cycleway.

3. 1.4 miles/2.3km Turn right and follow the lane uphill, crossing with care straight over the main road at the top and onto Slad Lane. Follow the lane, bearing right onto Flowers Bottom Lane at the horse sanctuary and following it around to the right between some houses and then down the hill. Take the footpath just after the former Old Plow pub on your right (not the one just before the pub).

4. 2.4 miles/3.9km Follow the footpath through fields with horses and sometimes cattle grazing – please keep dogs on leads here. Continue along the valley, keeping straight ahead at path junctions, until you reach the road in Upper North Dean village.

HOW TO GET HERE

By Public Transport The nearest station is 1 mile (1.6km) away at Saunderton on the Chiltern Railways line. Join the route at point 2.

By Car From the A4010, High Wycombe to Princes Risborough road, take Bradenham Wood Lane. Take the first right (Rectory Lane) along the edge of the village green, then next left along on a track on the southern edge of the village green for about 200 yards (180m). The designated car park is just after the cricket pavilion. For SatNav use postcode HP14 4HF.

By Bicycle The Chiltern Cycleway passes nearby, however cycling is not permitted on much of the run route.

OS Map Explorer 172

Start / End National Trust car park in Bradenham village near the cricket pavilion. OS grid reference: SU827969.

N

500 m

Lacey Green

Speen

4

Horse Trust Stables

3 P

5

Courns Wood

Park Wood

2

Walter's Ash

Bradenham

PH **6**

1 Bradenham Manor

Naphill Common

PH

Naphill

Hunt's Hill

A4010

Hearnton Wood

Great Cookshall Wood

---

5. **3.4 miles/5.5km** Turn right onto the lane and then right again onto Clappins Lane. After about 110 yards (100m) turn left onto a footpath and follow this diagonally uphill to reach a stile into Stocking Woods. Follow the white arrows through the woods, eventually emerging into a field. Follow the footpath diagonally across the field, then bear right onto an obvious path across a larger field to reach the road and buildings at Naphill village.

6. **4.5 miles/7.3km** Cross the road with care, taking the footpath straight ahead and following it through houses and into the woodland at Naphill Common. Continue straight ahead through the woods, joining a larger track and passing Lady Horse Pond on your left. Bear right at the fork then continue straight ahead along the footpath through oak woodlands and onto a track. Follow the track downhill, bearing left at the fork to reach Bradenham Manor. Run to the left of the wall to return to the car park.

Other trails nearby

There are several excellent trail to explore around the estate, or venture out into the Chilterns where the Ridgeway and Icknield Way National Trails await exploration.

Above: Trails at Bradenham estate.

40. Stowe

New Inn
Buckingham
MK18 5EQ

ABOUT THIS RUN

Distance **3.7** miles (5.9km)
Ascent **226ft** (69m)

Good trails and paths
Buggy/wheelchair-friendly
  alternative (paid entry/
  NT members)
Wildlife
History/culture
Dog friendly
Toilets available during café
  opening hours only

Said to be Capability Brown's masterpiece, Stowe is considered to be one of the greatest gardens in the world. With its shining lakes and more than 40 temples and monuments placed thoughtfully throughout its manicured grounds, it's a fascinating place to visit, whether you're running the upgraded multi-user lakeside path with a buggy or heading out into the fields, meadows and groves to explore the surrounding countryside. This run takes in a wide arc around the house (now home to Stowe School) and gardens, running on a mixture of grass and hard paths through glorious open fields and parkland, dotted with mature trees. Starting along a stretch of the Ouse Valley Way, it passes close to Stowe's famous Palladian Bridge – one of only three in the country – and the ornate, Grade I-listed Corinthian Arch with its uninterrupted views across the estate.

Above: Looking across parkland towards the Wolfe Obelisk at Stowe.

THINGS TO SEE

The lost village

A short distance from this route, the medieval church at Stowe is all that remains of a former medieval village, one of more than 2,000 across England. These villages, in some of which you can still see the doorways, rooms and fireplaces of the dwellings, were deserted for a number of different reasons. Some succumbed to natural forces, like Dunwich in Suffolk, which was destroyed by major storms in the 14th century and today is the largest medieval underwater site in Europe. Some suffered irrecoverable losses through disease or lack of local resources. And some, like Stowe and nearby Wimpole, were destroyed by landowners for aesthetic reasons during major landscaping operations or because they obscured an important view. The meaning of Capability Brown's expertly crafted landscapes to those that use them for recreation and relaxation today is an intriguing contrast to the vastly different uses, value and meaning of the same land in years gone by.

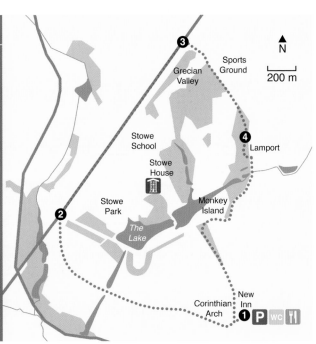

HOW TO GET HERE

By Public Transport Milton Keynes station 15 miles (24km). Arriva X60 bus runs between Aylesbury and Milton Keynes, stopping in Buckingham town. From here it is a very long walk – 1.5 miles (2.4km) – to complete the journey to Stowe.
By Car 2 miles (3.2km) north-west of Buckingham town, just off the A422 Buckingham to Banbury Road. From M40 take exits 9–11; from M1 exits 13 or 15a. SatNav use postcode MK18 5EQ.
OS Map Explorer 192
Start / End National Trust New Inn visitor centre.
OS grid reference: SP682363

N

200 m

Grecian Valley

Sports Ground

Stowe School

Stowe House

Stowe Park

The Lake

Monkey Island

Lampart

New Inn

Corinthian Arch

1. From the New Inn visitor centre, run past the Corinthian Arch, then turn right onto the main path, also the Ouse Valley Way, following the obvious path along a wide grove of trees. The path heads downhill, passes between two small lakes and then climbs to reach a path junction.

2. 1.1 miles/1.8km Continue straight ahead along the main drive. The Ouse Valley Way turns off left just after the house but don't take this and continue straight ahead, passing a car park on your right.

3. 2.1 miles/3.4km Where the surfaced path curves around to the right, follow it, running downhill to reach a path junction. Continue straight ahead here and continue alongside fields to reach some houses at Lamport.

4. 2.6 miles/4.2km Bear right before the houses and follow the edge of the park around to the right to return to the New Inn visitor centre.

Other trails nearby
The Ouse Valley Way runs for 142 miles (229km) along the River Great Ouse from its source in Syresham, Northamptonshire, to the sea at Kings Lynn in Norfolk, passing Stowe en route.

Right: The Oxford Bridge at Stowe.

Central England
and East Anglia

41. Brockhampton

Bringsty
Near Bromyard
WR6 5UH

ABOUT THIS RUN

Distance **3.7 miles (6km)**
Ascent **597ft (182m)**

Good trails and paths
May be muddy
Wildlife
History/culture
Family friendly
Dogs welcome

Lower Brockhampton Manor House lies at the heart of Brockhampton's 1,700-acre (688ha) estate. Many miles of paths and trails wind through the orchards, park and woodlands, making this an ideal place to escape for a peaceful, nature-filled adventure. Starting at the manor, this run follows the yellow waymarkers of the Carriage Rides walk around the estate, climbing up to the high ground at Warren Farm for outstanding views across the rolling Herefordshire countryside. From here there's an enjoyably long downhill run through the woods and back to the manor.

Above: The manor house and gatehouse at Brockhampton.
Opposite: The moat at Brockhampton.

THINGS TO SEE

Reimagining the orchards
Over the coming years the orchards at Brockhampton, once at the heart of the estate, will be reinstated and regenerated. Three fields – some 21 acres (8.5ha) – will be transformed back into orchard using imaginative and creative planting. The project is involving artists, architects and orchard experts, celebrating these special fruit trees and the wild flora and fauna that live alongside them.

The manor house
The rambling, moated timber-framed building of Lower Brockhampton Manor House was built in the late 14th century using wood from the estate and stayed in the same family for more than 400 years. The quirky and somewhat lopsided gatehouse was built in 1543, a miniature version of the manor; and, while there have been many renovations over the centuries, the bargeboards at the back entrance and the huge, studded door are original. Four species of bat live in the manor house: brown long-eared, common pipistrelle, soprano pipistrelle and lesser horseshoe bat.

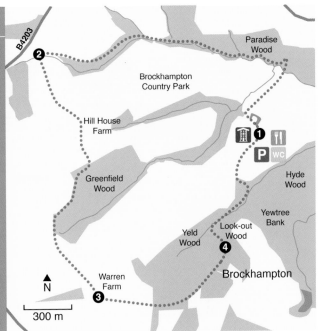

HOW TO GET HERE

By Public Transport Hereford train station 18 miles (29km), Worcester Foregate Street train station 12 miles (19.3km). Regular bus service passes near both stations.
By Car Follow the A44 west from Worcester or the A44 east from Bromyard and turn off at the Brockhampton estate sign. Follow the winding road to Lower Brockhampton and park in the main car park near the manor house.
OS Map Explorer 202
Start / End National Trust Manor house car park, Lower Brockhampton.
OS grid reference: SO687559

1. From the car park, run towards the manor, turning right before reaching the house and following yellow waymarkers through the orchard and across a meadow, continuing uphill to reach Paradise Wood. Turn left and run along the lower edge of Paradise Wood, following the course of the stream along Blews Ditch until you reach the top of the hill.

2. 1.4 miles/2.2km On reaching the ridge, turn left and continue following yellow waymarkers past Hill House Farm and along the ridge to Warren Farm, the highest point on the route.

3. 2.5 miles/4km Follow the waymarkers downhill through parkland, joining a surfaced driveway and continue on this past Brockhampton church.

4. 3.1 miles/5km Continue following the waymarkers along the drive through woodland, emerging onto parkland above Lower Brockhampton Manor. Follow the waymarkers back to the car park.

Other trails nearby
The Herefordshire Trail runs for 150 miles (241km), linking the five market towns of Ledbury, Ross-on-Wye, Kington, Leominster and Bromyard.

42. Croome

Near High Green
Worcester
Worcestershire
WR8 9DW

ABOUT THIS RUN

Distance **3.9 miles (6.2km)**
Ascent **141ft (43m)**

Good trails and paths,
  some grassy sections
Wildlife
History/culture
Family friendly
Buggy friendly
Dog friendly

Croome's 750 acres (304ha) of 'Capability' Brown landscaped parkland, dotted with follies and viewpoints, are set within picturesque Worcestershire countryside with great views out to the Malvern Hills on a clear day. Easily accessed from the M5, there's a wealth of running potential here, and the surfaced paths around the park are excellent for running buggies and wheelchairs. This route links up a triangle of footpaths around the edge of Croome, passing the pretty church of St Mary Magdalene and crossing the Croome river at the Chinese Bridge near Croome Court. The final stretch takes you through the historic Worcester Gates and along the Worcester Drive, with a challenging finish up the hill to the church.

Above: Bridge over the river at Croome Park.
Opposite: Buggy running at Croome.

THINGS TO SEE

Feathered friends
Croome is an amazing place for birdwatching, with a hide for quiet observation. The dense, scrubby shelter belt makes an ideal habitat for nightingales, a species that has declined by 90 per cent over the last 40 years and is now rare, particularly outside the south-eastern corner of Britain. Listen out for them singing from the leafy canopies of the trees – their varied songs can be heard during the day as well as in the evenings – and help to protect their nesting sites by keeping dogs on short leads. The ranger team at Croome is working hard to increase nightingale habitat by coppicing blackthorn and encouraging brambles to create dense scrub and erecting deer fences to prevent deer from clearing it. Other birds you might spot include nuthatches, treecreepers, woodpeckers, kingfishers, swallows and house martins. And don't forget to look up to catch a glimpse of kestrels and buzzards hunting and large flocks of Canada geese arriving over the autumn months.

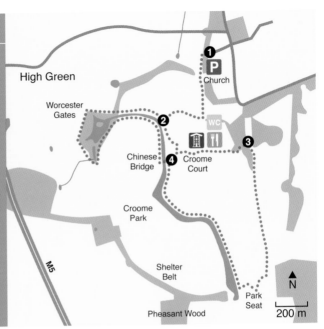

1. Leave the car park and head for the main entrance, passing the church on your right and running towards the main house. Follow the footpath as it curves right to reach the river.

2. 0.4 miles/0.7km Turn left and follow the path alongside the river and then continue following it around the house and up the hill. Bear right to reach a junction.

3. 0.9 miles/1.5km Turn right and follow the path through parkland to reach a belt of trees. Continue on the path down the hill past the Park Seat to reach the river. Turn right and follow the riverside path, keeping the water on your left.

4. 2.3 miles/3.7km Turn left, crossing the river over the Chinese Bridge and then turn right, following the path and keeping the water on your right. Continue along this path through the field, passing two pedestrian gates until you reach a field gate. Go through this gate and turn right onto the lane. Keep going until you see the Worcester Gates on your right. Go through the gates and follow the path through the park and back up the hill to the church where you started.

Other trails nearby
Explore further at Croome or head to the Malvern Hills where there's a fantastic network of trails to run. The Severn Way runs along the River Severn, just the other side of the M5 from Croome.

43. Hanbury Hall

School Road
Hanbury
Droitwich Spa
Worcestershire
WR9 7EA

ABOUT THIS RUN

Distance **4.9 miles (7.8km)**
Ascent **305ft (93m)**

Good trails and paths
Paid entry/NT members
Urban escape
History/culture
Dogs welcome on leads
Monthly Trust10 run

The imposing 18th-century, Grade I-listed Hanbury Hall stands in nearly 400 acres (162ha) of gardens and parkland, within easy reach of the M5 motorway south of Birmingham. The parkland and surrounding Worcestershire countryside is crisscrossed with a great network of footpaths, towpaths and bridleways, making for some thoroughly enjoyable running. This route begins at the Hall, heading across fields and through woodland to eventually join the Birmingham Canal for a stretch of pleasant waterside running. Heading back through fields brings you to the edge of the woodland at Piper's Hill, with the finishing miles taking you up and over Hanbury Church Hill with a good downhill back to the Hall to finish.

Above: Running through the estate at Hanbury Hall.

THINGS TO SEE

Piper's Hill
Also known as Hanbury Woods, Piper's Hill, a couple of miles north-east of Hanbury Hall, is one of the Wildlife Trusts' flagship nature reserves. Home to a nationally important area of wood pasture, the reserve contains some of the oldest trees in the county. In the past, livestock would have grazed in and around much of Britain's woodland, keeping trees well-spaced and fertilizing the foliage-rich woodland floor. As grazing by large herbivores has decreased, woodland has grown crowded, depriving its inhabitants of nutrients and light. Careful management, selectively removing new growth and introducing conservation grazing, is gradually restoring areas of wildlife-rich wood pasture to the country.

Other trails nearby
Wychavon Way is a 40-mile (64km) route between Droitwich and Broadway. The Worcester and Birmingham Canal runs for 30 miles (48.2km), linking the two cities.

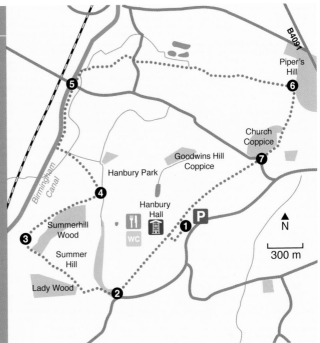

HOW TO GET HERE

By public transport
Droitwich Spa station is 4 miles (6.4km) away. Buses from Worcester to Birmingham (passing close to Droitwich Spa train station), alight Wychbold, 3.4 miles (5.5km)
By car from M5 exit 5 follow A38 to Droitwich; from Droitwich 4 miles (6.4km) along B4090.
OS Map Explorer 204
Start / End National Trust Hanbury Hall and Gardens car park.
OS grid reference: SO946637

---

1. From the car park follow the path around to the front of Hanbury Hall, then turn left onto a public footpath heading south-west across the parkland to reach School Road on a sharp bend.

2. **0.5 miles/0.8km** Go through the gate but don't go onto the road. Instead, turn sharp right and go through a second gate onto another footpath. Bear left after the trees and follow the footpath across fields to reach Summerhill Farm.

3. **1.1 miles/1.8km** Turn right at the farm and follow a track along the edge of an area of woodland, with this to your right.

4. **1.6 miles/2.6km** At the end of the woodland, follow the footpath across another field, then turn left and continue until you reach the canal. Turn right and follow the towpath to reach a road bridge.

5. **2.4 miles/3.8km** Go under the road bridge and continue on the towpath for about 110 yards (100m), then turn right onto a footpath, crossing a brook and Astwood Lane and continuing along the footpath along the edges of fields, heading east until you reach the woodland at Piper's Hill.

6. **3.7 miles/5.9km** Turn right, emerging from the woods and passing some houses, continuing straight on along the footpath up Hanbury Church Hill to reach the church at the top.

7. **4.1 miles/6.6km** Follow footpath signs past the church, then take the footpath to the left of the road and to the right of the graveyard, running downhill on grassy trails to return to Hanbury Hall.

44. Clent Hills

Nimmings Wood
Romsley
Worcestershire
B62 0NL

ABOUT THIS RUN

Distance **3.6 miles (5.7km)**
Ascent **800ft (244m)**

Good trails and paths
May be muddy
Urban escape
Family friendly
History/culture
Dogs welcome
Outdoor café and toilets
  (not NT) 10am–4pm

Just 10 miles (16km) south-west of central Birmingham, the Clent Hills offer a haven of green, rolling countryside in the heart of the busy West Midlands. Networked with footpaths, trails and bridleways they're great for exploring on foot or mountain bike. This run scribes a wide arc around the undulating ridge of the hills, taking in their highest points of Walton Hill at 1,036ft (316m) and Clent Hill at 1,014ft feet (309m), either side of the dividing valley of St Kenelm's Pass. On a clear day, the short, steep climbs are handsomely rewarded with views from the tops across to the Malvern Hills, the Cotswolds, the Shropshire Hills and the Black Mountains of the Welsh borders.

Above: Running through the Four Stones at Clent.
Opposite: Woodland trail at Clent.

THINGS TO SEE

Forts and follies

The Clent Hills are dotted with many fascinating echoes of those who have lived here over the centuries, including an Iron Age hill fort on Wychbury Hill and a number of 18th-century follies. These follies were commissioned by the Lyttelton family, builders of the neo-Palladian mansion of Hagley Hall to the north-west of the hills, whose ancestors still live there today. According to Tom Pagett's 1994 booklet *The Follies and other Features of Hagley Park*, the dual

purpose of the follies was to draw the eye to a point in the distance and to provide a talking point for visitors. While exploring the area, look out for some of the follies that remain intact today, including the atmospheric Four Stones on the summit of Clent Hill, the Rotunda, the much-vandalised remains of a Palladian bridge, Jacob's Well, Thomson's Seat, the Temple of Theseus and Hagley Castle, a mock-castle situated in Hagley Park and visible from the hills.

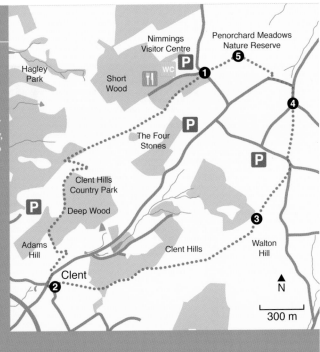

By Public Transport Trains to
Hagley, 3.5 miles (5.6km);
Stourbridge Town, 5 miles
(8km); Bromsgrove, 9 miles
(14.5km). Bus service 192,
Birmingham, Halesowen, Hagley
and Kidderminster. Alight Hagley,
then 20-minute walk up a steep
hill to Nimmings Wood car
park; 318, Stourbridge, Hagley
and Bromsgrove, then 0.5 miles
(0.8km) from Clent village.
By Car South-west of
Birmingham, between the
villages of Clent and Romsley.
South-east of Hagley and 6
miles (9.6km) from M5 (J4),
signposted off the A491 Sat
Nav B62 0NL
OS Map Explorer 219
Start / End National Trust
Nimmings Wood car park.
OS grid ref: SO938807

1. Follow the obvious zigzag track uphill and along the ridge to the Four Stones. From here continue on the path, dropping down slightly and bearing left through woodland to the road by the church in Clent.

2. 1.4 miles/2.3km Cross the road and follow the footpath east up the other side onto the ridgeline of the hills. Bear left at the path junction and continue to climb to the top of Walton Hill.

3. 2.5 miles/4km Bear right off the main ridge, running downhill to Walton Hill Road. Cross and continue straight ahead, following the footpath to St Kenelm's Road.

4. 3 miles/4.9km Turn left along St Kenelm's Road then turn left onto Chapel Lane. Turn right onto a footpath, then left, heading north-west across fields to Penorchard Meadows Nature Reserve (Wildlife Trust).

Other trails nearby
The North Worcestershire Path is a waymarked long-distance trail running 37 miles (59.5km) from Bewdley, Worcestershire to Major's Green, Birmingham.

5. 3.4 miles/5.5km Turn left at the nature reserve, following a footpath across fields back to the car park.

45. Kinver Edge

Holy Austin Rock Houses
Compton Road
Kinver
Near Stourbridge
Staffordshire
DY7 6DL

ABOUT THIS RUN

Distance **3.5 miles (5.7km)**
Ascent **626ft (191m)**

Some good paths and trails
Waymarked
Urban escape
History/culture
Dogs welcome
Free lay-by parking

Famous for its fascinating rock houses and hill fort, carved into the local red sandstone, Kinver Edge is also home to a beautiful area of wildlife-rich heathland and, further afield, mixed woodland. Running along the trails that wind through yellow gorse and purple heather offers glorious views out across the neighbouring towns and countryside. This route, crossing the border between Staffordshire and Worcestershire and back again, takes in an outstanding tour of the surprising variety of landscapes in this area, traversing open heathland, following woodland trails and a section of the Staffordshire Way and passing two of the rock houses. Follow the purple Rock House Trail waymarkers throughout.

Above: Rock houses at Kinver Edge.
Opposite: Estate trails at Kinver.

THINGS TO SEE

The Hill Fort and Rock Houses

Exploring Kinver you'll discover a soaring sandstone ridge topped with a hill fort, thought to date from the Late Bronze Age. Standing strong on the Worcestershire/Staffordshire border – once the boundary between two Iron Age tribes – the two huge earth ramparts visible today would originally have been even larger. Topped with a wall or fence, the enclosure would probably have contained a settlement of roundhouses, the circular impressions of which

are visible at certain times of the year when conditions are right (usually in winter).

Rising to 538ft (164m) above sea level, the fort towers over the intriguing Holy Austin Rock Houses, set deep into the red sandstone. The site of the last troglodyte dwellings in England, these houses were occupied until the 1960s and have been restored by the National Trust to give a taste of what life might have been like for the inhabitants over the centuries.

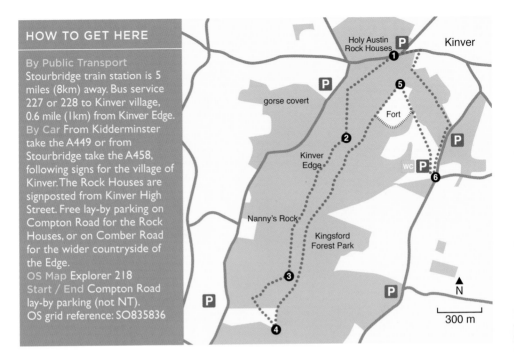

HOW TO GET HERE

By Public Transport
Stourbridge train station is 5 miles (8km) away. Bus service 227 or 228 to Kinver village, 0.6 mile (1km) from Kinver Edge.
By Car From Kidderminster take the A449 or from Stourbridge take the A458, following signs for the village of Kinver. The Rock Houses are signposted from Kinver High Street. Free lay-by parking on Compton Road for the Rock Houses, or on Comber Road for the wider countryside of the Edge.
OS Map Explorer 218
Start / End Compton Road lay-by parking (not NT).
OS grid reference: SO835836

Holy Austin Rock Houses

Kinver

gorse covert

Fort

Kinver Edge

Nanny's Rock

Kingsford Forest Park

N

300 m

Other trails nearby

The waymarked, 95-mile (153km) Staffordshire Way runs between Mow Cop in Staffordshire and the southern fringes of Kinver Edge, lying entirely in Worcestershire.

1. From the noticeboard at the start, follow purple waymarkers uphill through the woods.

2. 0.4 miles/0.7km Continue straight on below Kinver Edge, passing Nanny's Rock.

3. 1.1 miles/1.7km Passing open heathland on your right and Vale's Rock – a rock house that isn't open to the public – on your left, follow waymarkers through woodland to ascend to Kinver Edge.

4. 1.4 miles/2.3km Continue along the edge of the escarpment, following waymarkers – this is also a section of the Staffordshire Way.

5. 2.6 miles/4.1km Admire the views from the hill fort, then turn around and follow the purple waymarkers down past the ramparts, crossing grassland and heading through woodland.

6. 3 miles/4.8km Continue downhill, passing the rock houses and returning to the car park.

46. Carding Mill Valley

Church Stretton
Shropshire
SY6 6JG

ABOUT THIS RUN

Distance **5.5 miles (8.9km)**
Ascent **1,076ft (328m)**

Good paths and hill trails
May be muddy
Wildlife
Dogs welcome
Family friendly

Set deep within the Shropshire Hills Area of Outstanding Natural Beauty, the National Trust-managed Long Mynd and Carding Mill Valley cover nearly 5,000 acres (2,023ha) of rolling, heather-covered hills scored through with steep river valleys. There's plenty to see and do here, whether you're running or not, from wildlife watching and paddling in the stream to heading into the hills to discover the peace and solitude of the Long Mynd.

This run follows an adventurous loop, starting along the main path through Carding Mill Valley before climbing up into the hills on inviting trails with outstanding views. The final miles take you down a well-earned descent into Townbrook Valley, tracing the snaking course of the brook to return to Carding Mill. Please keep to the trails when running here to avoid damage to the sensitive landscape.

THINGS TO SEE

Bridleways
The Long Mynd is networked with bridleways, perfect for exploring on horseback or mountain bike. Maps of bike-friendly trails are available at the visitor centre and there's a fantastic range of trails with something to suit every level of rider.

Long Mynd wildlife
Amidst the gorse and heather there's a wonderful array of flora and fauna to spot here. Look for wildflowers such as birdsfoot trefoil, shepherd's cress, sheep's sorrel and heath bedstraw – once used to fragrance mattresses. Birdlife includes ravens, skylarks, grouse, snipe, wheatear and dipper, while green hairstreak, orange tip, copper and small heath butterflies can be spotted in late spring. The area is also popular with amphibians, including frogs, common toads and palmate newts, while common lizards can sometimes be seen basking on a warm rock on a sunny day.

Above: Running down Carding Mill Valley.
Opposite: Carding Mill Valley.

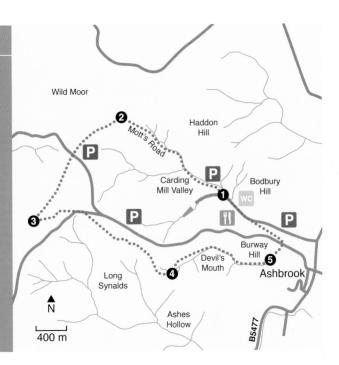

HOW TO GET THERE

By Public Transport Church Stretton train station is 1 mile (1.6km) away.
By Car West of Church Stretton Valley and A49; approached from Church Stretton or from Ratlinghope or Asterton.
OS Map Explorer 217
Start / End National Trust Carding Mill Valley car park.
OS grid reference: SO445945

Wild Moor

❷

Mott's Road

Haddon Hill

🅿

Carding Mill Valley

❶

WC

🅿

Bodbury Hill

❸

🅿

🍴

🅿

Burway Hill ❺

Devil's Mouth

Ashbrook

❹

Long Synalds

N

400 m

Ashes Hollow

B5477

1. From the start at the car park at the heart of Carding Mill Valley, follow the main track alongside the stream, climbing steeply through the valley towards the hills – this is also part of the Jack Mytton Way.

2. 1.1 miles/1.7km As the climb becomes less steep you'll reach a track junction. Turn left here and follow the main path, crossing a road and continuing to reach the viewpoint at Pole Bank.

3. 2.2 miles/3.6km From the viewpoint, turn sharp left, leaving the main track and following a footpath to reach the road. Turn left onto the road and then right onto a footpath, following this parallel to the road – with the road on your left – down into Townbrook Valley.

4. 3.7 miles/5.9km At the path junction, bear left and cross Town Brook, following its course down the valley, descending steeply until you reach the reservoir and a footbridge and an area of woodland.

5. 4.7 miles/7.5km Turn left before you enter the woodland and follow the footpath down to the road at Ashbrook. Cross the road and follow the footpath around the hill to the left, running back up the valley to return to the car park.

Other trails nearby
There's a vast network of trails to explore in the Shropshire Hills, including the Jack Mytton Way, nearly 100 miles (161km) of waymarked footpaths and bridleways around the Shropshire countryside.

47. Attingham

**Atcham
Shrewsbury
Shropshire
SY4 4TP**

ABOUT THIS RUN

Distance **3.1** miles (5km)
Ascent 105ft (32m)

Level grassy and surfaced
  paths
Paid entry/NT members
Wildlife
History/culture
Dogs welcome
Family friendly

The grand 18th-century classical mansion at Attingham was the home of the Berwick family and subject to its variable fortunes for more than 160 years before being bequeathed to the National Trust in 1947. Surrounding the house are 200 acres (81ha) of picturesque gardens, pleasure grounds and deer park, perfect for exploring on foot, while the wider estate, incorporating farmland and properties, extends to around 4,000 acres (1,619ha). Landscaped by Humphrey Repton, the parkland is dotted with areas of woodland and wound through with inviting paths and the rivers Severn and Tern. This run loops the parkland, following trails through the trees, with two river crossings, including Deer Park Bridge that opens out to the Repton-designed parkland, and some wonderful open sections across the springy grass of the parkland.

Other trails nearby

Waymarked trails around the estate include the World War II walk, the Wildlife Walk and the River Reflections walk, all of which are great for running, too.

THINGS TO SEE

The estate

There's a fascinating range of buildings and businesses scattered across the wider estate at Attingham, including 60 houses and cottages, 12 tenant farms, a cookery school, three Scheduled Ancient Monuments, one of which incorporates one-third of the Roman City of Viroconium (now known as Wroxeter), and Cronkhill – a beautiful Italianate villa designed by John Nash. Over 3,200 acres (1,295ha) of the estate are used for agriculture, growing a variety of crops and producing milk, beef and lamb. The Mansion and Stables Courtyard buildings are heated using woodchip and firewood, sustainably produced from 370 acres (150ha) of woodland. The deer park is also home to ancient trees, some of which are over 800 years old. There's a rich diversity of wildlife across the estate, including bats and birds such as barn owls, ravens, buzzards and woodpeckers; fungi from tiny waxcaps to giant puffballs; and around 180 fallow deer in the deer park.

By Public Transport
Shrewsbury train station
4.7 miles (7.6km). Then bus
service 81 or 96 Shrewsbury
to Telford, stopping at the
Mytton and Mermaid, directly
opposite main gates. There is a
1 mile (1.6km) walk from here
to the main entrance and
visitor reception.
By Car Attingham is on the
B4380, 4 miles (6.4km)
south-east of Shrewsbury
with good access from the A5.
OS Map Explorer 241
Start / End National Trust
visitor reception.
OS grid reference: SJ550098

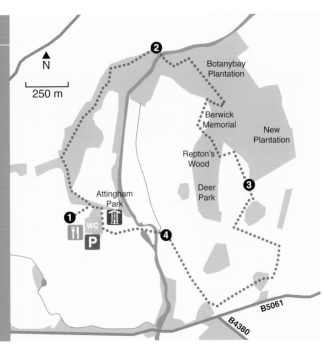

1. From the start, follow the waymarked Mile Walk signs through woodland, passing the walled garden on your left. Where the Mile Walk turns right, take the left fork marked Deer Park and Woodland Walk.

2. 0.9 miles/1.5km Cross the footbridge, joining the Deer Park Walk and following this up the gentle slope through Botanybay Plantation. At the top of the slope turn right, keeping on the Deer Park Walk and emerging onto the Deer Park itself. Pass the Berwick Memorial on your left and after 150 yards (137m) turn left entering Repton's Wood, following this path until the World War II Walk joins from the right.

3. 1.7 miles/2.8km Turn onto the World War II walk and follow this around the edge of the Deer Park, finishing along the riverside path, with the river on your left.

4. 2.7 miles/4.3km Turn left, crossing the footbridges to return to the house and car park.

Opposite: Deer in the
parkland at Attingham Park.
Below: Deer Park Bridge.

48. Calke Abbey

Calke Abbey
Ticknall
Derby
DE73 7JF

ABOUT THIS RUN

Distance **Up to 5.6 miles
(9km)**
Ascent **325ft (99m)**

Surfaced multi-user path
Waymarked
Running buggy/wheelchair
    friendly
Wildlife
History/culture
Dogs welcome on leads

Standing on the site of a Medieval religious building, Calke Abbey has a fascinating history and stands today, frozen in time, much as it has done for the past 150 years. Surrounding the house are 600 acres (243ha) of historic parkland to explore, networked by many outstanding footpaths and bridleways. This route follows the waymarked, multi-user Tramway Trail, taking you through woodland, farmland and rolling pasture, as well as following some of the old horse-drawn tramway that once linked Ticknall with Ashby. You can choose to start your run at the Abbey car park and combine it with a wander around the house and gardens, or discover the new Calke Explore outdoor hub, where you'll find great facilities and lots of ideas for adventurers of all ages. Suitable for running buggies, wheelchairs and accompanying kids on bikes, you can make your run longer or shorter to suit, with a figure-of-eight, single loop or two shorter loops to choose from.

THINGS TO SEE

Ancient trees
Calke Park is home to many ancient and fragile habitats and a National Nature Reserve. Some of Europe's oldest trees can be found on the estate, including the Old Man of Calke, a 1,200-year-old oak tree, and its young neighbour – another oak tree just 900 years old.

Above: The Avenue at Calke Abbey.

The un-stately home
With its peeling paintwork, eccentric collections amassed over many generations and overgrown courtyards, Calke Abbey tells the story of the dramatic decline of a country house estate. Little restoration work has so far been done on the house and stables, while areas overtaken by nature and the faded beauty of the walled gardens and orangery echo a period in the 20th century when many country houses did not survive to tell their story.

By Public Transport Nearest train stations at Derby, 9 miles (14.5km, then bus service 61, Derby to Swadlincote. Alight at Ticknall, then a 1.5 mile (2.5km) walk through the Park to the Ticket Office.
By Car 10 miles (16km) south of Derby on A514 at Ticknall. M42/A42 exit 13 and A50 Derby South. Brown signposts from A42.
OS Map Explorer 245
Start / End National Trust Calke Explore hub car park.
OS grid reference: SK359225.

Ticknall 4
A514
B5006
Clay Pit Plantation
Calke Park National Nature Reserve
Staunton Harold Reservoir
Mere Pond
Jubilee Plantation
P 1
Betty's Pond
Calke Abbey
WC
Poker's Leys
Heathend Plantation
Southwood
3
2
Pisternhill Plantation
N
South Wood
300 m

1. At Calke Explore, join the Tramway Trail just beyond the main car park, and then turn left onto the hard path. When you reach the trail map, turn left to follow the path through the woodland. At Hogg's Close corner, pass through the gate and bear left towards the driveway (be aware of cars approaching from the left). Take the track on the right, away from the driveway, with the dry stone wall to your right. Continue until you reach a bend in the track, then look for a gate to your right. Pass through the gate and follow the path until you reach two pedestrian gates near a brick barn. Pass through the gates and continue along the path through farmland and woodland.

2. **0.9 miles/1.4km** When you reach a squeezer stile on your left, do not cross the road but continue along the Tramway Trail to the right, which runs parallel to the road. Eventually, you'll reach a road crossing. Cross the road and continue along the trail under a small bridge. When you reach a sharp bend in the path, continue to your right along the Tramway Trail.

3. **2.7 miles/4.4km** Pass under another small bridge and continue along the trail until you reach a gravel track with some cottages on your right.

Continue along the path until you come to a road crossing. Cross over, then pick up the Tramway trail and continue until you reach a small tunnel. Pass under the tunnel, then continue to follow the path through another gate.

4. **4 miles/6.4km** When you reach another tunnel, take the right-hand pathway up to the trail (do not go under the tunnel this time). Turn right at the top, and pass a pond on your left. Continue to follow the trail alongside the main driveway until you reach Middle Lodge, where you will find two gates. Pass through the right-hand gate and continue along the hard track until you reach Calke Explore.

Other trails nearby

There's a great network of nearby trails, including many around the Calke estate. Long-distance trails include the National Forest Way, running 75 miles (121km) between the National Memorial Arboretum in Staffordshire and Beacon Hill Country Park in Leicestershire, and the Cross Britain Way, which stretches 280 miles (450km) across England and Wales from Boston to Barmouth.

49. Ilam Park & Dovedale

Ilam Park
Ilam
Derbyshire
DE6 2AZ

ABOUT THIS RUN

Distance 5.5 miles (8.8km)
Ascent 1,276ft (389m)

Good paths and grassy
trails
Dogs welcome
History/culture
Wildlife

Ilam Park and neighbouring Dovedale lie in the White Peak, the southern half of the Peak District, where grassy limestone hills have been cut through by the relentless passage of the River Dove to form a deep, sheer-sided gorge. The resulting running is brilliantly varied, with long stretches along a peaceful, flat riverside trail, edged by invitingly craggy fells where tough ascents and technical descents are interspersed with glorious views. This run begins at Ilam, where you'll also find a National Trust shop, café and car park, and heads across to explore Dovedale, following the river up past the famous stepping stones to Ilam Rock. From here there's a good climb through Dovedale Wood before an enjoyable, undulating stretch through limestone countryside returns you to Ilam Park.

Above: River Dove at Dovedale.
Opposite: Running across the Dovedale stepping stones.

THINGS TO SEE

The Peak District

In 1951 The Peak District became the first of Britain's National Parks, following decades of campaigning for access to open spaces for all. One of the most successful acts of civil disobedience in British history, the mass trespass to Kinder Scout paved the way for the National Parks legislation in 1949 and, eventually, the Countryside and Rights of Way Act in 2000.

Today, the Peak District remains true to its original purpose: an accessible area of open spaces and natural beauty where people can escape the surrounding cities and enjoy recreation in the great outdoors. It is also without a doubt one of the best places in the country for trail running, networked with hundreds of miles of well-maintained footpaths and bridleways. The character of the running here differs with its underlying geology. To the north, the Dark Peak lies on a bedrock of gritstone, giving the area its windswept high fells and prominent edges while, to the south, the White Peak boasts a landscape of steep limestone valleys, clear streams and open, fast-draining grassland.

By Public Transport Train to Matlock or Derby, from where there are regular buses to Ashbourne. Change to 442 bus to Thorpe near Ilam.
By Car Ilam village and Dovedale are near Thorpe village about 5 miles (8km) north-west of Ashbourne. Routes from the A52 and the A515.
OS Map Explorer OL24
Start / End National Trust Ilam Park car park.
OS grid reference: SK132507

Ilam Rock **4** Pickering Tor
▲ N
400 m
Weir
Sharplow Dale
5
Jacob's Ladder — Tissington Spires
Weir
Bunster Hill
Dovedale Castle
Ilam Country Park — Ilam
WC
P
1
2 Hotel
3
Thorpe Cloud
P

1. From the start, follow the footpath away from Ilam, with the car park on your right, heading up into the parkland. Follow the path as it curves around to the right to reach the road in Ilam village. Turn right onto the road, then bear left at the triangle. Follow the road as it curves to the right, then turn left onto a footpath after the buildings on your left.

2. 0.6 miles/1km Join the main path and turn right, following the path around the hillside and past the Izaak Walton hotel to reach the road and main car park for Dovedale.

3. 1.3 miles/2.1km Cross the road and the footbridge over the river and run up Dovedale with the river on your left. You'll pass the stepping stones, weirs and several caves as you go.

4. 3 miles/4.9km Cross the river over the footbridge and take the footpath opposite, climbing steeply straight up the hill through Dovedale Wood. At the top of the woodland, follow the footpath left and along the edge of the woods to reach a cottage and farm buildings at Ilam Tops.

5. 4 miles/6.4km At the path junction turn left and follow the footpath south, down Bunster Hill and continue straight ahead to reach the road just outside Ilam village. Turn right and rejoin your outward route through the village and back to Ilam Park.

Other trails nearby

The Manifold Way runs for 8.1 miles (12.9km) from Hulme End in the north to Waterhouses in the south, mostly through the Manifold Valley.

50. Kinder Reservoir

Hayfield Sett Valley Trail car park
Station Road
Hayfield
SK22 2ES

ABOUT THIS RUN

Distance 5.8 miles (9.4km)
Ascent 1,233ft (376m)

Stoney and grassy tracks
  and trails, steep sections,
  some road
Views
Wildlife
History/culture
Dogs welcome

The River Kinder rises on Kinder Scout, the highest point in the Peak District National Park, and flows 98ft (30m) over Kinder Downfall, a dramatic ice cascade (during a cold winter) that's popular with climbers and through Kinder Reservoir before joining the River Sett only 3 miles (4.8km) further on. Surrounded by dramatic Dark Peak scenery, this run takes in a full circuit of the reservoir, starting through the avenues of Hayfield before heading off-road and following the famous Snake Path up to reach the heather-clad moors surrounding Kinder. Surprise viewpoints and beautiful, peaceful moments make this varied, engaging run one you'll want to do again and again.

THINGS TO SEE

Fell racing
The Peak District has a strong tradition of fell racing, with many of the best in the sport coming from the local club Dark Peak Fell Runners. The Hayfield Fell running championships feature a number of races of differing distances around Kinder, from the appropriately named Kinder

Downfall to the amusingly named A Groovy Kinder Love. The High Peak Marathon is another famous local race, first run in 1972 and now an established classic on the fell-racing calendar. Taking place in early March, when snow often lies thickly on the ground, it sees teams of four self-navigating across 40 miles (64.3km) of rough terrain overnight.

Right to Roam
The Snake Path, along which this run begins, was opened in 1897 as the first in a series of successes for the Peak and Northern Footpaths Society in their mission to win public access to the moors. Then, on 24 April 1932, the Kinder Mass Trespass, an act of wilful trespass by a group of 400 ramblers, was undertaken to highlight the lack of access to areas of open country, arguably leading to the National Parks legislation in 1949.

Above: View across Kinder Reservoir.
Opposite: William Clough below Kinder Scout.

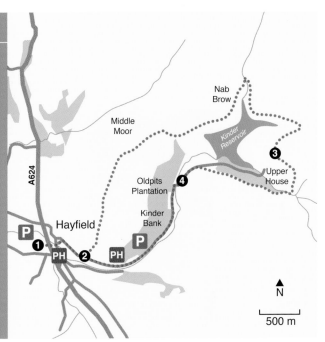

HOW TO GET HERE

By Public Transport New Mills train station, 3.2 miles (5.1km). Then bus service 62 or 358 to Hayfield, follow directions to the start of Snake Path.
By Car Hayfield Sett Valley Trail car park (not NT) is in the centre of Hayfield, postcode SK22 2ES.
OS Map Explorer OL1
Start / End Hayfield Sett Valley Trail car park (not NT), Station Road, Hayfield.
OS grid reference: SK036868

1. Leave the car park, crossing the road and running past the Conservative Club and church on your left. Turn left onto Church Street, then take the first turning right onto Kinder Road. Run past the library on your left, then look for the signpost to Snake Path on your left.

2. 0.4 miles/0.6km Turn left onto Snake Path and follow this as it climbs steadily across open grassland and around the northern shore of Kinder Reservoir. Where the path forks left for William Clough, stay right, rounding the northern point of the reservoir and heading back down its eastern side. Continue on the main path, crossing a footbridge and reaching an area of trees by Upper House.

3. 3.2 miles/5.1km Bear left at Upper House, then follow the track around to the right, passing to the left of the trees and keeping these and the reservoir on your right until you reach an access road. Turn left and then cross the river at Booth.

4. 4.3 miles/7km Turn left after the bridge, joining Kinder Road and following this back to Hayfield, rejoining your outward route to return to the start.

Other trails nearby
There's a wealth of excellent running right across the Peak District, including the Pennine Way, which starts in Edale, just east of Hayfield, and runs 268 miles (431km) northwards to Kirk Yetholm in the Scottish borders. The Limestone Way and the Pennine Bridleway also run past Hayfield.

51. Lyme Park

Disley
Stockport
Cheshire
SK12 2NR

ABOUT THIS RUN

Distance **3.7 miles (5.9km)**
Ascent **617ft (188m)**

Good paths and grassy
 trails
May be muddy
Parkrun and Trust10
Urban escape
Dogs welcome
Family friendly

Lying on the western fringes of the Peak District National Park, the National Trust's Lyme estate covers 1,400 acres (567ha) of gardens, moorland and deer park. Easily reached by train it's a glorious place to escape from the busy towns and cities nearby, including Manchester, Stockport and Macclesfield. The park is brilliantly set up for runners, with a weekly parkrun, monthly Trust10 and even a regular running group – Lyme Runners – ideal if you're keen to explore the area further in the company of other runners with good local knowledge.

This run at Lyme takes in a loop of the park, making the most of its varied landscape and setting with plenty of opportunity to pause for breath and admire the views and trails through woodland, across open moor and along a section of the Gritstone Trail.

THINGS TO SEE

The Cage

Lyme Park's iconic, Grade II-listed tower, the Cage, complete with its three impressive sundials, stands overlooking the main entrance road to the estate. Originally built in the 16th century, it was demolished and rebuilt in 1737 by Peter Platt for Peter Legh XII. Used as a hunting lodge and banqueting hall, it has a long and varied history. For a time it is said to have been used as a prison for poachers caught on the estate and during the Second World War it housed children evacuated from nearby Manchester. More recently it was used in the filming of the 2011 thriller *The Awakening*. Exploring the tower is free, however dogs are not allowed inside.

There are several other unusual structures to be discovered as you explore the park, including the three-storey, octagonal-spired belvedere, known as the Lantern, hidden in Lantern Wood near to the house.

Bollinhurst Bridge

Mudhurst Lane

Cage Hill

Crow Wood

Kennel Wood

4

1

🏛 🍴 WC

P
Lyme Park

Lantern Wood

Hampers Wood

3

Knightslow Wood

Higher Moor

Higher Lane

Gritstone Trail

▲ N

Bow Stones **2**

200 m

1. Turn left out of the car park and follow the main drive around to the left. Where the path forks, stay left, following the waymarked Gritstone Trail across grassland and then over the wooded hill at Knightslow. Emerging onto open moorland, continue on the Gritstone Trail until you reach a road at a T-junction.

2. 1.2 miles/2km Turn left onto the road and run along this, passing a couple of buildings and continuing until you reach a larger road.

3. 2.1 miles/3.4km Don't join the road but turn left and head between the buildings and out onto a footpath the other side. Follow the footpath first alongside a wall and then bearing slightly left across scrubland to reach a stone track.

4. 2.7 miles/4.3km Turn left and follow the stone track all the way back to the car park.

Opposite: Runners at Lyme Park in front of the Cage.
Right: Deer at Lyme Park.

Other trails nearby
The Peak District is one of the best places in the country for off-road running, with trails to suit every runner. The Gritstone Trail runs from Disley station for 35 miles (56km) through Lyme Park to Kidsgrove in Staffordshire.

52. Clumber Park

Worksop
Nottinghamshire
S80 3AZ

ABOUT THIS RUN

Distance 5.2 miles (8.4km)
Ascent 239ft (73m)

Multi-user surfaced path,
  woodland trails
Can be made suitable for
  bikes and buggies
Family friendly
Parkrun and Trust10
Wildlife
History/culture
Dogs welcome

Once the country estate of the Dukes of Newcastle, Clumber Park is a wide expanse of open grass and farmland, heaths, woods and a majestic lake, in total covering an area of more than 3,800 acres (1,538ha). One of just a few Grade I-listed parks in the country, it is networked by well-maintained trails, paths and roads, making exploring the wider estate enjoyable and accessible for all. The diversity of landscapes means a great variety of wildlife flourishes here, a peaceful haven just a short way from Nottingham and the busy East Midlands. This run loops the northern half of the estate, following winding woodland paths and finishing with a long stretch alongside the lake. It also crosses the famous Lime Tree Avenue, planted in 1840 and the longest of its kind in Europe, which stretches for 2 miles (3.2km) and comprises 1,296 common lime trees.

Above: Lime Tree Avenue at Clumber.
Opposite: View across the lake at Clumber Park.

Other trails nearby
Visiting places associated with the legendary outlaw, the Robin Hood Way runs for 107 miles (172km) between Nottingham and Edwinstowe, in Sherwood Forest.

THINGS TO SEE

The Lake
The long, shining serpentine of Clumber Lake covers 87 acres (35.2ha), south of the site of Clumber House. It was built in 1772 by damming the River Poulter at the bottom end of the estate and excavating the river bed to form a wide expanse of water, a project that took 15 years to complete and cost £6,612. An ornamental bridge was built at the western end of the lake, a Grade II-listed structure consisting of three arches topped by ornate balustrades. In 2018 the bridge was severely vandalised and is, at the time of writing, undergoing rebuilding and restoration.

Outdoor activities
There's a fantastic range of activities to get involved in at Clumber, including a weekly 5km parkrun, Trust10 monthly 10km (6.2-mile) runs, a Run Further running group, Nordic walking, a dog-walking group, volunteer ranger-led walks, bike hire and a beginner-friendly cycling group.

By Public Transport Worksop train station is 4.7 miles (7.6km) away. Stagecoach 'The Sherwood Arrow' Worksop to Ollerton, alight Carburton.
By Car 4.5 miles (7.2km) south-east of Worksop, 7 miles (11.3km) south-west of Retford, 3 miles (4.8km) from A1/A57, 12 miles (19.3km) from M1 exit 30.
By Bicycle National Cycle Network route 6 and several bridleways run through the estate.
OS Map Explorer OL270
Start / End National Trust Clumber Park car park.
OS grid reference: SK625745

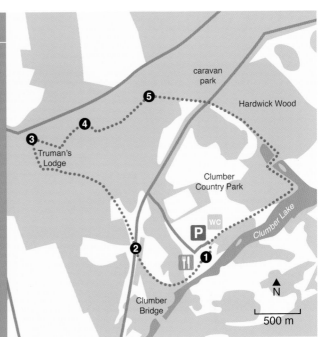

1. Leave the main car park and follow the signs for the café and toilets. Go past the toilets and at the signpost follow the path to reach the lakeside. Follow the path with the lake on your left. Cross the minor road and continue to Lime Tree Avenue.

2. **0.7 miles/1.1km** Cross with care, turning right and running along the road for a short distance until you can turn left onto National Cycle Network Route 6, following this and bearing right at a path junction to reach Clumber Lane, just in front of Truman's Lodge.

3. **1.9 miles/3km** Turn right onto the driveway and follow it until you can turn left onto a footpath, just before Clumber Cottage. Follow this for a short distance to reach the Robin Hood Way.

4. **2.4 miles/3.8km** Turn right onto the Robin Hood Way. Take the first footpath left, following this straight ahead to a T-junction with a bridleway.

5. **2.9 miles/4.7km** Turn right onto the bridleway and follow this back to the lake, running past the first, smaller lake and then turning right before the larger lake. Follow the path with the lake on your left, and continue on to the car park.

53. Lyveden

Near Oundle
Northamptonshire
PE8 5AT

ABOUT THIS RUN

Distance **5.8 miles (9.4km)**
Ascent **279ft (85m)**

Grassy fields and tracks,
   quiet lanes and surfaced
   path
Mostly waymarked route
History/culture
Wildlife
Dogs welcome on leads

Lyveden New Bield is an unfinished Elizabeth lodge and
moated garden, standing amidst rolling Northamptonshire
countryside. Begun as an ambitious project by Sir Thomas
Tresham, a prominent Elizabethan Catholic landowner,
the lodge stands intriguingly suspended in time, left where
construction had reached when Tresham died in 1605.
With the exception of a short stretch of track to shorten
its length slightly, this run follows the waymarked Lyveden
Way, a circular path through beautiful meadows, woodland
and villages.

Above: Lyveden New Bield.
Opposite: Purple emperor
butterflies can be seen at
nearby Fermyn Woods.

THINGS TO SEE

Lyveden Manor
Take the time to explore Lyveden's Elizabethan
earthworks and moats as you make your way
to the garden lodge (also known as Lyveden
New Bield) to start your run. Built by Thomas
Tresham's son, Lewis, in c.1620, Lyveden Manor
was in private ownership until it was acquired
by the National Trust in 2013. The building is
believed to have replaced an older structure
located at the entry point of Tresham's
Elizabethan garden. Many of the building's original
features have been removed or damaged over
the years. In 2019, an extensive renovation
project begun to transform the building into a
new visitor hub with café, visitor reception and

interpretation spaces. For the first time, visitors
can discover the wonder of this rare Elizabethan
garden with its 390ft (120m) of grass paths,
viewing mounts and moat leading upwards
from the Manor House to the New Bield.

Lyveden wildlife
The official start of the Lyveden Way is at
nearby Fermyn Woods, a good place to spot the
rare and beautiful purple emperor butterfly over
the summer months. While you're out exploring
the countryside look out for dragonflies and
damselflies and birds including swallows,
skylarks and red kites.

HOW TO GET HERE

By Public Transport Corby train station, 7.5 miles (12.1km).
By Car Lyveden is just off the A6116 between Islip and Corby.
OS Map Explorer 224
Start / End From the National Trust Lyveden car park there is a 390ft (137m) walk through the Elizabethan garden to Lyveden New Bield.
OS grid reference: SP984853

N

500 m

Bearshank Wood

Lyveden New Bield **1**

Lilford Wood

Lady Wood **4**

2

Souther Wood

Green Side Wood

Titchmarsh Wood

3

Oxen Wood

1. From Lyveden New Bield, take the left fork of the Lyveden Way along a bridleway into Lilford Wood. Continue following the bridleway, emerging from the wood, crossing a stream and joining a main track to reach a track junction just before Wadenhoe Lodge.

2. 1 mile/1.6km Continue straight on, following waymarkers past the lodge to reach a lane. Turn right onto the lane and follow this, carrying straight on where the Lyveden Way turns off left to the village of Wadenhoe. On reaching a sharp right-hand corner in the road, carry straight on, following a green lane straight ahead – the Lyveden Way also re-joins at this point.

3. 2.5 miles/4.1km Turn right off the green lane and onto a footpath across fields, staying on the Lyveden Way. Follow this path along the edge of the woods, eventually bearing left and running through woodland to reach a path junction where the Lyveden Way heads left to Fermyn Wood and right to Lyveden.

4. 4.8 miles/7.7km Turn right and follow the Lyveden Way back to Lyveden and the end of the run.

Other trails nearby
The full, waymarked Lyveden Way covers a distance of approximately 9.5 miles (15.3km) and makes an excellent longer run.

54. Belton

Grantham
Lincolnshire
NG32 2LS

ABOUT THIS RUN

Distance **3.2 miles (5.2km)**
Ascent 131ft (40m)

Good paths and grassy
  trails
Parkrun
Dogs welcome on leads
Family friendly

Belton Park estate covers 1,300 acres (526ha) of wildlife-rich countryside, including formal gardens, pleasure grounds and 750 acres (303ha) of designated deer park, home to around 300 fallow deer. A perfect place to bring the family, the playground is the National Trust's largest, with plenty of fun – and coffee for grown-ups, too. This run follows the Park Walk around the estate, starting at the impressive 17th-century decorative Carolean mansion and winding through leafy woodland, across open grassland and alongside a golf course. The return trip traces the gentle meanders of the River Witham – keep an eye out for kingfishers and green woodpeckers as you go – before finishing through the Wilderness and returning to the house.

Other trails nearby
The Viking Way, just to the west of Belton, runs for 147 miles (237km) between the Humber Bridge in the north of Lincolnshire and winds its way through the county to Oakham in Rutland in the south.

THINGS TO SEE

Towthorpe medieval village
Running alongside the River Witham you'll pass the deserted medieval village of Towthorpe. Mentioned in the Doomsday Book of 1086, there's evidence of much earlier settlement including Saxon and prehistoric findings. If you look carefully you can spot the remains of earthworks and the ridges and furrows of medieval farming methods visible between the meadow and the river.

Sustainability matters
At the time of writing, Belton is in the process of having the National Trust's largest biomass boiler installed, designed to provide renewable heat for 16 properties on the site. Fuelled by sustainable, local woodland management, the boiler will burn 373 tons of woodchip each year. This will generate 1,100,000kWhs of heat, reducing Belton's CO_2 emissions by 200 tons per year.

Above: Belton House.
Opposite: Fallow deer at Belton House.

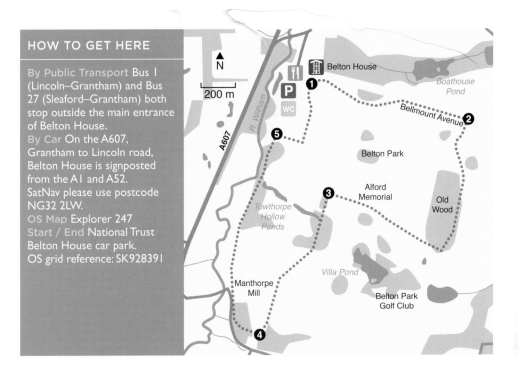

HOW TO GET HERE

By Public Transport Bus 1 (Lincoln–Grantham) and Bus 27 (Sleaford–Grantham) both stop outside the main entrance of Belton House.
By Car On the A607, Grantham to Lincoln road, Belton House is signposted from the A1 and A52. SatNav please use postcode NG32 2LW.
OS Map Explorer 247
Start / End National Trust Belton House car park.
OS grid reference: SK928391

N

200 m

Belton House

Boathouse Pond

Bellmount Avenue

Belton Park

Alford Memorial

Old Wood

Towthorpe Hollow Ponds

Villa Pond

Manthorpe Mill

Belton Park Golf Club

R. Witham

A607

1. From the start, looking at the front of the house, head around to the right and follow the small gravel path along the edge of the estate with the railings on your left. Continue straight on, following the line of trees, until you reach a wooden gate.

2. 0.6 miles/0.9km Go through the wooden gate and follow the path as it bears right along the line of the avenue. Towards the top of the hill, bear right again in front of the deer sanctuary fence to take you along the back of Old Wood. Bear right at the end of the woods before the golf-course fence and run downhill to reach the 19th-century Grade II-listed Conduit House and then the Alford Memorial.

3. 1.6 miles/2.5km Turn left at the corner of the golf course, passing Towthorpe Hollow Ponds and following the path along a line of trees to reach the Lion Gates at the far end of the park.

4. 2.1 miles/3.4km Turn right, following the main avenue from the gates towards the house. After 55 yards (50m), turn left onto a footpath

across to the River Witham. Turn right and run with the river on your left past the site of the deserted medieval village of Towthorpe.

5. 2.9 miles/4.7km Bear right across to the main path back to the front of the house.

55. Gunby Estate

Spilsby
Lincolnshire
PE23 5SS

ABOUT THIS RUN

Distance **3.8 miles (6.1km)**
Ascent **112ft (34m)**

Grassy fields and tracks,
some surfaced road
and path
History/culture
Wildlife
Dogs welcome

Modest, characterful and homely, Gunby Hall is an 18th-century country house surrounded by 8 acres (3.2ha) of picturesque gardens and nestled at the foot of the rolling Lincolnshire Wolds. This run explores the parkland and grounds, heading for the nearby hamlet of Bratoft. Along the way it passes the atmospheric remains of the house and garden of Bratoft Manor (not NT), a moated medieval site that was once home to the Massingberd family, prior to building Gunby. A short loop around Bratoft, on peaceful, wide-verged lanes with views out across open fields dotted with mature oaks and ashes, brings you to the homeward stretch along a section of path that was formerly the East Lincoln railway and operated between 1848 and 1971.

Above: The park at Gunby Hall.
Opposite: Gunby Hall.

THINGS TO SEE

Bratoft Manor
The name of the local hamlet and former manor, 'Bratoft' comes from the old Scandinavian *breithr* meaning 'homestead'. The moat, still clearly visible today, would have surrounded a medieval manor and gardens, most likely to have been built during the mid- to late 13th century. Bratoft Manor was originally the home of the de Braytoft family before being acquired by the Massingberds. The manor was demolished around 1700 by Sir William Massingberd, on the completion of Gunby Hall.

The Lincolnshire Wolds
The Lincolnshire Wolds Area of Outstanding Natural Beauty covers some 220 sq. miles (570 sq. km) of low hills formed from chalk, limestone and sandstone rock, laid down in the Cretaceous period, and characteristic open valleys, created through the actions of glaciation and meltwater during the last glacial period. The peaceful, rolling countryside, dotted with market towns and small settlements and networked with long-distance footpaths, makes it a particularly nice place to explore on foot.

HOW TO GET HERE

By Public Transport Skegness train station, 7.5 miles (12.1km), then bus service 6 from Lincoln and Skegness. Layby at Gunby roundabout is a request stop.
By Car On A158 off Gunby roundabout between Spilsby and Skegness. Signposted from A158, 14 miles (22.5km) east of Horncastle.
OS Map Explorer 274
Start / End National Trust Gunby Hall car park.
OS grid reference: TF466669

N

500 m

Gunby Estate Hall and Gardens

Gunby

A158

Island Pond

Hunger Hill

Bratoft Manor

1. From the courtyard at Gunby Hall, follow the path through the white gate, past the carp pond and through the gate on your left before the church. Follow the footpath across the parkland, bearing left after the second stile and following the fence line along the edge of the field and then along the green lane. At the end of the lane turn left, crossing a field to reach the disused railway.

2. **1 mile/1.6km** Cross the railway path and continue following the footpath along the edge of the next field to reach the medieval moat, all that remains above ground of Bratoft Manor. Continue straight ahead after the moat to reach a road.

3. **1.4 miles/2.3km** Turn left onto the road, then right and right again, running past the church and through the pretty hamlet of Bratoft. On

re-reaching the road, turn left and follow this for about 0.5 miles (0.8km) until you can turn right onto the railway path. Run along this for just over 0.5 miles (0.8km), passing Island Pond on your left.

4. **2.9 miles/4.6km** Reaching the footpath on your left on which you crossed the railway line at point 2, turn left to rejoin your outward path back across the fields and parkland to Gunby.

Other trails nearby
The Lincolnshire Wolds are great for gentler running. Try one of many circular routes based on the Viking Way, a long-distance trail that runs for 147 miles (237km) between the Humber Bridge in North Lincolnshire and Oakham in Rutland.

56. Wimpole

**Wimpole estate
Cambridgeshire
SG8 0BW**

ABOUT THIS RUN

Distance 3.1 miles (5km)
Ascent 174ft (53m)

Good trails and paths,
   some grassy sections
Wildlife
History/culture
Dog friendly
Parkrun and junior parkrun

Wimpole Hall, given to the National Trust by Rudyard Kipling's daughter Elise Bambridge in 1976, is a grand mansion dating back to the mid-1600s. Set within a wider estate covering 3,000 acres (1,214ha), Wimpole's 600-acre (243ha) parkland is edged by belts of ancient woodland and dotted with open-grown trees, a wonderfully peaceful place to explore. This run follows the route of the weekly parkrun, looping the main area of the park on a mixture of surfaced paths, gravel trails and grass underfoot. Starting out along a section of the Harcamlow Way, it follows a line of a woodland belt to reach the lakes, winding back through the parkland to finish in style at the front of the house.

Above: Autumn colour at
Wimpole estate.
Opposite: Running at Wimpole.

THINGS TO SEE

Home Farm
Set within 2,500 acres (1,012ha) of arable and grazing land, Wimpole Home Farm is one of the country's largest rare-breeds centres. The farm is home to Shire horses, Longhorn and White Park cattle, Bagot goats and rare-breed pigs and sheep and there's lots to do for visitors of all ages, from taking a ride in a carriage pulled by a Shire horse and meeting the newborn lambs in spring, to learning how to take care of the animals. The farm also produces organic and Freedom Foods-accredited food for the estate's shop and restaurant.

Wimpole wildlife
The woodland belts and ancient woodland surrounding the park are home to a wide variety of wildlife and the area is a designated Site of Special Scientific Interest. Look out for birds including jackdaws, treecreepers, nuthatches, woodpeckers, marsh tits and hawfinches; butterflies such as the speckled wood and dark green fritillary; and, if you're walking at dusk, badgers, rare Barbastelle bats and at least eight other bat species.

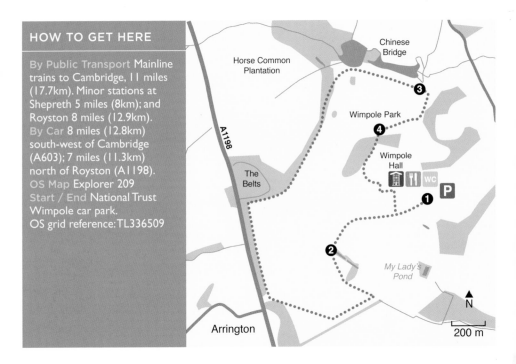

Horse Common Plantation

Chinese Bridge

Wimpole Park

Wimpole Hall

The Belts

My Lady's Pond

Arrington

A1198

N

200 m

1. From the start, follow the main path (also the Harcamlow Way) across the park with the house on your right.

2. 0.4 miles/0.7km Just after two small ponds on your left, turn left, following a minor path across the grass to reach a belt of trees. Bear right as you reach the trees and follow the path alongside these, curving to the right and then crossing the main path at right angles. Continue following this path along the border of trees all the way around the park.

3. 2.3 miles/3.7km Just after the two lakes on your left, bear right along another belt of trees, staying right to run to the right hand side of Wimpole Hall.

4. 2.7 miles/4.4km Bear left around to the front of the house, running down the main driveway immediately in front and then turning left back onto your outward path to return to the start.

Other trails nearby
The Wimpole Way runs 11 miles (18km) from central Cambridge to Wimpole Hall; the Harcamlow Way runs for 141 miles (227km) in a figure-of-eight around the counties of Cambridgeshire, Hertfordshire and Essex. Wimpole hosts a weekly parkrun, suitable for all-terrain buggies and dogs, junior parkrun and introduction to running group.

57. The Lodes Way

Wicken Fen National
Nature Reserve
Lode Lane
Wicken
CB7 5XP

ABOUT THIS RUN

Distance Up to 6.2 miles
(10km) each way
Ascent 85ft (26m)

Multi-user surfaced path
Wildlife
History/culture
Dogs welcome

The Cambridgeshire Lodes are six artificial waterways connecting the villages on the edge of the fens to the River Cam. Running through this intriguing landscape, the Lodes Way is an 8-mile (12.9km) multi-user trail linking Wicken Fen and Anglesey Abbey, forming part of the National Cycle Network route 11. This run begins at the National Trust's Wicken Fen visitor centre and follows the Lodes Way south towards Anglesey Abbey, stopping at the Lug Fen Droveway, where the cycle route heads towards Waterbeach. An out-and-back route that's perfect for the kids on their bikes or simply to enjoy the fens countryside without worrying about navigation, hills or rough ground, this is a thoroughly enjoyable route for everyone. Bicycles can be hired at the Cycle Hire Centre opposite the visitor centre.

THINGS TO SEE

Wicken Fen

The National Trust's oldest nature reserve, Wicken Fen is one of Europe's most important wetlands. Covering an area of nearly 2,000 acres (785ha) of wildflower meadows, lush grasslands, sedge and reedbeds, networked by boardwalks, there's an abundance of wildlife here. The reserve is home to more than 9,000 different species: this includes a vast array of plants; birds, such as rare hen harriers, barn owls and bitterns; mammals including water voles, badgers and bats; and insects such as dragonflies. An ongoing, ambitious landscape-scale conservation project is opening up new areas of land to explore, with grazing herds of Highland cattle and Konik ponies helping to create a diverse range of new habitats.

Above: Baker's Fen.
Opposite: Free-ranging Konik horses
help to manage the vegetation at
Baker's Fen.

HOW TO GET HERE

By Public Transport Ely train
station 9 miles (14.5km) away.
By Car South of Wicken
(A1123), 4 miles (6.4km)
west of Soham (A142), 9 miles
(14.5km) south of Ely; 17 miles
(27.3 miles) north-east of
Cambridge via A10.
By Bicycle National Cycle
Network 11 from Ely; Lodes
Way from Anglesey Abbey
and local villages.
OS Map Explorer 226
Start / End National Trust
Wicken Fen car park and
visitor centre.
OS grid reference: TL565706

N

1000 m

Upware

WC

Wicken Fen

Wicken
A1123

PH

Wicken Lode

New River

Reach Lode

Burwell Lode

Swaffham Prior Fen

Swaffham Bulbeck Lode

PH Reach

Bottisham Fen

Lug Fen Droveway

Swaffham Prior

1. Leave the visitor centre and follow the National Cycle
Network (NCN) route 11 signs south, away from Wicken Village.
Continue following route 11 signs, weaving your way through the
fens on long, straight trails. As an out-and-back run, you can turn
around at any point. From here, either continue, with some road
sections, to Anglesey Abbey, or turn around and run back to
Wicken Fen.

Other trails nearby
The Rothschild Way
(38 miles/61km) and the Fen
Rivers Way (50 miles/80km) are
two long-distance paths that
run near to Wicken Fen, great
for exploring further afield.

58. Flatford

**Station Approach
Manningtree
CO11 2LE**

ABOUT THIS RUN

Distance **7 miles (11.3km)**
Ascent **246ft (75m)**

Gravel and grass trails and
paths, riverside, some
quiet road
May be muddy
Wildlife
History/culture
Dogs welcome on leads

'The sound of water escaping from Mill dams ... Willows, Old rotten Banks, slimy posts, & brickwork. I love such things ...' wrote John Constable in a letter to a friend of the place that inspired some of his greatest works of art. This run explores Constable Country, tracing trails along the Stour Valley and Dedham Vale. Starting at Manningtree train station, it visits the pretty hamlet of Flatford, which provides the setting for Constable's work *The Hay Wain* where there is a National Trust tea room. It then takes the Stour Valley Path to Dedham village, where Constable went to school, and back out again along peaceful riverside trails. Perfectly positioned for arriving by train, you could also run from the National Trust car park at Flatford, a circular route of about 4 miles (6.4km).

THINGS TO SEE

Explore the River Stour

Between April and October, regular 30-minute boat trips run between Dedham and Flatford, a great way to see the river from a completely different perspective. The Stour was one of the first rivers in England to be converted into a navigation system following an Act of Parliament in 1705, however this did not include rights of passage for horses to travel on the towpaths. Agreement could not always be reached for the same side of the river, meaning on occasion horses needed to be transported across the river on specially designed platforms mounted on the boats in order to continue their journey.

Flatford

The pretty hamlet of Flatford is a delightful place to explore, or to relax for a post-run scone at the National Trust riverside tea room. Its fascinating buildings – many straight out of Constable's painting – include the Grade I-listed mill; Willy Lott's house, as depicted in *The Hay Wain*; Flatford Bridge Cottage; the former wool store of the Granary; and the beautiful, timber-framed, 15th-century Valley Farm.

Above: River Stour near Flatford.
Opposite: Trails at Flatford.

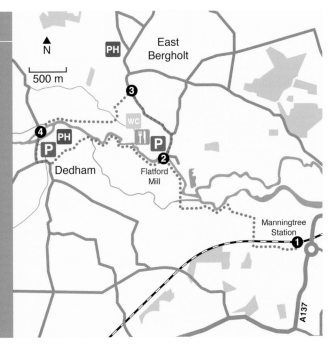

By Public Transport Route begins at Manningtree station (London Liverpool Street to Ipswich).
By Car Off A137 Harwich to Ipswich road. Car parks at Manningtree station, National Trust Flatford and Dedham.
By Bicycle The Painter's Trail cycle route passes through Stour Valley to Manningtree station. Cycle hire is available from Manningtree station.
On foot Along Station Road (B1352) from Manningtree town centre.
OS Map Explorer 196
Start / End Manningtree rail station.
OS grid reference: TM093322

1. Leave Manningtree rail station exit and descend the ramp to the right. The footpath starts from the end of the ramp in the car park. After leaving the car park, turn right along a track, then right again under a railway bridge. Follow the path until you reach the river and turn left through the Cattawade Marshes. Continue along this path until you cross the bridge into Flatford.

2. 1.8 miles/2.9km After crossing the river, continue straight ahead, following the lane past a car park on your left. Bear left at the junction and either run along the next section of lane or follow the footpath to the right of the lane for about 0.5 miles (0.8km).

3. 2.5 miles/4km Turn left onto a footpath just before you reach the outskirts of East Bergholt. Follow this straight ahead and over a bridge, crossing the river to meet the Stour Valley Path. Turn right onto this and follow it to reach the road at Dedham Bridge.

4. 3.5 miles/5.7km Turn left, crossing the bridge and following the road into the village. Turn left at the T-junction and then left again at the sharp right-hand-bend, leaving the road and following a

lane to Dedham Hall. Where the lane turns left into the hall, continue straight ahead, following a footpath to reach the river. Turn right here and follow the riverside path back to Flatford, turning right onto your outward path to return to Manningtree station.

Other trails nearby
The Stour Valley Path runs for 60 miles (96km) through Suffolk from Cattawade to Newmarket and is used for the annual Stour Valley Path 50km (31-mile) or 100km (62-mile) ultramarathon race.

59. Dunwich Heath

Dunwich Heath
Suffolk
IP17 3DJ

ABOUT THIS RUN

Distance **3.6 miles (5.8km)**
Ascent **102ft (31m)**

Footpaths and short
  stretches of road
Family friendly
Dogs welcome on leads
History/culture
Wildlife
Coastal

Set within the Suffolk Coast and Heaths Area of Outstanding Natural Beauty, Dunwich is a peaceful, atmospheric place, and is great for running, with many miles of trails that loop their way across the open heathland, through nature reserves and along the wave-washed pebbled edge of the sea. This run takes you through the varied landscape around Dunwich, starting just above the beach and following trails through open grassland and out in a wide loop around the heather-clad heath, edged with delicate silk ribbons of silver birch. The final stretch heads through woodland, finishing back at the beach, perfect for a relaxing post-run paddle.

Other trails nearby
The 60-mile (97km) Stour Valley Path, venue for an annual ultramarathon that takes in its entire length but with plenty of opportunities for shorter, circular excursions. The Little Ouse Path follows the winding river for 10 enjoyable miles (16km) from Brandon to Thetford.

THINGS TO SEE

In and around Dunwich
Legend has it that on a quiet day with a certain tide, the bells of the churches from the submerged old town of Dunwich can still be heard echoing along the Suffolk coast. Dating back to Anglo-Saxon times, the pretty village that stands here today was once part of a major port town, until storm surges during the 14th century reclaimed much of the land.

The wildlife-rich Dunwich Heath is a surviving fragment of lowland heath and one of the rarest habitats in Britain. Making their homes within the heather, gorse, sandy soil and acid grassland are Dartford warblers, nightjars, woodlarks, antlion flying insects and adders, while at neighbouring RSPB Minsmere there are avocets, bitterns and otter. Much of this fascinating and important area is officially designated a Site of Special Scientific Interest, a Special Area of Conservation and a Special Protection Area.

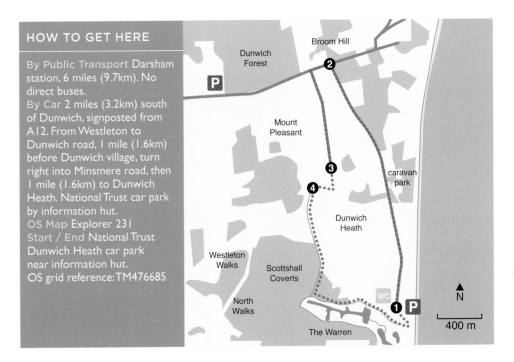

HOW TO GET HERE

By Public Transport Darsham station, 6 miles (9.7km). No direct buses.
By Car 2 miles (3.2km) south of Dunwich, signposted from A12. From Westleton to Dunwich road, 1 mile (1.6km) before Dunwich village, turn right into Minsmere road, then 1 mile (1.6km) to Dunwich Heath. National Trust car park by information hut.
OS Map Explorer 231
Start / End National Trust Dunwich Heath car park near information hut.
OS grid reference: TM476685

Broom Hill

Dunwich Forest

Mount Pleasant

caravan park

Dunwich Heath

Westleton Walks

Scottshall Coverts

North Walks

The Warren

N

400 m

1. From the car park, follow Minsmere Road, parallel to the coast, with the sea on your right, until you reach Westleton Road.

2. **1.4 miles/2.3km** Turn left onto Westleton Road, then left again onto a footpath, continuing along this past some buildings at Mount Pleasant on your left.

3. **2.1 miles/3.4km** Go straight on over a bridleway crossroad to reach a T-junction at the edge of the heath. Turn right here.

4. **2.2 miles/3.6km** Take the next left turn, before you reach the woods, following a footpath down the edge of the heath. Take the steps to the right and turn left at the bottom, following the course of the stream as it bears left just before Docwra's Ditch, heading for the coast. Continue until you reach the path junction above the beach, running up and over some steps. Turn left on the bridleway, then left again to return to the car park at the top of the bridleway.

Above: Take a diversion from the route to run along the sand at Dunwich Beach.
Opposite: Running across Dunwich Heath.

60. Blickling

Aylsham
Norwich
Norfolk
NR11 6NF

ABOUT THIS RUN

Distance 4.2 miles (6.7km)
Ascent 210ft (64m)

Multi-user surfaced trail
Waymarked
Suitable for bikes and
 buggies
Family friendly
History/culture
Dogs welcome on leads

The grand Jacobean mansion at Blickling stands grandly amidst striking formal gardens and 4,600 acres (1,862ha) of glorious parkland simply crying out for exploration. The undulating estate is filled with intriguing landmarks, stunning views and fascinating wildlife. Many of the trails that wind through the estate are suitable for bikes, buggies and wheelchairs as well as runners and walkers; maps of waymarked routes are available from visitor reception.

This run follows the multi-use, all-weather trail all the way around the perimeter of Blickling Park. Along the way, you'll run through woods and across open grassland, passing the Tower and Blickling Great Wood. Perfect for running buggies, wheelchair-users and cyclists, it's a great place to head for a family run. Visit in spring to see Great Wood carpeted in bluebells.

THINGS TO SEE

The house and garden

Built on the foundations of a Tudor manor house, thought to have been the birthplace of Anne Boleyn, the imposing Jacobean hall at Blickling was constructed by successful London lawyer Sir Henry Hobart after he purchased it in 1616. Many family portraits of the Hobarts, including works by Gainsborough and Reynolds, and watercolours by Humphry Repton, hang within the hall. The unique 18th-century Long Gallery library contains over 12,500 volumes and is the most prestigious book collection held by National Trust. Blickling's formal gardens cover some 55 acres (22.3ha) of grounds and are fascinating to explore. Things to see include the Parterre with its topiarised yew trees, the temple, orangery and the beautiful walled kitchen garden in which produce for the estate has been grown for over 400 years.

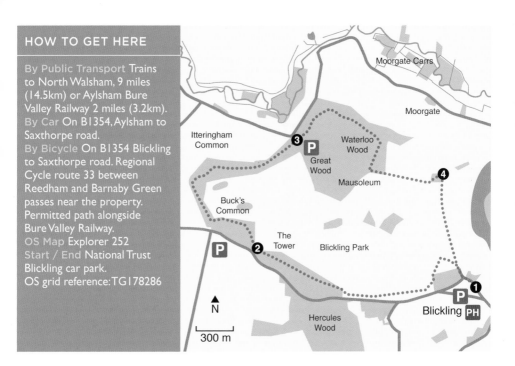

HOW TO GET HERE

By Public Transport Trains to North Walsham, 9 miles (14.5km) or Aylsham Bure Valley Railway 2 miles (3.2km).
By Car On B1354, Aylsham to Saxthorpe road.
By Bicycle On B1354 Blickling to Saxthorpe road. Regional Cycle route 33 between Reedham and Barnaby Green passes near the property. Permitted path alongside Bure Valley Railway.
OS Map Explorer 252
Start / End National Trust Blickling car park.
OS grid reference: TG178286

Moorgate Carrs

Moorgate

Itteringham Common

Waterloo Wood

Great Wood

Mausoleum

Buck's Common

The Tower

Blickling Park

N

300 m

Hercules Wood

Blickling

1. The multi-use trail is waymarked throughout. With the visitor centre behind you, run past the car park and follow the fence around to the road. Turn left and then bear right through the gate into Blickling Park to reach the start of the multi-use trail. Follow waymarkers right and then alongside the Aylsham road.

2. 1.4 miles/2.2km Run through the woodland at Long Plantation, passing The Tower on your right and continuing around Hyde Park and then alongside Bunker's Hill.

3. 2.4 miles/3.9km Enter Great Wood and follow the path through the woodland until you emerge near to the Pyramid of the Mausoleum on your right. Turn left and follow the path until it emerges into The Beeches.

4. 3.5 miles/5.7km At the path junction, turn right, go through the gates and follow the path back to the car park and Muddy Boots Café.

Other trails nearby
There's a great network of trails around the estate or, further afield, the Weavers' Way runs for 61 miles (98km) between Cromer and Great Yarmouth, passing Blickling along the way.

Above: View of the garden, house and lake at Blickling.
Opposite: Running through the estate at Blickling.

Northern
England

61. Formby

Victoria Road
Freshfield
Formby
Liverpool
L37 1LJ

ABOUT THIS RUN

Distance 3.2 miles (5.2km)
Ascent 95ft (29m)

Soft, steep dunes; sandy
  beach; uneven paths
Coastal
Wildlife
History/culture
Family friendly
Dogs welcome

Just 12 miles (19.3km) north of Liverpool city centre, Formby is a wonderful place to escape, where a vast crescent of sandy beach is edged by rolling dunes and sweeping coastal pine forest. A network of trails allows easy exploration of the area, where there is a fascinating, ever-changing coastal landscape to discover. This run follows an enjoyable loop of Formby, taking in a bit of everything to be found here. Starting and finishing at the National Trust's main information board, it heads through pine-scented shady woodland and up to the high point of the dunes for amazing views before a steep, sandy descent brings you out onto the beach. A long, glorious run along firm, flat sand – take your time to explore right down to the edge of the waves or come back at the end for a paddle – is followed by a second trip through the dunes and trees, this time picking up the Asparagus Trail with its intriguing history as you wind your way back to the start.

Above: The inviting beach at Formby.
Opposite: A family run on the beach at Formby.

THINGS TO SEE

Red squirrels
Formby lies within one of 17 strongholds for the native red squirrel in northern England. Active in the pinewoods year-round, autumn and spring are the best times of year to see them – visit first thing in the morning or at dusk to catch them foraging for natural food that is abundant in the woodlands.

Coastal landscape
The landscape at Formby has been shaped by both human and natural influences. The flat fields were levelled for asparagus, a crop that had its heyday back in the 1930s; the ridge and furrow of the planting lines can still be seen in places. Like everything else on this special stretch of coast, the paths themselves are subject to the relentless forces of weather and waves and may change as they migrate through the dunes. The marram grass that grows around the dunes is key to their stabilisation and its conservation is a particularly important part of the work here.

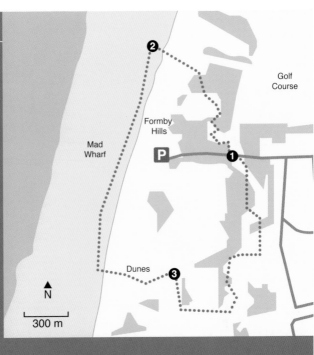

HOW TO GET HERE

By Public Transport
Freshfield station, on
Merseyrail Northern Line,
I mile (1.6km) walk to
National Trust Formby.
On Foot Sefton Coastal Path
passes through Formby.
By Car 2 miles (3.2km) off
A565. Follow brown tourist
signs from roundabout at the
north end of Formby bypass
(by BP garage). Park at the
National Trust car park at
Victoria Road, Formby (charges
apply for non-NT members).
By Bicycle National Trust
Formby 3 miles (4.8km) from
National Cycle Network
route 62.
OS Map Explorer 285
Start / End Main National
Trust noticeboard, Formby.
OS grid reference: SD280082

Golf
Course

Formby
Hills

Mad
Wharf

Dunes

▲
N

300 m

1. From the start, follow Cornerstones Path until you reach a T-junction next to a natural play area. Turn right here, heading to Gypsy Path. This will take you through the woodland, passing a caravan park on your left and then into dune grassland. Climb up through open sand on the dunes ahead to avoid trampling marram grass and then head down to the beach.

2. 0.8 miles/1.3km Turn left and run along the beach, parallel to the dunes. After almost 1 mile (1.5km) turn left at the beach marker for Blundell Path and pick a route with the sea behind you towards the woodlands.

3. 2.1 miles/3.4km Turn right to join the main Sefton Coastal Path and follow it past St Joseph's Hospice on your left. Leave the path and turn left as the trees open up. Run towards the tall pine stand at the end of the field. Keep left through the tall pines, towards the next pine area, then follow the narrow path with a bench to your left. Head down, keeping the fenced field to your right, and follow around the field. Turn left to

follow the Asparagus Trail across Blundell Avenue. The path will bring you to an open field. Keep right and contine along the path, returning to the start.

Other trails nearby
The Sefton Coastal Path runs for 21 miles (33.8km) between Crossens and the Crosby Lakeside Adventure Centre passing the Ainsdale National Nature Reserve, Formby and Antony Gormley's *Another Place*.

62. Dunham Massey

Altrincham
Cheshire
WA14 4SJ

ABOUT THIS RUN

Distance **6.5 miles**
(10.4km)
Ascent 174ft (53m)

Grass, towpath, surfaced
paths and short sections
of quiet road
Wildlife
History/culture
Dogs welcome but not
permitted in the Winter
Garden.

Set in 300 acres (121ha) of beautiful parkland, Dunham
Massey Hall was built in the 18th century and has had a
long and interesting history, including being turned into
the Stamford Military Hospital to house the injured from
the First World War from April 1917 to January 1919.

Above: Dunham Massey is
surrounded by parkland
and waterways.

   This route starts and finishes in the magnificent deer park,
dating back to the 14th century, which has been designated a
Site of Special Scientific Interest (SSSI) and is home to some
of the UK's rarest beetles as well as the fallow deer herd.
Remaining within the wider 3,000-acre (1,214ha) Dunham
estate, the route includes sections of towpath on the
Bridgewater Canal, as well as a disused railway track, now
part of the Trans Pennine Trail, and paths across one of the
many estate farms, with views across the Bollin Valley.

THINGS TO SEE

The Winter Garden
If you visit at the right time of year, the Winter
Garden at Dunham Massey is a perfect spot to
relax after a run. Open seasonally, it covers 7
acres (2.8ha), making it the largest of its kind in
the country. It is home to an incredible 700
different plant species, including over 1,600
winter shrubs, trees and evergreens, each of
which has been carefully chosen for its scent,
colour and texture. Before work began on the
garden in 2007 it was a wilderness of weeds and
brambles, yet today it is filled with an abundance
of wildlife. Officially opened in 2009, having
allowed the garden some time to establish, paths
weave through the various areas, giving great
views of the contrasting plants. Thousands of
winter-blooming bulbs, such as snowdrops, white
cyclamen and irises, flourish in the shelter offered
by mature beech, birch and oak trees, remnants
of former woodland. An intriguing and inspiring
place to visit, at its finest on a peaceful, frosty
winter morning when most gardens lie dormant.

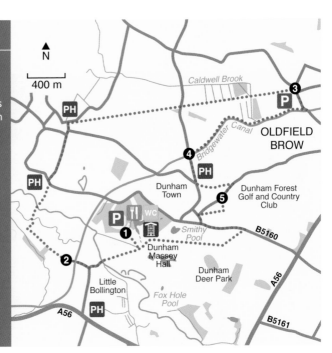

HOW TO GET HERE

By Public Transport
Altrincham station and Metro
3 miles (4.8km), Hale station
3 miles (4.8km). Altrincham bus
station/interchange, Warrington
Borough Transport, No. 5 bus,
alight by the main entrance
gates to Dunham Massey.
By Car M6 motorway exit 19,
M56 motorway exit 7,
A56 towards Altrincham/
Manchester, B5160 Charcoal
Road.
By Bicycle National Cycle
Network Route 62, 1 mile
(1.6km) away.
OS Map Explorer 276
Start / End National Trust
Dunham Massey car park.
OS grid reference: SJ731874

1. Leave the car park and visitor centre, passing the hall and lake on your left, to reach the main path running in front of the hall. Turn right here, leaving the deer park and crossing fields and a footbridge to reach the village of Little Bollington. Bear right in the centre of the village, where the main road curves left, and follow a footpath under the tranquil Bridgewater Canal.

2. 0.6 miles/1km After crossing under the canal, bear right at the path junction and then right again to cross the River Bollin and reach the road at Dunham Woodhouses. Turn left and follow the road as it curves to the right, following Station Road until it reaches the Trans Pennine Trail. Turn right and drop on to the path, following this for 1.5 miles (2.5km) to reach a road junction and houses on the outskirts of Altrincham.

3. 3.3 miles/5.3km Turn right and follow the road between houses to reach the Bridgewater Canal. Don't cross the bridge – instead turn right and join the towpath, running along this with the canal on your left until you reach a bridge.

4. 4.3 miles/7km Turn left and cross the bridge. Follow the road through Dunham Town and, shortly after the church, turn left onto a footpath across fields to reach Oldfield Lane. Turn right onto the lane and follow it for a short distance until you can turn left onto another footpath across fields.

5. 5 miles/8km Follow this footpath to reach a path junction, turning right here to reach a road in Dunham Town. Turn left onto the road, then left again onto Charcoal Road, following this for a short distance until you can turn right onto a footpath across the Dunham Massey deer park. Head straight for the front of the hall, turning left onto the path as you reach it to return back to the start.

Other trails nearby
The Trans Pennine Trail, a 207-mile (333km) coast-to-coast route between Southport and Hornsea, and the Bridgewater Canal with its excellent towpath for running both pass through the estate.

63. Stubbins Estate

Lumb Carr Road car park
Holcombe
Bury
BL8 4NN

ABOUT THIS RUN

Distance 5 miles (8km)
Ascent 689ft (210m)

Uneven moorland
    tracks and trails,
    some surfaced road
May be muddy
Wildlife
History/culture
Dogs welcome

Nestled in the South Pennines, just north of Manchester, Bolton and Rochdale, the Stubbins estate and Holcombe Moor were given to the National Trust in 1948 by Colonel Porritt in memory of his son Richard, who died at Dunkirk. A place of contrasts where wild, open moorland meets lush, wooded river valley, the area includes the only grassland Site of Special Scientific Interest in the West Pennines. This enjoyable run begins in pretty Holcombe village and heads for the moor on a clear bridleway, returning over the moors along a well-used track. This upland section is well marked by yellow marker posts, with a series of flags marking the boundary of the MOD training area – the route runs alongside this but does not enter it. Along the way you'll pass Robin Hood's Well, the Ellen Strange Memorial Stone, the Moor Stone and finally Peel Tower, a great place to pause for a moment to take in the extensive views over the varied surrounding landscapes.

Above: Gawthorpe Hall.

THINGS TO SEE

Peel Tower

The final stretch of this run takes in the distinctive Peel Tower on Holcombe Hill. It was built in 1852 and commemorates Sir Robert Peel, Prime Minister of Britain from 1841–46. The tower stands 128ft (39m) high and is a fantastic viewpoint across Manchester to the Peak District and even to the mountains of North Wales on a clear day. The tower is open to the public when the flag is flying.

Gawthorpe Hall

Sometimes referred to as the 'Downton of the North', nearby Gawthorpe Hall was redesigned in the 1850s by Sir Charles Barry, who also designed the Houses of Parliament and Highclere Castle – Downton Abbey in the TV series. Home to the North West's largest collection of portraits, on loan from the National Portrait Gallery, Gawthorpe is also the final stop on the Brontë Way, a long-distance route visiting places associated with the writing of the Brontë family. Run in partnership with Lancashire County Council, Gawthorpe Hall is a great place to visit with the family, with gardens, including a fine parterre, and woodland to explore.

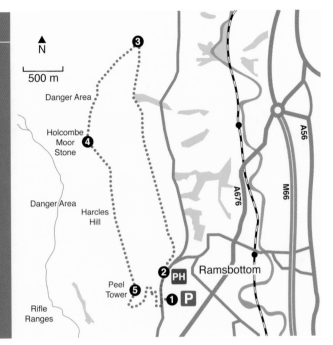

By Public Transport The East Lancashire Steam Railway runs from Bolton Street station, Bury to Ramsbottom station, 1.2 miles (1.9km) from the start. Trains run weekends and Bank Holidays all year round, Wed–Sun and May–September.
By Car The Lumb Carr Road car park is just outside Holcombe village; nearest postcode BL8 4NN. Driving through Holcombe village, the car park is a short distance on the left after the Shoulder of Mutton pub.
OS Map Explorer 287
Start / End Lumb Carr Road car park (not NT).
OS grid reference: SD781161

1. Turn right out of the car park, crossing the road with care and running on the pavement up Lumb Carr Road into Holcombe village. After the first set of terraced houses on your left, Cross Lane turns off left. Don't follow Cross Lane but take the bridleway that runs up behind the houses to the right of the benches.

2. 0.2 miles/0.4km Follow the bridleway as it climbs up onto the moor and continue following it northwards, with Holcombe Moor rising to your left and the Stubbins estate, River Irwell and the motorway to your right.

3. 2.1 miles/3.4km Where the bridleway reaches a stone walled enclosure, turn sharp left, leaving the bridleway and following a footpath, first alongside the wall but then bearing left away from the wall, climbing Beetle Hill and heading over Holcombe Moor, with the firing range on your right, to reach the Moor Stone.

4. 3.1 miles/5km Bear left at the Moor Stone, which marks the site of Pilgrims Cross, heading straight for Peel Tower and running along the vague ridge of the moor, over Harcles Hill.

5. 4.3 miles/6.9km From Peel Tower, follow the main zig-zag path down towards the car park, turning right where it emerges onto a lane next to some houses and then left down a footpath, bringing you out at Lumb Carr Road, opposite the car park where you started.

Other trails nearby
The South Pennines have a fantastic network of footpaths and bridleways to explore, including the 41-mile (66km) Rossendale Way, which crosses Holcombe Moor, and the 9-mile (14km) Weighver's Way, the Pennine Way and Pennine Bridleway, the Irwell Valley Path alongside the river and the 43-mile (69km) Brontë Way linking Oakwell Hall near Birstall with Gawthorpe Hall.

64. Hardcastle Crags

Hardcastle Crags
Near Hebden Bridge
West Yorkshire
HX7 7AA

ABOUT THIS RUN

Distance **4 miles (6.4km)**
Ascent **689ft (210m)**

Waymarked
Mostly even gravel trails,
 some uneven sections
May be muddy
Unfenced drops and water
History/culture
Wildlife
Dogs welcome

This adventurous run takes you through the heart of Hebden Dale, following a combination of two waymarked trails along steep, densely wooded hillsides overlooked by craggy tops. Hebden Water is a constant companion, its character changing with each meander, from roaring rapids to the glassy stillness of the millpond. Halfway along the valley the 19th-century Gibson Mill is entirely powered by its own renewable energy sources.

Above: Crossing Hebden Water.
Opposite: Exploring the crags at Hardcastle Crags.

THINGS TO SEE

The Crags
To make the run even more of an adventure, take the upper route that traverses the high ground along the top of Hardcastle's millstone grit crags. This detour offers glorious views of the tree-lined valley and some tricky hands-on sections (see step 2).

Go #OffTheGrid
Stop at the fascinating Gibson Mill visitor centre for tea and cake and to discover the power of renewables. The former cotton mill is completely off-grid in its remote river valley, being 100 per cent self-sufficient in energy, water and waste treatment (it has no rubbish collections). Energy generation is balanced between a hydro-electric system, solar photovoltaic panels and a biomass boiler.

Wonderful wildlife
The river and its wooded valley provides a rich habitat for a wide variety of plants and creatures. Look out for roe deer; any of the eight resident species of bat; green woodpeckers, dippers, herons and songbirds; rare mosses and lichens; and the northern hairy wood ant.

HOW TO GET HERE

Walshaw Wood

Turn Hill

Abel Cote Wood

Hardcastle Dale

Gibson Mill

Middle Dean

Shackleton

Hebden Dale

New Bridge

Hebden Wood

Crimsworth Dean Brook

N

250 m

1. From Midgehole car park follow the red 'Mill Walk' waymarkers west through woodland, descending to Hebden Water at Gibson Mill and passing the millpond on your left. From Gibson Mill follow the green 'Crags Constitutional' waymarkers north along the eastern bank of Hebden Water, descending to reach a footbridge.

2. 1.4 miles/2.2km Either continue following the green waymarkers or take the adventurous steps leading up to the left and follow the upper path through the crags (optional – CAUTION steep, slippery ground).

3. 1.9 miles/3km Cross Hebden Water using the footbridge and run southwards, continuing to follow the green waymarkers along the western bank of the river until re-reaching Gibson Mill. From here a path leads steeply uphill to Clough Hole car park, an alternative starting point for the run.

4. 2.7 miles/4.4km Cross the footbridge at Gibson Mill and rejoin the 'Mill Walk' trail, following red waymarkers along the river to return to the car park at Midgehole.

Other trails nearby
The Pennine Way National Trail runs parallel to this section of Hebden Dale, easily reached about half a mile west of the National Trust Clough Hole car park at the top of the valley. This 268-mile (431km) route from Edale in Derbyshire to Kirk Yetholm in the Scottish Borders has seen many record attempts by some of the finest distance runners.

65. Nostell

Doncaster Road
Nostell
Near Wakefield
West Yorkshire
WF4 1QE

ABOUT THIS RUN

Distance **2.8 miles (4.5km)**
Ascent **200ft (61m)**

Surfaced paths, grassy trails
Wildlife
Family friendly
History/culture
Parkrun
Dogs welcome on leads

A masterpiece of 18th-century Palladian architecture, built on the site of a 12th-century Augustinian priory, Nostell was a grand statement of wealth and importance by its creators, the Winn family. Approaching the magnificent frontage of the house, it's easy to imagine the elite of society at the time coming up the sweeping drive in all their finery. Exploring the 300 acres (121ha) of gardens and parkland surrounding the mansion takes you through open meadows and grassland, through leafy woodland and around the lakes. This run loops the estate, taking in a bit of everything it has to offer. Starting at the car park, it follows paths and grassy trails to the obelisk, at the furthest point of the estate, before running back down through park and woodland to skirt the lakes and pass the house to finish. Please note: there are electric fences in places and livestock grazing during the summer.

Other trails nearby

There's a great network of footpaths and bridleways spanning out around Nostell, perfect for exploring the surrounding area. The Trans Pennine Trail, a 215-mile (346km) coast-to-coast route between Southport and Hornsea, also runs near to the park.

THINGS TO SEE

Inside Nostell

The house is a trove of fascinating treasures, including paintings by Brueghel, Hogarth and Kauffmann and a longcase clock by John Harrison, the man who solved the problem of calculating longitude at sea. Most of the original furniture, much of it by Thomas Chippendale, is still in place. Nostell also boasts one of the finest of the Trust's libraries, housing over 4,000 books, combining four smaller collections brought together by Charles Winn (1795–1874) in the 19th century.

The Obelisk Lodge

The impressive pyramid of Obelisk Lodge, built in the 18th century, was inhabited up to the late 1950s and the rooms and fireplaces can still be seen inside. The arched lodge was the main entrance to the parkland up to 1866, until the building of Nostell train station changed it to its current position.

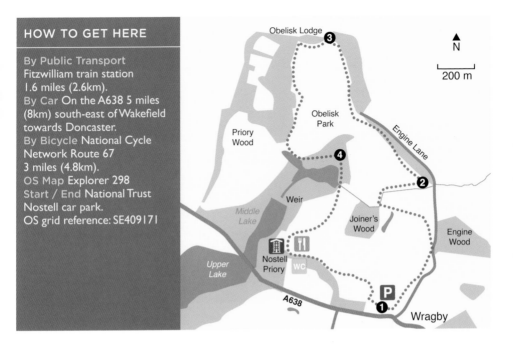

HOW TO GET HERE

By Public Transport
Fitzwilliam train station
1.6 miles (2.6km).
By Car On the A638 5 miles
(8km) south-east of Wakefield
towards Doncaster.
By Bicycle National Cycle
Network Route 67
3 miles (4.8km).
OS Map Explorer 298
Start / End National Trust
Nostell car park.
OS grid reference: SE409171

1. Leave the car park from its entrance furthest from the house, following the grassy trails along the eastern edge of the park to reach a surfaced path. Turn left onto this, following it past a small lake on your left and through a gate onto a larger surfaced path. Turn right onto this and follow it for a short distance as it curves to the right and continues to reach a band of trees.

2. 0.7 miles/1.2km Turn left, off the surfaced path, and follow a mown path alongside trees on your right. Continue straight ahead, running up a gentle incline, until you reach the Obelisk Lodge at the top of the park.

3. 1.3 miles/2.1km After exploring the lodge, continue following the grassy paths around the edge of the parkland, running down the hill back towards the lake with the trees on your right. Go through a wooden gate and turn left onto a wide surfaced track. Follow the track through the bluebell woods until you reach a junction.

4. 2 miles/3.2km Turn right and follow the path past the lake on your righ and over the Boathouse bridge, through the trees to emerge near the main house. Follow the path as it runs past the front of the house, bearing left and running back up past the stable and onto the welcome cabin and car park.

Opposite: **Exploring the estate at Nostell.**
Right: **Running past the Obelisk Lodge at Nostell.**

Watersinks car park
Malham Tarn
Settle
North Yorkshire
BD23 4DJ

ABOUT THIS RUN

Distance **6.3 miles**
(10.2km)
Ascent 613ft (187m)

Trails along lakeside and
moorland and fell
Dogs welcome on leads,
apart from boardwalk
and Nature Reserve
Wildlife

The Malham estate, deep in the Yorkshire Dales, covers a dramatic, open area of limestone pavement and grassland, rugged high peaks and rocky outcrops. Nestled within this classic limestone landscape, the gleaming scoop of Malham Tarn reflects the weather day by day: serenely calm one moment, wind-whipped and brooding the next. An integral part of the Malham Tarn National Nature Reserve, this area is internationally important for its abundance of wildlife.

Above: Running across the dales above Malham Tarn.
Opposite: Running on the Pennine Way at Malham.

This run begins right by the tarn and follows the Pennine Way around its shore to reach the north-western point. From here, it heads across stone-walled fields and up onto high, open moorland from where there are beautiful views out across the Dales on a clear day. After joining the clear path of the Pennine Bridleway, the final stretch descends back into the dry valley, following the Pennine Way once again to return to the tarn.

THINGS TO SEE

In and around the tarn
Malham Tarn is a natural hollow in the boulder clay, overlying a bedrock of slate. The water from the tarn flows underground for over 2 miles (3.2km), reappearing at Aire Head. It's a great place to visit to watch birds; from the hide, just off the boardwalk section of the route, you can see great crested grebes, tufted ducks, pochard, wigeon, teal, goosander and sometimes peregrine falcons. There are also a number of species of bat

here, and regular expert-led bat walks with National Trust rangers start at Malham Tarn House (pre-booking required). Within running distance of the tarn there is also the beautiful waterfall at Janet's Foss, the exciting scramble up Gordale Scar and the fascinating limestone pavement that tops the great scoop of Malham Cove, once a vast waterfall and now a destination for the best rock climbers.

HOW TO GET HERE

By Public Transport Settle
train station 7 miles (11.3km);
Skipton train station 13 miles
(20.9km). Buses from Skipton:
210/211 Mon–Fri, 75 Sat;
873/884 summer Sundays
and Bank holidays; from Settle:
881 summer Sundays and
Bank Holidays.
By Car Close to the A65
and Settle; 4 miles (6.4km)
west of Malham. Follow signs
from Malham.
OS Map Explorer OL2
Start / End Watersinks
car park (not NT).
OS grid reference: SD895658

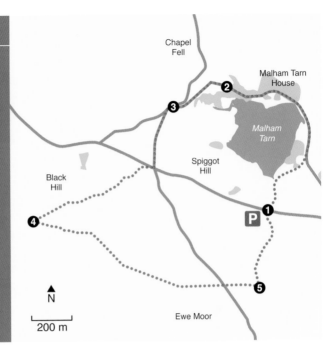

Chapel
Fell

Malham Tarn
House

Malham
Tarn

Spiggot
Hill

Black
Hill

P

N

200 m

Ewe Moor

1. Join the Pennine Way and
head northwards along the
grassy path towards Malham
Tarn. The Pennine Way continues
to the overflow of Malham Tarn
before joining the track to Tarn
House. Continue along the
track, passing Great Close Scar
and then Malham Tarn House
Field Centre on your right.

2. 1.7 miles/2.7km At
Sandhills Cottage on your
left, leave the Pennine Way
and follow signs to the
Nature Reserve, following the
boardwalk through the woods.

3. 2.1 miles/3.4km Where
the boardwalk ends, join the
road, turning left, and following
the road, bearing left at the
junction. At the crossroads,
take the footpath diagonally
opposite and follow this
straight across fields to reach
the Pennine Bridleway.

4. 3.7 miles/6km Turn left onto
the Pennine Bridleway and
follow it, crossing a road and
descending into the steep valley
to reach the Pennine Way.

5. 5.7 miles/9.1km Turn left
onto the Pennine Way and
follow this back to the car park.

Other trails nearby
The Dales is perfect off-road
running country, and the
Pennine Way, Pennine
Bridleway and Dales Way
all pass Malham, ideal for
exploring further afield.

67. Brimham

Brimham Moor Road
Summerbridge
Harrogate
North Yorkshire
HG3 4DW

ABOUT THIS RUN

Distance **3.2 miles (5.2km)**
Ascent **466ft (142m)**

Grassy trails, tracks and
   surfaced paths
Wildlife
History/culture
Family friendly
Dogs welcome, keep on
   leads around livestock

Set on a picturesque, heather-clad hillside within the
Nidderdale Area of Outstanding Natural Beauty, Brimham's
natural rock sculptures draw visitors from far and wide to
admire their otherworldly shapes. Carved by millennia of
Yorkshire weather, the stacked gritstone rocks started life
in an expansive river delta more than 300 million years ago.
This run follows, for the most part, the Boundary Trail,
looping the 400-acre (162ha) estate and discovering its
wonderful variety, as well as visiting the rocks themselves, of
course. Alternating between shady trees and open moorland
clearings with grand views out across the Dales, this route is
best run during less busy times, such as weekdays, mornings
and evenings, to fully appreciate its tranquil beauty.

Above: Exploring the rocks
at Brimham.

THINGS TO SEE

Exploring the rocks

Brimham's weird and wonderful rock
formations have captured the imagination of
many throughout history and today it's a popular
place with runners, walkers, climbers and families
alike. It's said you can spot a dancing bear, a gorilla,
an eagle and turtle hiding around the heather
moorland, or try crawling through the Smartie
Tube or balancing on the Rocking Stones – a
natural obstacle course. Brimham Rocks and
its heather moorland are both Sites of Special
Scientific Interest and home to a rich diversity

of wildlife. If you're visiting in summer, look for
wild bilberries and lingonberries – a perfect snack
on the go – growing amidst several different
species of heather. There are many species of
insect here, including the green tiger beetle and
solitary ashy mining bees, together with birds
such as red grouse and meadow pipits on the
open moorland, and robins, tits and finches in
the woodland. Swallows and house martins also
make their nests in the crevices of the rocks and
surrounding buildings.

HOW TO GET HERE

By Public Transport Daily
bus service 24 from Harrogate
to Pateley Bridge passes
Summerbridge, 1.5 miles
(2.4km) from Brimham Rocks.
Sundays and Bank Holidays
(May–September); 825 Eastern
Dales Bus runs between
Harrogate, Brimham Rocks
and Fountains Abbey.
By Car 11 miles (17.7km)
from Harrogate off B6165;
4 miles (6.4km) from Pateley
Bridge off B6265.
By Bicycle Cycling welcome
on main track.
OS Map Explorer 298
Start / End Brimham Rocks
car park (not NT).
OS grid reference: SE208645

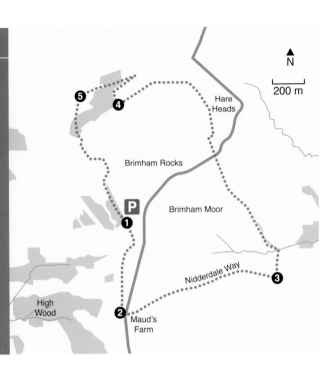

1. Turn left out of the car park and follow
the road as it curves around to the right,
signed 'Private road to Druids Cave Farm'.
Just before the National Trust boundary marker,
turn left onto a footpath and follow this straight
ahead, running parallel to the road over the
moorland.

2. **0.4 miles/0.6km** Reaching the track junction,
turn left, crossing the road with care and joining
the footpath opposite. Follow this across
moorland to join the more obvious path of the
Nidderdale Way. Turn right onto the Nidderdale
Way and follow this until you reach a wall
where the Nidderdale Way continues straight
ahead towards farm buildings.

3. **1 mile/1.6km** Turn left before the wall,
leaving the Nidderdale Way and following
a footpath north. Bear left where the path
divides, staying on the left of the wall and
following the footpath generally north-west
to reach a road. Cross with care and continue
following the footpath, first bearing right and
then, with the road to your right, contouring
around to the left below Hare Heads to reach
an area of woodland.

4. **2.2 miles/3.6km** Turn right and follow the
zigzag path downhill through trees to reach the
main track. Turn left onto this and follow it until
you reach a fork.

5. **2.7 miles/4.3km** Take the footpath to the
left of the left fork, heading uphill through trees
to reach the main area of Brimham Rocks where
there's also the visitor centre, toilets and café.
Once you have finished exploring, continue
straight on, following the main path back to
the car park.

Other trails nearby
The Nidderdale Way runs for 53 miles
(85.3km), starting and finishing at Pateley
Bridge and taking in many of the highlights
of the Yorkshire Dales along the way.

68. Fountains Abbey & Studley Royal

Fountains Abbey and
Studley Royal Water
Garden
Ripon
HG4 3DY

ABOUT THIS RUN

Distance 5.3 miles (8.6km)
Ascent 512ft (156m)

Bridleways, footpaths,
 roadways and gravel
 tracks
Waymarked trail
Family friendly
Dogs welcome on leads
History/culture
Wildlife

With its 900-year old abbey and Georgian water garden surrounded by 800 acres (324ha) of estate, the World Heritage Site of Studley Royal, including the ruins of Fountains Abbey, is an extraordinary place. Balancing manicured grandeur and fascinating history with a feeling of wildness and escape, running on the trails here is a real journey with something new and intriguing around every corner. Run across the medieval deer park and through Seven Bridges Valley; follow winding trails through ancient deciduous woodland; and spot herds of red, fallow and sika deer along the way. This run follows the Walk on the Wild Side trail in an enjoyable loop of the rivers, lanes, villages, woods and open parkland surrounding Fountains Abbey.

Above: There are plenty
of deer to spot on your run.
Opposite: Estate trails at
Fountains Abbey.

THINGS TO SEE

The Abbey

The majestic ruins of Fountains Abbey are the largest monastic ruins in the country. The abbey was founded in 1132 by 13 Benedictine monks seeking a simpler and more peaceful existence. Over the years, with the help of lay brothers, the abbey raised money to build the monastery through lead mining, stone quarrying, wool production and livestock rearing. However, its fortunes turned for the worse in the 14th century when it was hit by both the Black Death and raids by the Scots. The abbey was closed in 1539 during the Dissolution of the Monasteries ordered by Henry VIII. Today, the ruins are wonderfully atmospheric to explore, throwing fascinating shadows onto the grass on a sunny day or a pale silhouette rising against a dark, stormy sky.

HOW TO GET HERE

By Public Transport Nearest main railway station is Harrogate, 12 miles (19.3km) from Fountains Abbey. Some buses from Ripon and Harrogate – seasonal variations apply, check timetable. Pleasant 4-mile (6.4km) walk from Ripon city centre to Fountains Abbey.

By Car 4 miles (6.4km) west of Ripon off B6265 to Pateley Bridge, signposted from A1; 12 miles (19.3km) north of Harrogate (A61). National Trust car park at the visitor centre.

OS Map Explorer 298

Start / End National Trust Fountains Abbey visitor centre.

OS grid reference: SE272687

▲ N

|———| 400 m

A6265

Studley Roger

Studley Royal Deer Park

Ripon Rowel Walk

2

P WC

Banqueting House

Octagon Tower

Water Garden

Temple of Fame

Gillet Hill

Plumpton Hall

Whitcliffe **4**

3 Whitcliffe Hall

5 Rose Bridge

1 **P**

WC Fountains Abby

1. From the visitor centre follow signs for St Mary's Church, along the bridleway.

2. 0.4 miles/0.7km At the church, bear right across the deer park towards the lake. Follow the path around the lake and cross the footbridge, continuing to follow the path through Seven Bridges Valley, then up the hill to reach the lane at Whitcliffe Hall.

3. 2.2 miles/3.6km Turn left and follow the lane for 0.3 miles (0.5km).

4. 2.5 miles/4.1km Turn left off the lane into woodland, emerging into fields and continuing to follow the footpath until you reach Hell Wath Cottage. Bear left here, down the steps and over the footbridge and continue along the footpath to reach a path junction.

5. 3.4 miles/5.5km Turn left and follow the path to Studley Roger village. Cross the road and follow the footpath straight ahead across the deer park and back to the church, turning left onto the bridleway and rejoining your outward route to the finish.

Other trails nearby

There are numerous excellent paths and trails around Fountains Abbey. Further afield, the Ripon Rowel Walk covers 49 miles (79km) of waymarked trail, taking in villages, historic sites, wooded valleys, rivers, lakes and streams.

69. Roseberry Topping

Newton-under-Roseberry
North Yorkshire
TS9 6QR

ABOUT THIS RUN

Distance 2.9 miles (4.7km)
Ascent 699ft (213m)

Surfaced and gravel paths,
 steep trails on hillside
Dogs welcome
History/culture
Wildlife

With its distinctive, appealing outline and intriguing history, Cleveland's most famous hill, Roseberry Topping, is a fascinating place to explore. Rich in history, geology and wildlife, there's something to amaze everyone here, and the challenging climb to the top is rewarded with outstanding views and a fun, fast descent. This route runs through open fields and peaceful woodland before taking you up and over Roseberry Topping. From here it's downhill all the way home, starting with the steep northern flanks of the hill, diving into Newton Wood and emerging to join Roseberry Lane to finish. It can easily be started from Great Ayton station, following the footpath through Undercliffe to join the route at Rye Hill, approximately half a mile south-east of point 2.

Above: The path towards
Roseberry Topping.
Opposite: Roseberry Topping.

THINGS TO SEE

Roseberry Topping

Sometimes referred to as Yorkshire's mini Matterhorn, Roseberry Topping's distinctive conical shape has made it a well-known landmark, rising from the edge of the North York Moors and visible from many miles around. From the summit you can see as far as 50 miles (80km) on a clear day, out across the Cleveland plain and to the Pennines. Once a more symmetrical sugarloaf shape, the sharp cliff on its western slope was carved by a landslip in 1912, possibly due to a combination of a geological fault and mining

works on its lower slopes. The hill has a long history of human fascination and was named by the Vikings. There is evidence of Bronze Age and Iron Age occupation and, in the 18th century, it was a favourite stomping ground of explorer Captain James Cook, who, as a young boy, lived in nearby Great Ayton. Even today there's something about Roseberry Topping that inspires people to climb it, and it's a perfect day out whether you're running, walking or out exploring with the family.

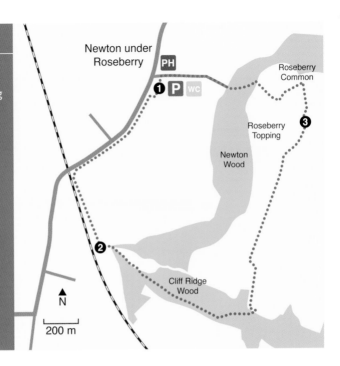

HOW TO GET HERE

By Public Transport Great Ayton station is 1.5 miles (2.5km) from the route, joining half a mile (0.8km) south-east from point 2.
By Car On the A173 between Guisborough and Great Ayton. Car park (not NT) at Newton-under-Roseberry (a charge applies). SatNav use postcode TS9 6QR.
OS Map Explorer OL26
Start / End Public car park in Newton-under-Roseberry (not NT).
OS grid reference: NZ570128

1. From the car park, follow the footpath that runs alongside the main road with the road on your right (don't cross the road). Turn left just before the railway, continuing along the footpath.

2. 0.7 miles/1.2km Turn left and then bear right into Cliff Ridge Wood, following the footpath along the edge of the woodland. Bear left around Cliff Rigg Quarry, then run straight across fields, following the footpath to the summit of Roseberry Topping.

3. 2.2 miles/3.5km From the summit, continue in the same direction, following the footpath down the northern side of the hill. On reaching woodland at the base of the hill, turn left and follow the footpath, then bridleway, back to the car park.

Other trails nearby

The Roseberry Romp running trail follows the route of the popular annual fell race, organised by the National Trust, and is an excellent alternative tour of Roseberry Topping. The Cleveland Way runs for 109 miles (175km) between Helmsley and Filey, skirting heather-clad windswept moorland and rugged, castle-topped coast along the way.

70. The Bridestones

| Staindale |
| Dalby |
| Pickering |
| North Yorkshire |
| YO18 7LR |

ABOUT THIS RUN

Distance 6.1 miles (9.9km)
Ascent 577ft (176m)

Forest tracks, moorland,
   some surfaced roads
Views
Dogs welcome on leads
History/culture
Wildlife

Situated on the edge of Dalby Forest, the Bridestones are a fascinating group of wind, frost and rain-sculpted sandstone rocks set in a nature reserve and designated Site of Special Scientific Interest. The stones are the remains of a cap of Jurassic sedimentary rock, deposited around 150 million years ago. Today they're an intriguing and beautiful place to explore, with a network of excellent trails and plenty of spots to stop to catch your breath and take in the stunning views. Our run here starts along an easy stretch of Stain Dale before a good climb through forest takes you up onto the escarpment. A glorious section along the Tabular Hills Walk, from where the views stretch for miles across the moors to the North Sea, finishes with an enjoyable descent back into Stain Dale.

Above: One of the naturally sculpted formations that make up the Bridestones.
Opposite: Woodland trail near the Bridestones.

THINGS TO SEE

Bridestones wildlife

The 300-acre (121ha) nature reserve around the Bridestones is abundant in fascinating flora and fauna. A landscape of open heather-clad moorland, rough pasture, wooded hills and grassy dales filled with wild flowers in summer, there's a great diversity of habitats. Because the moor in the reserve escapes the burning required for grouse shooting or sheep grazing, there's a wealth of mosses, lichens and insects here including heather, rare dwarf cornel – usually found only in the Scottish Highlands – and sundew. Keep an eye out for adders, basking on rocks in the sun, although these shy creatures will usually have disappeared before you spot them. They give their name to the area of trees that line the starting point of the run – Adderstone Wood.

HOW TO GET HERE

By Public Transport Moors Bus weekend service to Dalby Forest, Easter–October. Regular buses to/from Thornton Le Dale to major towns and cities.
By Car Car park just south of Bridestones, postcode YO18 7LR. Please note: road access is via Dalby Forest, toll payable to Forestry Commission.
OS Map Explorer OL21
Start / End Bridestones car park (not NT).
OS grid reference: SE878904

Thompson's Rigg

Crosscliff Wood

The Bridestones

Yondhead Rigg

P Dargate Dikes

P ❶ High Staindale

Peathead Rigg

P

Adderstone Rigg

P **P** Jingleby Thorn

Ebberston Low Moor

Forest Drive

❷

❸

▲ N

500 m

Other trails nearby

Dalby Forest has an excellent network of dedicated running, walking and cycling trails and is great for families, too.

1. From the start, turn right and head east along Stain Dale, passing Staindale Lake on your right. Bear right after the lake and house and follow the main track – marked as a cycle path – through the woods to reach the buildings at Jingleby Thorn. Carry straight on to reach a road.

2. **1.4 miles/2.3km** Turn left and follow the road, joining the Tabular Hills Walk and bearing left where it forks to reach the viewpoint at the edge of the escarpment. Follow the Tabular Hills Walk along the escarpment to a path junction at the edge of the forest.

3. **4.7 miles/7.6km** Turn left and follow the track across moorland to reach the Bridestones. Explore the trails that wind around the stones before continuing and descending back into Stain Dale to finish.

71. Cleveland coast

Old Saltburn and
 Warsett Hill
North Yorkshire
TS12 1HF

ABOUT THIS RUN

Distance **4.4 miles (7.1km)**
Ascent **545ft (166m)**

Paths over grassland and
 fields; coastal trails; may
 be muddy
Easily accessible by train
Wildlife
Dogs welcome on leads
History/culture

The stretch of coast at Old Saltburn in Cleveland is part of the Yorkshire Heritage Coast, a landscape sculpted by the sea and a long history of human use. From the Roman defensive sight station on Warsett Hill, a series of locally-inspired sculptures and the remnants of an industrial and mining past, to the blaze of colourful coastal wildflowers in summer, this is a place of fascinating contrasts. Starting on the seafront at pretty Saltburn-by-the-Sea, this run explores the open fields and farmland across the headland to start, making its way up and over Warsett Hill, from where there are outstanding panoramic views of coast and countryside. The home stretch takes you along part of the Cleveland Way back to Old Saltburn.

Above: View towards Warsett Hill.
Opposite: Sculpture at Warsett Hill.

THINGS TO SEE

Coastal wildlife

The grasslands and boulder-clay cliff slopes along this stretch of the coast support a stunning variety of coastal flora, including wildflowers that bloom over the summer months. Running along Hunt Cliff on the homeward section of the route, you might spot some of the area's many breeding seabirds, including kittiwakes and fulmars.

Ironstone mining

The Cleveland Hills are a rich source of ironstone, a sedimentary rock containing a substantial amount of iron ore that can be smelted commercially. During the late 19th and early 20th centuries the Huntcliffe Mine, based on this stretch of the coast, produced vast quantities of ironstone which was transported to the Teesside blast furnaces for smelting. The Guibal fan house, named after its Belgian inventor and passed on the eastern edge of the run route, would once have housed a huge fan, some 30ft (9m) in diameter. Powered by a static steam engine, the fan drew foul air up the vertical shaft while clean air was drawn in through the drift (horizontal) entrances.

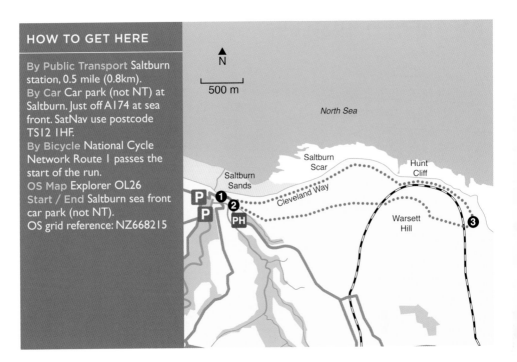

HOW TO GET HERE

By Public Transport Saltburn station, 0.5 mile (0.8km).
By Car Car park (not NT) at Saltburn. Just off A174 at sea front. SatNav use postcode TS12 1HF.
By Bicycle National Cycle Network Route 1 passes the start of the run.
OS Map Explorer OL26
Start / End Saltburn sea front car park (not NT).
OS grid reference: NZ668215

N

500 m

North Sea

Saltburn Scar

Hunt Cliff

Saltburn Sands

Cleveland Way

Warsett Hill

1. From the car park, cross the road to the seafront and turn right, following the road as it curves around to the right.

2. **0.2 miles/0.3km** Just after the right-hand corner, turn left off the road onto a footpath marked with a National Trust sign. Follow the path uphill, passing a row of cottages on your left. The path will widen to a gravel track. Follow this track and continue straight on, past a farmhouse on your left. Cross the railway line and run up to the top of Warsett Hill and bear left up to the trig point. With your back to the stone trig point head back down the hill across two fields to cross the railway at the two styles.

3. **2.2 miles/3.5km** Turn left and follow the coastal path all the way back to Old Saltburn. Come down the steps to The Ship Inn and turn right onto the road to return to the car park.

Other trails nearby
The Cleveland Way runs for 109 miles (175km) from Helmsley in the south of the North York Moors, around the western edge of the National Park and along the coast from Saltburn to Filey.

175

72. Tarn Hows

**Ambleside
LA21 8AQ**

ABOUT THIS RUN

Distance 1.9 miles (3km)
Ascent 266ft (81m)

Surfaced trail, undulating
  in places
Suitable for buggies
  and wheelchairs
Wildlife
Dogs welcome on leads
History/culture

Set in a low-level valley between Coniston and Hawkshead, surrounded by stunning mountain views, Tarn Hows is a perfect place for a day out, whether you're running, walking or exploring with friends or family. This run follows the gently undulating surfaced trail around the tarn, an enjoyable introduction to running in the Lake District and ideal for buggies and wheelchair users, although cycling is not permitted.

Other trails nearby
Nearby trails include the Hawkshead to Wray off-road trail and the west shore of Windermere.

THINGS TO SEE

The tarn through time
At the start of the 19th century Tarn Hows looked very different, with three separate tarns set within classic Lake District lowland. As part of an ambitious project to reshape the landscape in the popular picturesque style, the owner of the estate, James Garth Marshall, dammed the outflow creating one larger ornamental lake. Around the lake he planted hundreds of trees to enhance the landscape. Beatrix Potter bought the land to protect it from development in 1929 and today the National Trust manages this special place for the enjoyment of thousands of visitors each year.

There is ongoing conservation work at Tarn Hows to re-establish elements of Marshall's original plan for the landscape and protect the area's rare habitats, including tree thinning using traditional horse logging techniques, which reduce damage to the fragile and boggy terrain. The tarn is a registered Site of Special Scientific Interest (SSSI), supporting a particularly diverse range of plant species in the wetlands that create exceptional water quality in the tarn. Small herds of Belted Galloway cattle are contributing to conservation through their grazing, which significantly improves the diversity of wildlife.

By Public Transport Bus service 505, Hawkshead–Coniston. Alight at Hawkshead Hill Chapel and follow road signs to Tarn Hows (approx. I mile/I.6km).
By Car From Ambleside take the A593 and then the B5286 towards Hawkshead, and then the B5285 towards Coniston. From Hawkshead Hill follow signs to Tarn Hows. Do not follow SatNav, follow signs for Tarn Hows from B5285, Coniston or Hawkshead Hill.
OS Map Explorer OL7
Start / End National Trust Tarn Hows car park.
OS grid reference: SD326995

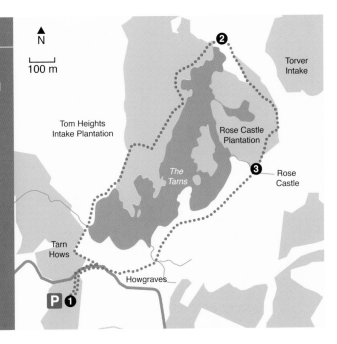

1. From the car park, cross the road and bear left, following the track down to the lake side. Pass through the gate and continue on the track in a clockwise direction around the Tarns.

2. **0.9 miles/I.4km** On reaching the furthest point of the lake, continue on over a footbridge and follow the path down the opposite side.

3. **I.5 miles/2.4km** At this point a path crosses the main route, extending the route with a loop that takes in more great views. However, this section is not suitable for buggies or wheelchairs, which should continue following the main lakeside path back to the car park. To extend the route, go through the gate to the left of the track and proceed uphill to an upper track. Otherwise, continue on this track in the

direction signposted to Coniston, Hawkshead and Old car park until reaching the car park.

Opposite: Coniston Tarn Hows, or The Tarns, is an unmissable beauty spot.
Opposite: Running around The Tarns.

73. Great Langdale

Sticklebarn
Near Ambleside
Cumbria
LA22 9JU

ABOUT THIS RUN

Distance **3.9 miles (6.3km)**
Ascent **410ft (125m)**

Undulating, rough trails,
    short sections of road
    and road crossings
Wildlife
History/culture
Dogs welcome, keep on
    leads around livestock

Lying at the heart of the Lake District National Park, Langdale takes its name from the Old Norse for 'long valley'. A classic, U-shaped glacial valley, this landscape was beloved by Victorian historian George Macaulay Trevelyan. He protected it from private ownership and development, donating it to the National Trust to ensure it could be enjoyed by everyone.

The mountains encircling Great Langdale create an awe-inspiring jagged skyline, including the inviting challenges of the Langdale Pikes, Bowfell and Crinkle Crags. This run takes in a spectacular low-level route, traversing both sides of the valley, immersed in breathtaking mountain scenery. Starting at the National Trust owned Sticklebarn, it follows the Cumbria Way beneath Raven Crag, a popular spot with rock climbers, as far as the Old Dungeon Ghyll. Crossing the river it rejoins the Cumbria Way on the opposite side, contouring around the hillside below Side Pike and Lingmoor Fell. The final stretch follows the flat riverside trail back to the Sticklebarn.

THINGS TO SEE

Sticklebarn pub
The National Trust-owned and run Sticklebarn is a hydroelectric-powered pub that sources as much as possible from the valley itself and reinvests every penny into the local community. Brilliantly situated amidst a wealth of outstanding running, walking, climbing and cycling routes, it's a perfect place to relax and refuel after a long day out in the fells. You'll find hearty food and warming fires on colder days, and a sunny terrace with views of the mountains for summer evenings. There's always a packed calendar of events and entertainment, including bat walks, night runs, live music, theatre and quiz nights.

Stickle Tarn
Follow the long, uphill footpath to Stickle Ghyll, straight from the rear of the Sticklebarn and you'll eventually reach Stickle Tarn, a peaceful, silver circle backed by the imposing crag of Pavey Ark and looking out over spectacular mountain scenery. An engaging walk with a couple of hands-on sections, it's a great mini adventure for foot-sure runners, walkers and families.

Opposite: Stickle Tarn and Pavey Ark from Harrison Stickle.
Above: The Sticklebarn at Great Langdale.

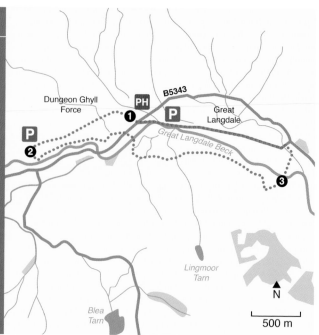

1. Leave the car park via its top entrance, heading uphill past the hostel towards Stickle Ghyll. At the first path junction, turn left onto the Cumbria Way. Follow this until you reach the Old Dungeon Ghyll hotel.

2. **0.7 miles/1.1km** Turn left and descend between the buildings towards the road. Before you reach the road, take the footpath on the left that runs back the way you have just come, parallel to the road. When you reach the bottom end of the car park, rejoin the Cumbria Way, crossing the road with care and taking the footpath opposite. Cross two bridges and run past Side House on your right, continuing straight ahead and uphill until you reach a path junction. Bear left here, staying on the Cumbria Way and following it onwards around the hillside.

3. **2.6 miles/4.2km** Just after the buildings at Oak Howe, the Cumbria Way turns left, running down to the stream. Follow it over the footbridge and across a field to a second footbridge. Cross this and turn left, following a footpath across fields to reach a larger, surfaced path. Turn left onto this and follow it all the way back along the valley to the road opposite the Sticklebarn, crossing with care to return to the car park.

Other trails nearby
The Cumbria Way offers a relatively low-level crossing of the Lake District, running 70 miles (113km) between Ulverston and Carlisle, and passing through Great Langdale en route.

74. Buttermere

Buttermere
Near Cockermouth
Cumbria
CA13 9UZ

ABOUT THIS RUN

Distance **4.7 miles (7.6km)**
Ascent **361ft (110m)**

Lakeside trails, some
     uneven ground
Wildlife
Dogs welcome

Towards the north-west of the Lake District National Park, the deep valley at Buttermere is approached via the steep and snaking road over the Honister Pass. The lake, which is 1.5 miles (2.4km) long and 0.5 miles (0.8km) wide, was once joined to Crummock Water until silting divided it into two. This is a magical place to run, surrounded by dramatic fells, waterfalls, farms and woodland. Whether you're keen to explore the airy ridgelines or happiest circumnavigating the serene lakes, there's something to suit every runner here.

This run takes in a loop of Buttermere from the village, with just one short stretch of road. It's a popular walking route, so best run in the early morning or evening, when you may have the place to yourself. Part of the trail is closed during the sandpiper nesting season – April to the end of June – to protect these special birds, who lay their eggs on the shore. Still an outstanding run, diversion signs, taking you through Buttermere village, will be in place during this time.

THINGS TO SEE

Scale Force
The truly spectacular waterfall at Scale Force, to the south of Crummock Water and near to Buttermere, is the highest waterfall in the Lake District. It consists of a single drop of water of 121ft (37m), plunging into a wooded ravine. The return distance from Buttermere village is about 4 miles (6.4km).

Below the surface
The clear, deep water, well away from agricultural runoff and other pollutants, is home to some fascinating fish, well adapted to the conditions. As well as brown trout, sea trout and salmon, the Arctic charr, a glacial relict fish, is found nowhere else in England.

Above: Snow-dusted fells around Buttermere.
Opposite: Exploring Great Langdale.

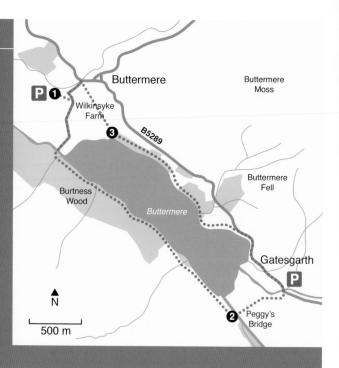

HOW TO GET HERE

By Public Transport
Workington station, 20 miles
(32.2km) to the west, or
Penrith station 26 miles
(41.8km) to the east. Honister
Rambler bus service 77 from
Keswick to Buttermere
(April–October).
By Car For Buttermere and
Crummock Water, take B5289
from Keswick or B5292 from
Cockermouth, forking right
onto the B5289 at Lorton.
National Trust Buttermere
village car park CA13 9UZ.
By Bicycle National Cycle
Network route 71 (C2C)
skirts nearby Loweswater.
OS Map Explorer OL4
Start / End National Trust
Buttermere village car park.
OS grid reference: NY172169

1. Facing the Bridge Hotel in the centre of the village, take the lane to the left of the hotel and bear left into the lane alongside the Fish Hotel. Continue along the lane until you reach a field. Keep on the main path through the fields until you reach the lakeside, bearing right to a bridge. Cross the bridge and carry on along the path, keeping the lake on your left.

2. 2 miles/3.3km At the far end of the lake, cross Peggy's Bridge and run through Gatesgarth Farm to reach the road. Turn left onto the road and follow it for a short distance until you can turn left, dropping down to the lake shore and following the rough path. Shortly after the path goes around a promontory and through Crag Wood, there's a short tunnel to go through.

3. 4 miles/6.3km Bear right, following the bridleway back to Buttermere village rather than continuing around the north shore of the lake, which is often closed to encourage nesting birds.

Right: Buttermere valley, best seen in the early morning or late in the day when it's quiet.

Other trails nearby
Buttermere's neighbouring lake, Crummock Water, is also a wonderful place to run. Often quieter than Buttermere itself, the loop is longer at 9 miles (14.5km), with the same starting point. Further afield, the Lake District is home to some of the best off-road running in the world, with a vast range of outstanding trail and fell-running routes to explore.

75. Aira Force & Gowbarrow Fell

3 **P** **👥** **🍴**

Near Watermillock
Penrith
Cumbria
CA11 0JS

ABOUT THIS RUN

Distance 4.2 miles (6.8km)
Ascent 1,365ft (416m)

Trails, off-road paths, steps,
   some quiet road
Wildlife
Dogs welcome on leads
History/culture

At 9 miles (14.5km) long by 0.5 miles (0.8km) wide, Ullswater is the second-largest body of water in the Lake District. This gleaming stretch of water snakes through the fells from Pooley Bridge in the north, a peaceful patchwork of fields edged by dry-stone walls, to Glenridding in the south, where the ridges and summits of St Sunday Crag, Dollywaggon Pike and Helvellyn rise impressively on the skyline. Along Ullswater's northern shore, the mighty falls of Aira Force channel water from the fells to the lake over a 65ft (nearly 20m) drop, greeting you with a thunderous roar and spray that fills the air. This run begins with a tour of the falls before following the course of Aira Beck upstream to explore the peaceful open grasslands of Gowbarrow Fell with its superb Lakeland views.

Other trails nearby

The Lake District is home to some of the best off-road running in the world. Nearby, the Ullswater Way is excellent and easy to follow; it is 20 miles (32.2km) long in its entirety, however divided up into sections it makes for a fantastic yet achievable adventure.

THINGS TO SEE

Red squirrels

Here in the UK there are an estimated 2.5 million grey squirrels yet fewer than 140,000 red squirrels – our native breed – of which three-quarters are found in Scotland. Grey squirrels were introduced from North America in the 1800s and, through competition for food and habitat and the diseases they carry, have drastically reduced the red squirrel population.

With their russet fur, bright eyes and fluffy ears, red squirrels are a delight to see and the Lake District is one of their few remaining strongholds in England, along with the Isle of Wight, the Isles of Scilly, Brownsea Island, Formby and parts of Northumberland. Anglesey in Wales and Ireland also have stable red squirrel populations. Look for them among the branches as you run through the woodlands at Aira Force, and also at Grasmere and Borrowdale further afield in the Lake District.

Above: View across Ullswater.
Opposite: Stone bridge at Aira Force.

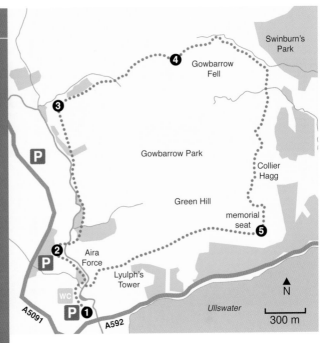

1. From the car park take the waterfall path up through the picnic field. Follow the path and head through a gateway in the wall into a grassy area known as the Glade. Continue to follow this path until you reach the woodland.

2. 0.4 miles/0.6km Follow the path down the steps to the viewing platform in front of the waterfall, crossing the footbridge and climbing the steep steps to the left. Follow the path of the river upstream, keeping the river on your left, until you emerge into open farmland.

3. 1.1 miles/1.8km At the boundary dry-stone wall, turn right and go through the gate onto the open fell, following the main path parallel to the stone wall on your left to reach the trig point at the summit of Gowbarrow Fell.

4. 1.7 miles/2.8km From the summit, continue on the path with the wall on your left, descending and bearing right to reach an old shooting lodge. Stay right, following the path around the eastern flank of Gowbarrow, descending to reach an obvious cairn, near to the memorial seat.

5. 3.1 miles/5km Detour over to the gate to take in the views from the memorial seat if you wish. Then continue along the same path, descending back into the woods and bearing left to cross the river. From here the outbound path leads downhill back to the car park.

76. Gibside

**Near Rowlands Gill
Gateshead
Tyne and Wear
NE16 6BG**

ABOUT THIS RUN

Distance **5 miles (8km)**
Ascent **882ft (269m)**

Surfaced paths and grassy
  trails
Waymarked route
Paid entry/NT members
Family friendly
History/culture
Wildlife
Dogs welcome on leads

Designed to showcase its spectacular Derwent Valley views
and the imagination of its creators, Gibside is a rare example
of a Georgian-designed landscape. Exploring the 600-acre
(243ha) estate, there are many surprises to be discovered,
from shy deer and sudden open vistas to a Neo-classical
chapel and grand ruin. This run follows the Wonders of
Nature route, fully waymarked to allow you simply to enjoy
running on well-maintained trails through Gibside's gardens,
woodland and countryside – a beautiful and peaceful escape.
From the bustling Market Place it heads straight through the
walled garden with its neat vegetable plots, emerging into
open parkland and tracing the course of the River Derwent.
The remainder of the route links up the areas of woodland
dotted around the estate, starting through Snipes Dene
Wood and finishing through West Wood.

Above: Runners at Gibside, where
there is a weekly parkrun and other
organised runs.

THINGS TO SEE

Outdoor activities

Gibside has an excellent range of activities for
everyone to enjoy, whether you need an exciting
adventure playground for the kids to enjoy while
you take it in turns to run or you're after some
music, good food and a beer afterwards. As well
as a play area in the café at the Market Place
there's the popular and extensive Strawberry
Castle playground which has plenty to keep little
ones entertained for hours. You could challenge

your running partner to a game of boules or
table tennis – equipment is available for a small
deposit. Or, throughout the summer months,
Gibside hosts regular Friday evening and Sunday
lunchtime events with food, live music and a bar,
perfect for relaxing after a run. There are also
weekly groups offering expert-led walking and
running in a supportive and encouraging
environment.

By Public Transport Blaydon station 5 miles (8km); Metrocentre 6 miles (9.7km); Newcastle 9 miles (14.5km). Frequent bus services from Newcastle (passing train station and Metrocentre) to Consett, alight Rowlands Gill, 0.8 miles (1.3km).
By Car Entrance on B6314 between Burnopfield and Rowlands Gill; follow brown signs from A1, taking exit on to A694 at north end of Metrocentre.
By Bicycle National Cycle Network Route 14 passes within 0.5 miles (0.8km); however, no cycling on the estate.
OS Map Explorer 307
Start / End Market Place.
OS grid reference: NZ171583

1. To find the start of the route, from the car park go through the visitor reception and up the wooden boardwalk, crossing the road to reach the Market Place. The run follows the Wonders of Nature route, waymarked with green arrows throughout. From the start, go straight ahead with the walled garden on your left. Turn left into the walled garden and follow the path straight ahead, turning right once you have passed through the gates. Turn left and run alongside The Avenue and then through a section of woodland, descending to reach the River Derwent. Follow the riverside path, entering another area of woodland and following the path around to the right.

2. 1.2 miles/1.9km Where the path joins a forestry road, turn right and follow a trail uphill through the woods, passing the lily pond and the Column to Liberty. Where the track emerges into a clearing, take the smaller path sharp left, signed to the Column. Continue past the column and follow the waymarkers as the trail turns right then left to bring you to another forestry road.

3. 2.1 miles/3.4km Turn right and follow the forestry road, following it uphill to the top of Snipes Dene. Continue on this track around a right-hand bend and then follow it downhill to reach the Octagon Pond. Follow the track to the right of the pond to reach the stables. Turn left here and follow the trail into West Wood.

4. 4.2 miles/6.8km Nearing the southern edge of the woods, turn right and follow Leapmill Burn downhill, emerging at the Strawberry Castle play area. Follow the path to the right of the play area and around to the right to return to Market Place and some well-earned refreshments.

Other trails nearby
The Derwent Walk is popular 12-mile (19.3km) linear route between Consett and Swalwell that also makes an excellent, level running trail.

77. Souter Lighthouse

**Coast Road
Whitburn
Sunderland
Tyne and Wear
SR6 7NH**

ABOUT THIS RUN

Distance 6.2 miles (9.9km)
Ascent 403ft (123m)

Surfaced paths and grassy
  trails
Coastal
History/culture
Wildlife
Dogs welcome on leads

Standing proud on a grassy coastal headland midway between the rivers Tyne and Wear, its red and white stripes vibrant against a backdrop of sky and sea, Souter Lighthouse is an impressive sight from many miles around. Opened in 1871, it was the first lighthouse in the world designed and built to be powered by electricity. This run traces inviting trails through the coastal grasslands, taking a loop from the lighthouse along a stretch of sheer, limestone cliffs. To the north, at point 3, you will run through the finish line of the Great North Run. A shorter loop, to the south, explores Whitburn Coastal Park and Nature Reserve, once colliery land but since reclaimed to create a haven for wildlife. Look out across to the many rocky outcrops just offshore and up into the sky to spot kittiwakes, fulmars, cormorants, shags and guillemots amongst other seabirds.

Above: Marsden Bay.
Opposite: Running past
Souter Lighthouse.

THINGS TO SEE

The lost village

Just north of Souter Lighthouse stretches a large, flat field, popular with dog walkers and families. Looking across the grassy expanse today, it's hard to imagine that, less than 70 years ago, there was a bustling village on the site, housing the miners from nearby Whitburn Colliery. With 135 houses and around 700 residents, Marsden village was well-serviced with a Co-op store, Miners' Institute, Post Office and school, children's playground, bowling green, tennis courts, football and cricket pitches. A combination of the closure of the colliery in 1968 and coastal erosion threatening many of the buildings forced residents to move away and the village was demolished. The site is now looked after by the National Trust, forming part of the Whitburn Coastal Park.

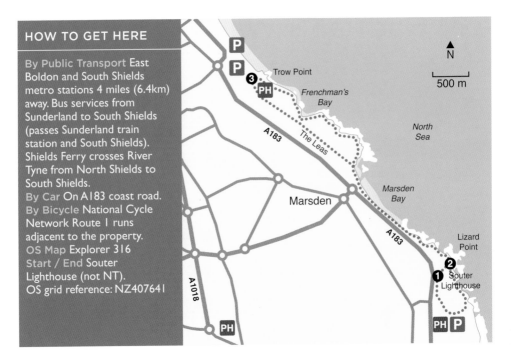

HOW TO GET HERE

By Public Transport East Boldon and South Shields metro stations 4 miles (6.4km) away. Bus services from Sunderland to South Shields (passes Sunderland train station and South Shields). Shields Ferry crosses River Tyne from North Shields to South Shields.
By Car On A183 coast road.
By Bicycle National Cycle Network Route 1 runs adjacent to the property.
OS Map Explorer 316
Start / End Souter Lighthouse (not NT).
OS grid reference: NZ407641

1. From the car park, with the green hut on your right, join the path that heads towards the sea. Turn right onto the tarmac path and run along the western edge of Whitburn Coastal Park to reach the car park at its southern end. Run around the edge of the car park on the grass and pass through the gate. Follow the path with the sea on your right and pass between the lighthouse and the coast.

2. 1 mile/1.6km Continue on the coastal path and pass The Grotto Café (not NT) on your right. After the car park, use the steps to cross the concrete path and remain on the coastal path. Continue along the path and pass Frenchman's Bay.

3. 3.7 miles/5.9km Bear round to the left, ignoring the black path to the right. You will see the Bambrough Pub on the main road. At this point, turn around and follow the path running parallel to your outward path, or return on the coast path as far as point 2 for grand coastal views in the opposite direction. Continue until you arrive back at the lighthouse when you can head towards the car park.

Other trails nearby

The South Tyneside Heritage Trail is a 26-mile (41.8km) circular route from South Shields along the coast to Whitburn then inland to reach the Tyne at Hebburn, returning via Jarrow. The heritage and history of the places it passes through are explained on 32 panels along the way. The coast path continues in either direction, providing outstanding seaside running.

78. Hadrian's Wall

**Near Housesteads Fort
Bardon Mill
NE47 6NN**

ABOUT THIS RUN

Distance **4.8 miles (7.7km)**
Ascent **754ft (230m)**

Undulating, rough trails,
    short sections of road
Wildlife
History/culture
Family friendly
Dogs welcome, keep on
    leads around livestock

Stretching 85 miles (137km) across northern England, marking the northernmost limits of the Roman province of Britannia, Hadrian's Wall is a monumental structure and a UNESCO World Heritage Site. Taking six years and three legions of 15,000 men to build, it makes use of the natural Whin Sill escarpment, rising and falling with the rolling countryside, a true feat of engineering set amidst Northumberland's breathtaking scenery. This run traces an enjoyable circuit a short distance west of the famous Housesteads Fort. Starting at Steel Rigg, with its high viewpoint, it visits peaceful Crag Lough and finishes along a stretch of the wall path, a National Trail in its own right, passing the famous and much-photographed Sycamore Gap along the way.

*Above and opposite: Running
at Hadrian's Wall.*

THINGS TO SEE

Housesteads Roman fort
Built in the 2nd century, midway along Hadrian's Wall, Housesteads is the most complete example of a Roman fort in Britain. Garrisoned by 800 soldiers until the end of the 4th century, it offers a fascinating insight into Roman military life. Wandering around the maze of stone walls, you can discover the stories behind the archaeological remains and explore the village south of the fort. Entering rooms where people once lived, including some of the oldest toilets in Britain, you really can imagine you're back in the days of the Romans. Please note: the fort is owned by the National Trust but maintained by English Heritage.

The Sill
Its striking design mirroring its dramatic surroundings, The Sill National Landscape Discovery Centre is Northumberland National Park's visitor hub (not NT). Here you'll find exhibitions, learning spaces, a local food café, YHA hostel and a shop selling local crafts and produce.

HOW TO GET HERE

By Public Transport
Haltwhistle station, 4.6 miles
(7.4km). Connections to
AD122 bus to Once Brewed
0.5 miles (0.8km) from the
start.
By Car North of the river
Tyne, 4 miles (6.4km) north of
Haltwhistle onto the B6318
turning off at the Twice Brewed
Inn following road up for 0.5
miles (0.8km) to car park,
postcode NE47 7AN.
By Bicycle National Cycle
Network route 68.
OS Map OL43
Start / End Steel Rigg
car park (not NT).
OS grid reference: NY749676

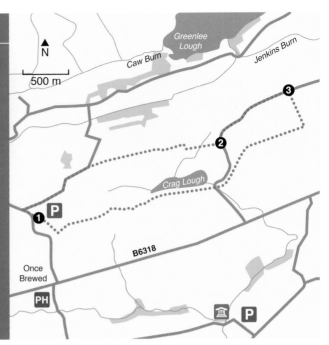

1. Leave the car park, heading
away from Hadrian's Wall and
follow the footpath on the right
of the road for a short distance
until you can turn right onto an
obvious track running parallel
to the wall. Continue to follow
the footpath over open
grassland after the track peters
out, passing Peatrigg Plantation
on your left and Crag Lough
on your right.

2. 1.7 miles/2.7km At the
path junction, turn left, following
the track around to the right
and then following the footpath
that carries straight on, passing
to the left of a plantation.

3. 2.3 miles/3.7km Turn right,
crossing to the wall path. Turn
right and follow the wall path
all the way back to the car park
at Steel Rigg.

Other trails nearby
Designated a National Trail in 2003, the Hadrian's
Wall Path runs between Wallsend on the east
coast of England and Bowness-on-Solway on the
west coast.

79. Cragside

Rothbury
Morpeth
Northumberland
NE65 7PX

ABOUT THIS RUN

Distance 6.1 miles (9.9km)
Ascent 836ft (255m)

Surfaced path, quiet road
Waymarked route
Family friendly
Wildlife
History/culture
Dogs welcome on leads

Over 40 miles (64km) of footpaths, including 14 waymarked routes, wind through the 1,000-acre (405ha) estate at Cragside. An extraordinary place, from the grand Victorian house – the first in the world to be lit by hydroelectricity – to the maze of drives and paths that meander through forests of rhododendrons, around wildlife-rich lakes and past one of the largest rock gardens in Europe. This run follows the fully waymarked Trust10 route on an adventurous exploration of the estate, starting from the visitor centre, looping the lakes and taking you past the house for a real taste of the wonders of Cragside. If you fancy adding something a bit different to your run you can even swing, climb and jump your way around the Trim Trail on Canada Drive.

Above: Lakeside trails at Cragside.
Opposite: Running at Cragside.

THINGS TO SEE

The estate
Described in 1880 as 'a palace of the modern magician', the Victorian mansion at Cragside, standing high on a rocky crag above Debdon Burn, was the home of Lord Armstrong and his wife, Lady Armstrong. A prolific inventor, Lord Armstrong filled the house and gardens with intriguing contraptions, including the first system in the world to light a house by hydroelectric power, an early design for a washing machine, fire alarm buttons, telephones, a passenger lift, Turkish bath and the country's first flushing loo. The

estate was created over a period of 20 years by the Armstrongs and architect Norman Shaw, adding Tudor-style features to the house, landscaping the grounds, constructing five lakes, planting contrasting areas of garden and some 7 million trees. Today, it is just as intriguing, powered once again by hydroelectricity since its reintroduction in 2013. Wandering the estate, look out for the tallest Scots pine in Britain, standing at 131ft (40m), rare red squirrels and the rock garden bursting into a riot of colour in late spring.

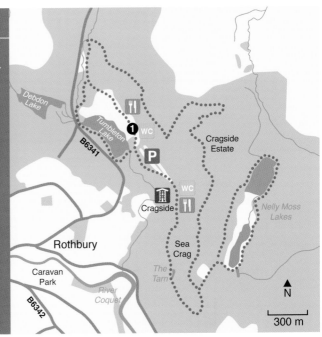

HOW TO GET HERE

By Public Transport Morpeth train station, 17 miles (27.4km).
By Car on B6341, 15 miles (24.1km) north-west of Morpeth on Coldstream road (A697). Turn left on to B6341 at Moorhouse Crossroads, entrance 3 miles (4.8km) on left.
OS Map Explorer 16 and 42
Start / End National Trust visitor centre.
OS grid reference: NU073022

1. From the visitor centre, follow Trust10 waymarkers throughout, starting around Tumbleton Lake then heading out past the house for a circumnavigation of Nelly Moss Lakes. From here you'll take on the Trim Trail along Canada Drive before skirting the northern edge of the estate, finishing alongside Tumbleton Lake and back to the visitor centre.

Other trails nearby
Explore the vast network of footpaths extending around the Cragside estate or head further afield to discover Northumberland's wealth of outdoor adventures, from the Cheviot Hills to the dramatic coast dotted with awe-inspiring castles.

80. Northumberland coast

Low Newton by the Sea
Alnwick
Northumberland
NE66 3ED

ABOUT THIS RUN

Distance 4.3 miles (7km)
Ascent 157ft (48m)

Grassy trails, surfaced path,
  sandy beach
Coastal
Family friendly
Wildlife
History/culture
Dogs welcome on leads

The National Trust looks after a 20-mile (32.2km) stretch of the spectacular north-east coast, including the castles at Dunstanburgh and Lindisfarne. An Area of Outstanding Natural Beauty, this stretch of coastline is also of European importance for its nature, in particular the incredible variety of birds. Beadnell village is set at one end of the wide, sandy crescent of Beadnell Bay, a popular place for watersports that boasts the only west-facing harbour on the east coast. This run makes the most of the bay, starting at Newton Links at its southern end and winding through dunes and coastal grassland all the way to Beadnell before taking to the beach for the return leg. From May until July access to the beach is restricted as it is a nationally important breeding site for terns. Runners are still welcome but please follow diversion signs.

THINGS TO SEE

Birdlife

This stretch of the coast is a fantastic place to see birds of many different varieties. Little terns, Arctic terns and ringed plovers nest at Long Nanny nature reserve in Beadnell Bay; puffins, shags, kittiwakes, razorbills, eider ducks, fulmars and guillemots can be seen on the Farne Islands; while at Newton Pool, a freshwater reserve, you might spot waders such as oystercatchers and rarer migrant birds including red-backed shrike, red-breasted flycatcher, yellow-browed warbler, and greenish and barred warblers.

Castles

The Northumberland coast is dotted with impressive castles, reminders of the Border wars that raged from the 14th to the 16th century. Some remain today, brooding on their rocky outcrops overlooking peaceful stretches of coastline and sandy beaches. Dunstanburgh was one of the most impressive castles of its time, but today stands as an atmospheric part-ruin and is an intriguing place to explore. The castle is owned by the National Trust and managed by English Heritage – entry is free for NT members.

By Public Transport
Alnmouth train station 11
miles (17.7km), then bus
service 418.
By Car Off the A1 between
Newcastle and Berwick-upon-
Tweed. Turn off on to the
B1340 from Alnwick or the
B6347 both towards Christon
Bank. The B1339 then runs
parallel to the coast, with
minor roads leading to the sea
at Newton and Embleton.
By Bicycle National Cycle
Network route 1 runs between
Newcastle and Berwick-upon-
Tweed via Alnmouth, Craster
and Seahouses, mostly on
minor roads.
OS Map Explorer 340
Start / End Newton Links
car park (not NT).
OS grid reference: NU235260

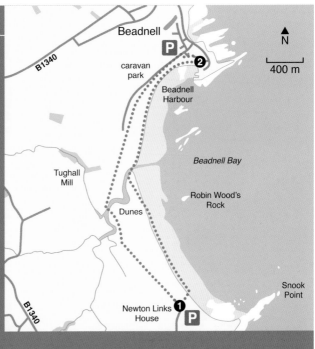

1. From the car park follow
the coast path, also St Oswald's
Way, through the coastal
grassland with the sea on your
right. Follow the curve of the
bay around and you'll eventually
reach the village of Beadnell.

2. **2.2 miles/3.6km** From
Beadnell, drop down to the
sandy beach and run back to
Newton Links along the beach.

Above: Running on the Northumberland coast
near Seahouses.
Opposite: Running past Dunstanburgh Castle.

Other trails nearby
Linking places associated with
St Oswald, a 7th-century King
of Northumbria, St Oswald's
Way runs 97 miles (156km)
between Holy Island
(Lindisfarne) in the north and
Hadrian's Wall in the south.

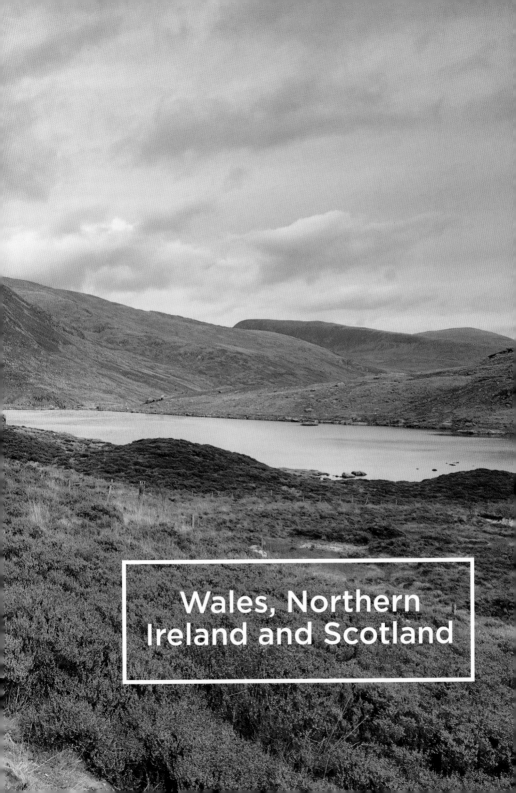

Wales, Northern
Ireland and Scotland

81. Stackpole

**Stackpole Quay
Pembrokeshire
SA71 5LS**

ABOUT THIS RUN

Distance **6 miles (9.5km**
Ascent **719ft (219m)**

Beach, grassy clifftop,
   lakeside paths, steps
Coastal
Wildlife
Dogs welcome on leads
Take care on coastal cliffs

Stackpole boasts some of the finest wildlife habitats in Pembrokeshire, including limestone cliffs, home to thousands of breeding seabirds. There are sandy beaches backed by rolling dunes, wooded valleys and freshwater lakes to explore. It's also a fantastic destination for those seeking outdoor adventures, from surfing in the wide bays to running the winding coastal trails. This run traverses the intricate and inspiring section of coastline around Stackpole Head, taking in everything this beautiful, special place has to offer; from the stunning beaches at Barafundle and Broad Haven South to the tranquil Bosherston lily ponds. There is plenty of accomodation in the area if you wish to extend your visit.

Above: Stackpole Warren. The enticing beaches beaches here offer great places to relax after a run.
Opposite: Night run at Stackpole.

THINGS TO SEE

The Stackpole estate

The estate once radiated from Stackpole Court, an early Georgian mansion in the Palladian style, built in the 1730s on the site of the earlier fortified house. Sadly, the requisition of much of the estate by the military over the course of the two World Wars caused irreparable damage to the house and it was finally demolished in 1963. Today the estate is celebrated for its wildlife and the Bosherston Lakes, created in the late 1800s by flooding a valley, are a link to its more opulent days. These spring-fed lakes are filled with rare freshwater plants; fish including eels, pike, perch, roach and tench; and, the star of the show for many, a healthy population of otters. They are also home to breeding birds such as herons, kingfishers, little grebes and moorhens, while over the winter months you might spot goosanders and gadwalls. Away from the lakes there are 12 species of bat and at least 30 species of butterfly on the estate, along with an abundance of birds, from tiny wrens and goldcrests to the impressive buzzards and sparrowhawks. Conservation grazing by cattle and Welsh Mountain sheep helps keep the vegetation under control.

HOW TO GET HERE

By Public Transport Pembroke station 6 miles (9.7km), then bus service 387 Coastal Cruiser from Pembroke stops at Stackpole Quay car park.
By Car B4319 from Pembroke – follow signs for Stackpole Village. Brown tourist sign for Stackpole Quay from coast road between Stackpole and Freshwater East.
By Bicycle Pembrokeshire Tourist Route to Stackpole Village.
On Foot The route follows a section of the Pembrokeshire Coast Path.
OS Map Explorer 308
Start / End Car park at Stackpole Quay (not NT).
OS grid reference: SR990958

B4319
Lodge Park
P Stackpole
Stackpole Park
Stackpole Centre
❹
Shippingback Wood
❶
P WC
Lorts Cave
Dunes
The Devil's Quoit
Bosherston
❸
P WC
Stackpole Warren
Dunes
❷
Saddle Point
Trefalen P WC
Stackpole Head
▲ N
400 m

1. From Stackpole Quay car park, follow the coast path to Barafundle, going down the steps onto the beach. Run straight across the sand and climb up the steps through woodland on the opposite side. Continue along the coast path around Stackpole Head and Saddle Point, then head inland along the edge of Broad Haven South beach to reach the lake outlet.

2. 3 miles/4.8km Cross the stone bridge and bear left, following the Western Arm path towards Bosherston, where there is a café.

3. 3.7 miles/6km Cross the Bosherston Causeway and the Central Causeway, looping the lily ponds. Follow the path to the Grassy Bridge but don't cross it – instead carry straight on through woodland with the lake on your right to reach the Eight Arch Bridge.

4. 4.9 miles/7.9km Cross the Eight Arch Bridge and follow the Deer Park track back to the car park at Stackpole Quay.

Other trails nearby

Numerous other waymarked running trails loop around Stackpole, perfect for on-foot exploring. The Pembrokeshire Coast Path continues in either direction, part of the 870-mile (1,400km) Wales Coast Path.

82. Marloes Peninsula

Marloes
Haverfordwest
Pembrokeshire
Nearest postcode
SA62 3BH

ABOUT THIS RUN

Distance 4.9 miles (7.9km)
Ascent 735ft (224m)

Coastal trails, field paths and quiet road; rough and uneven terrain in places
Wildlife
Coast/beach
Dogs welcome; keep on leads around livestock
History/culture
Take care on coastal cliffs

The Marloes Peninsula lies at the very western reaches of Pembrokeshire, a hidden haven of sandy beaches, a wealth of wildlife, fascinating history and outstanding coastal trails. This route loops the very end of the peninsula, starting with a run down towards Marloes Sands, a stunning golden crescent at low tide and one of Pembrokeshire's best beaches. From here it traces a long stretch of the dramatic, undulating coast path, rounding Wooltack Point from where there are spectacular views across St Bride's Bay to the islands that dot the sea. The final stretch heads back inland, crossing rolling farmland to return to the car park.

Above: View down to Marloes Sands. Opposite: Haven Point.

THINGS TO SEE

Wildlife watching
Marloes Mere is a birdwatching hotspot, boasting marsh harriers, teal, snipe, stonechat and whitethroat. Wooltack Point, visited on this run, is a great vantage point for seeing seabirds and a popular breeding ground for choughs, with their glossy black plumage and bright red legs and beaks. Vast colonies of guillemots, puffins and razorbills can be found on Skomer – day boats sail from Martin's Haven – while Grassholm is one of the largest gannetries in the world. If you look carefully you might also spot seals (the best time for seal spotting is during the

pup season in mid-November) and porpoises out amongst the waves.

Away from the sea, look for Welsh Black cattle, whose grazing is essential for conserving the coastal heathland vegetation.

Back in time
Marloes is home to some incredible geology, featuring both sandstones and volcanic rocks with folds, faults and pinnacles, while an Iron Age fort at Watery Bay overlooks Marloes Sands and Gateholm.

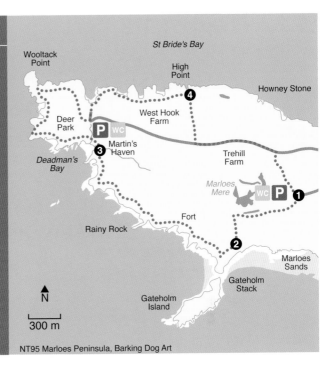

By Public Transport Trains to Haverfordwest, 14 miles (22.5km); Milford Haven, 9 miles (14.5km); Pembroke Dock, 16 miles (25.7km). Bus 315, Haverfordwest to Marloes, daily May to September.
By Car B4327 from Haverfordwest, then country roads. SatNav use postcode SA62 3BH
On Foot The route is on the Pembrokeshire Coast Path.
OS Map Explorer OL36
Start / End Marloes Sands car park (not NT).
OS grid reference: SM789082

St Bride's Bay

Wooltack Point

High Point

Howney Stone

4

Deer Park

West Hook Farm

P WC

Martin's Haven

3

Deadman's Bay

Trehill Farm

Marloes Mere

WC **P** **1**

Fort

Rainy Rock

2

Marloes Sands

Gateholm Stack

Gateholm Island

N

300 m

NT95 Marloes Peninsula, Barking Dog Art

1. From the south end of Marloes Sands car park turn right and follow the lane past Marloes Mere, at the end turning left towards the coast path and Marloes Sands.

2. 0.4 miles/0.7km At a footbridge, shortly before a white cottage, take the left fork towards the Iron Age ramparts of the Deer Park fort. Follow the path around the coastline of the Deer Park.

3. 2.2 miles/3.5km Bear left, running around the edge of the headland and passing Wooltack Point. Turn left just before you reach the Martin's Haven car park, following the surfaced road past the toilets towards the cove at Martin's Haven and then bearing right onto the coast path.

Other trails nearby
The Pembrokeshire Coast Path runs for 186 miles (299km) around Britain's only coastal National Park. It is a section of the Wales Coast Path which stretches 870 miles (1,400km) around the whole coast of Wales from Chepstow in the south to Queensferry in the north.

4. 3.9 miles/6.3km After just over 1 mile (1.6km) leave the coast path, turning right through a self-closing gate by a West Hook Farm National Trust omega sign, then cross three fields to the road. Turn left and follow the road past Trehill Farm. Turn right by two semi-detached cottages and down the lane leading back to the car park.

83. Treginnis

Porth Clais Harbour
Pembrokeshire
SA62 6RR

ABOUT THIS RUN

Distance 6.2 miles (10km)
Ascent 823ft (251m)

Coastal trails, off-road
  paths, some quiet roads
Wildlife
Coast/beach
Dogs welcome – on leads
  around livestock
History/culture
NT kiosk open in summer
  10am–4pm
Take care on cliffs

St David's Head is a dramatic headland northwest of
St David's – Britain's smallest city. The area is dominated
by the volcanic peak of Carn Llidi, one of many fascinating
geological features, from where, on a clear day, you can spot
the mountains of Wicklow in Ireland.

This run traces a loop around the Treginnis peninsula,
south-west of St David's. Starting at Porth Clais Harbour,
it crosses the peninsula to reach the lifeboat station at
St Justinian's. From here it follows the Pembrokeshire
Coast Path all the way back to Porth Clais, with
breathtaking coastal views throughout.

*Above: Running on the coast path
at Treginnis.
Opposite: There is a good possibility
of seeing grey seals in the area,
especially in November and
December.*

THINGS TO SEE

Ancient foundations
The Treginnis peninsula is formed from Wales'
oldest rocks, laid down during the Precambrian
era some 600 million years ago. The oldest rock is
the result of volcanic activity, in places covered by
a younger, sedimentary layer. Rounding the corner
and heading for the coast path on this run,
Ramsey Island, an RSPB reserve, comes into
view across the Ramsey Sound, its twin peaks
the remains of ancient extinct volcanoes.

Porth Clais
The pretty, 12th-century miniature harbour at
Porth Clais was once a busy port trading timber,
grain, coal and limestone – the old limekilns are
still visible either side of the harbour and the
former pump room for the gasworks is an
excellent tea kiosk. These days it is a popular spot
with kayakers and those exploring the dramatic
coast, walking, running or rock climbing on the
impressive cliffs.

By Public Transport Train stations at Haverfordwest and Fishguard, both 17 miles (27.3km). Bus routes 342 and 411, Haverfordwest to St David's; Puffin Shuttle 400, Solva, Marloes and Milford Haven to St David's; Strumble Shuttle 404, Fishguard and Newport to St David's. Then catch Celtic Coaster shuttle bus from St David's to Porth Clais (May–September).
By Car 1.5 miles (2.4km) south-west from St David's, follow signs for Porth Clais. SatNav postcode SA62 6RR. Please park at Porth Clais and not St Justinian's car park as it is much larger and has facilities.
On Foot Porth Clais is situated right on the Wales Coast Path.
OS Map Explorer OL35
Start / End Porth Clais Harbour (not NT).
OS grid reference: SM741242

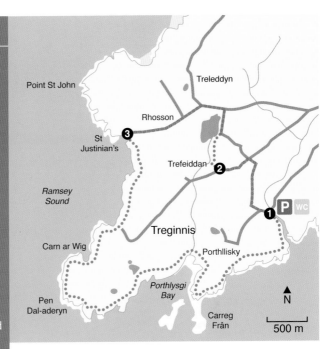

Other trails nearby
The Pembrokeshire Coast Path continues enjoyably in either direction, part of the Wales Coast Path which stretches some 870 miles (1,400km) around the whole coast of Wales from Chepstow in the south to Queensferry in the north. There are also excellent runs around many of the neighbouring Pembrokeshire peninsulas.

1. Turn right out of the car park and follow the lane to reach a crossroads. Turn left here, signed to Treginnis.

2. 0.8 miles/1.3km Turn right onto a footpath, shortly before Treginnis Lodge, and follow the footpath past a narrow stretch of water on your right and then the larger Pwll Trefeiddan. On reaching the lane, turn left and then left again at the T-junction, following this road to reach the coast at St Justinian's.

3. 2.1 miles/3.3km Turn left onto the coast path and follow it all the way around the spectacular Treginnis Peninsula for 4 miles (6.4km), eventually returning to Porth Clais.

84. Rhossili

**National Trust
visitor centre
Rhossili village
Gower
SA3 1PR**

ABOUT THIS RUN

Distance 4.4 miles (7.1km)
Ascent 725ft (221m)

Grassy trails – may be
slippery after rain, sandy
beach, quiet roads
Wildlife
Coast/beach
Dogs welcome; keep on
leads around livestock
History/culture

The 3-mile (4.8km) sandy sweep of Rhossili Bay edges
the Gower Peninsula, designated Britain's first Area of
Outstanding Natural Beauty in 1956. Backed by rolling
downland and framed by the rocky promontories of Worms
Head to the south and Burry Holms to the north. At low
tide, the remains of the wreck of the ship Helvetia rise from
the sand where it ran aground in a storm in 1887. This run
begins at Rhossili village with a steady climb to The Beacon,
the highest point on Gower and a perfect place to stop and
admire the glorious views out over the Bristol Channel to
Lundy. From here, there's an inviting trail along the ridge
before an enjoyable descent to the beach. The final stretch
back to Rhossili village across the firm, flat sands is best
run barefoot right at the water's edge.

Above: Rhossili Bay.
Opposite: Running across
Rhossili Bay.

THINGS TO SEE

Worms Head

Worms Head, whose name comes from the
Nordic 'Wurm', meaning serpent or dragon, is a
tidal island reaching out into the Bristol Channel
at the westernmost point of Gower. A rocky
causeway links the mainland to the island, which
has a large, flat-topped section known as 'Inner
Head', a natural rock bridge – the 'Devil's Bridge'
– and the smaller 'Outer Head'. The Outer Head

is a breeding ground for seabirds, including gulls,
guillemots, razorbills, kittiwakes and occasionally
puffins, and is therefore out of bounds during the
nesting season between 1 March and 31 August.
At about 1 mile (1.6km) in length, this is a
fascinating place to explore but visits must be
carefully timed as access is only possible for
approximately 2.5 hours either side of low tide.

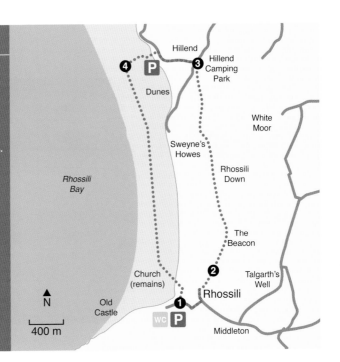

HOW TO GET HERE

By Public Transport Swansea train station 19 miles (30.6km) way. Bus 118 to Rhossili.

By Car From Swansea (J42) take the A483 to Swansea. Continue on to the A4067. At Black Pill, turn on to the B4436. Turn right to keep on the B4436 at Pennard before turning left on to the A4118. At Scurlage, take the B4247 to Rhossili.

On Foot Rhossili is situated right on the Wales Coast Path and at the end of the Gower Way.

OS Map Explorer 164

Start / End National Trust visitor centre, Rhossili.

OS grid reference: SS414880

Hillend

Hillend Camping Park

④ P ③

Dunes

White Moor

Sweyne's Howes

Rhossili Down

Rhossili Bay

The Beacon

N

400 m

Church (remains)

Old Castle

② Talgarth's Well

Rhossili

①

wc P

Middleton

1. Follow the road back through the village, taking the footpath by the bus stop as it bears left past the church. At the track junction turn left and continue until you reach a gate signed to Rhossili Down. Follow the main path as it climbs the hill towards the top of the downs.

2. **0.4 miles/0.7km** Stay left, continuing to follow the main path along the ridge to reach the trig point-topped summit of The Beacon, the highest point on Gower. Continue following the path as it descends steeply towards Hillend campsite.

3. **2 miles/3.2km** Go through the site, past Eddie's Café and turn onto the beach.

4. **2.6 miles/4.2km** Head left and enjoy running the full length back to Rhossili. The running is often easiest and most enjoyable where it is firmest, nearer to the sea.

Other trails nearby

The Gower and Swansea Bay Coast Path runs for 97 miles (156km) between Loughor, Swansea and Kenfig Dunes near Port Talbot. It is a section of the Wales Coast Path which stretches around the whole coast of Wales from Chepstow in the south to Queensferry, Flintshire, in the north.

85. Clytha

**nr Clytha
Monmouthshire
NP7 9BW**

ABOUT THIS RUN

Distance 3.1 miles (5km)
Ascent 371ft (113m)

Woodland and field paths
Waymarked route
May be muddy
History/culture
Wildlife
Dogs welcome on leads

Set within Monmouthshire's beautiful Usk Valley, the Clytha estate boasts an 18th-century landscaped park dotted with a number of fine buildings and glorious views across the surrounding rolling, verdant countryside. This run follows the waymarked circular route around the estate, starting alongside the River Usk before heading north, crossing open parkland, winding along woodland trails and passing the ruined, 12th-century Capel Aeddan and the site of a deserted medieval village. The final section takes you right around the remarkable folly of Clytha Castle and back to the start. This route does include several road crossings – please take care.

Above: Clytha Castle, a delightful castellated confection.

THINGS TO SEE

Clytha Castle
Considered to be one of the most outstanding 18th-century follies in Wales, Clytha Castle was designed by John Davenport and built by William Jones, owner of Clytha House, in 1790 as a memorial to his late wife Elizabeth. Standing proudly at the top of Clytha Hill, on the edge of a chestnut grove, the folly is currently looked after by the Landmark Trust and is available to book as holiday accommodation.

Clytha House
Grade I-listed Clytha House was rebuilt in the classic Greek style in the 1830s by architect

Edward Haycock and is one of the last remaining Greek-style houses in Wales. Faced in honey-coloured Bath stone, the grand oval entrance hall with its concave ceiling supported by seven Tuscan pillars is a truly impressive sight.

Capel Aedan
Heading back across the fields from furthest point of the run, look out for a number of stones on your left. These are the ruins of St Aeddan's Church – also known as Capel Aedan – founded in 1188 by Aedan of Gwaethfoed. Surrounded by a deserted medieval village this may also be where the original manor stood.

By Public Transport
Abergavenny train station
5 miles (8km), then bus service
83 to reach the start.
On Foot The Usk Valley Walk
runs between Newport and
Brecon, passing through Clytha.
By Car From the east, head
west along the A40 to Raglan.
Take the fourth exit at the
Raglan roundabout, signposted
Clytha and follow the National
Trust signs. From the west,
follow the B4598 from the
Hardwick roundabout just
outside Abergavenny. Continue
for 4.7 miles (7.6km), turn
right onto the Bettws Newydd
road and follow the National
Trust signs.
By Bicycle National Cycle
Network Route 42 passes
the start.
OS Map Explorer OL13
Start / End National Trust
Clytha riverside car park.
OS grid reference: SO361085

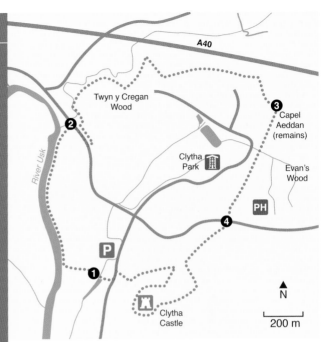

Other trails nearby

There's a wealth of footpaths
to explore around the estate,
or the Usk Valley Walk runs
for 50 miles (80km) between
Caerleon, Newport and
Brecon, Powys.

1. This run follows the waymarked circular estate route
throughout. From the car park go through the gate towards
the river. On reaching the river, turn right and follow the Usk
Valley Way. After about 0.5 miles (0.8km) bear right through
a gate, heading up hill to reach a road.

2. 0.6 miles/1km Cross the road with care. Go through
the gate then through the next gate on your left. Follow
waymarkers across the field and past the back of Rose
Cottage and through the woodland. Continue until you
pass the back of Chapel Farm, then cross the fields to reach
a path junction where a number of stones mark the remains
of Capel Aeddan.

3. 1.7 miles/2.7km Bear right at the junction then
follow waymarkers across fields and continue to reach
a road, passing the drive to the Clytha Arms pub on
your left.

4. 2.1 miles/3.3km Carefully cross the road, climb the steps
and go through the gate at the top. Keep right, following the
waymarkers over a couple of stiles into a field on a hill.
Follow the line of lime trees diagonally down to the track.
When you reach the track, turn left and follow it up, taking
the right fork up to the castle. After exploring the area (the
castle isn't open to the public) follow the waymarkers back
to Clytha.

86. Sugar Loaf

Llanwenarth car park
Abergavenny
Monmouthshire
NP7 7LA

ABOUT THIS RUN

Distance 3.3 miles (5.3km)
Ascent 895ft (273m)

Rough mud and grassy
  paths with some rocky
  sections; steep climbs
  and descents
Summit
Wildlife
History/culture
Dogs welcome on leads

Flanked by ancient oakwood valleys, the distinctive ridge
of the Sugar Loaf rises majestically from its place in the
Black Mountains on the eastern edge of the Brecon Beacons
National Park. With its summit an airy 1,955ft (596m) it
falls just short of official classification as a mountain, but
its height relative to its surroundings makes it a fantastic
viewpoint from which to see out across the Beacons to
the summit of Pen y Fan to the west, over the Usk Valley
towards the Bristol Channel in the south and to the rolling
countryside of Herefordshire and the Malvern Hills to the
east. This run begins at the Llanwenarth car park, well over
halfway from sea level to the summit, and which must be a
contender for having the best car-park views in the country.
From here, it follows clear, inviting paths up the grassy
hillside to reach a wild and rugged summit ridge, with a
splendid white-painted trig point. Now it's downhill all
the way, as fast as you dare, back to the finish.

Above: Running along the
summit ridge of Sugar Loaf.
Opposite: Running the trails
below Sugar Loaf.

THINGS TO SEE

Upland wildlife
The Sugar Loaf is a great place to spot upland
birds: from skylarks with their bubbling song, rising
from the grassland, to circling buzzards, red kites
and swooping swallows and house martins. You
might also see red grouse hiding in the heather.

Ancient woodland
Beneath the high, open hillsides of Sugar Loaf,
St Mary's Vale is a peaceful, wooded haven
nestled between the hills of Llanwenarth and
Rholben. An extensive area of oak and beach
woodland, cut through by the gentle stream –
the Nant Iago – much of the area is a Site of
Special Scientific Interest and Special Area of
Conservation, and home to a rich diversity of
wildlife, including the rare red wood ant.

HOW TO GET HERE

By Public Transport
Abergavenny train station
4 miles (6.4km). X43 bus
service from Cardiff to
Abergavenny.
By Car From the west follow
the A40. Just before you reach
Abergavenny, and just after the
Lamb and Flag pub, turn left
where the Sugar Loaf Vineyards
are signposted. Take the first
left and follow the road up.
Turn left again and the road
bends sharply round to the
right. Continue uphill around a
sharp left-hand bend, then take
the right-hand fork shortly
after. Continue along this road,
past some small parking areas,
until you reach the main
tarmac car park with stone
trig point.
OS Map Explorer OL13
Start / End Llanwenarth car
park (not NT).
OS grid reference: SO268166

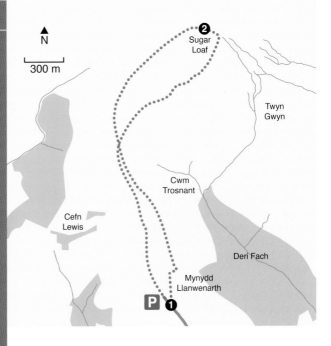

1. From the car park turn left onto the surfaced road then take one of the clear paths to the right, following this up the hillside until you reach the summit plateau of the Sugar Loaf. Aim for the trig point and stop to catch your breath and admire the views.

2. **1.7 miles/2.7km** Turn around and head back the way you came, but bear right, following a parallel path back down the hillside to the car park.

Other trails nearby

There's a great network of footpaths to explore across the Sugar Loaf and down into the surrounding valleys. For some excellent waterside running, head to for the pretty trail along the River Usk or the towpath of the wildlife-rich Monmouthshire and Brecon Canal.

87. Skirrid Fawr

Llanddewi Skirrid
Abergavenny
NP7 8AP

ABOUT THIS RUN

Distance **3.1 miles (5km)**
Ascent 1,256ft (383m)

Gravel tracks, mud and
   grass paths; steep climbs
   and descents
Summit
Wildlife
History/culture
Dogs welcome on leads

The distinctive jagged shape of the Skirrid is visible from many miles around in its setting in the Black Mountains on the eastern edge of the Brecon Beacons National Park. A mini mountain that feels wild and rugged at its summit, despite only reaching a height of 1,594ft (486m) above sea level, the views from the top rival many that make the official list of mountains. This run makes the most of the dramatic and varied landscape of the Skirrid, starting out with a steady climb through dense woodland before emerging onto open hillside. The run up the main ridge to the trig point-topped summit is well rewarded with panoramic views out across the Beacons, the Severn Estuary and the rolling countryside of Herefordshire. From here there's a fun, fast descent into the valley and winding woodland trails to the finish.

Above and opposite: Running on Skirrid Fawr.

THINGS TO SEE

Skirrid myths and legends

A result of its sandstone geology, the shape of the Skirrid has been much determined by landslips over its history, including a large one that created the distinctive jagged outline of its north-western slope. Before its cause was known, however, the fact that the mountain looked as though it had been hewn in two (its Welsh name, Ysgyryd, meaning 'split' or 'shattered') was the subject of many a legend. Long considered a spiritual place, Skirrid is known locally as Holy Mountain as it was believed that the split occurred at the moment of Christ's crucifixion. The medieval St Michael's Chapel, still part standing at the top of the hill, was used for services until the late 17th century. Another local story is of Jack O'Kent the giant and his bet with the Devil that the Sugar Loaf in the Black Mountains was higher than the Malvern Hills over the English border. On discovering Jack was right, the Devil picked up a huge apron of soil, intending to use it to add height to the Malverns. Unfortunately for the Devil, his apron strings snapped before he crossed the border and instead he piled the soil at the northern end of the Skirrid.

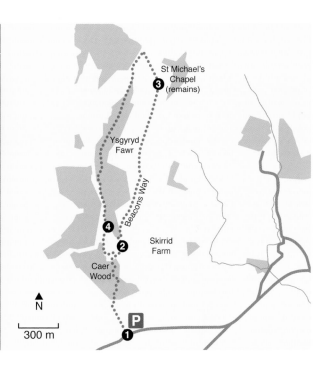

HOW TO GET HERE

By Public Transport
Abergavenny train station
4 miles (6.4km). Bus from
Abergavenny 3 miles (4.8km).
By Car A465 Hereford road
bypassing Abergavenny, turn
onto B4521 Old Ross Road.
Car park is 1.5 miles (2.4km)
on left.
On Foot The Beacons Way
passes over the Skirrid.
OS Map Explorer 13
Start / End Car park on
the B4521 (not NT).
OS grid reference: SO328164

St Michael's
3 Chapel
(remains)

Ysgyryd
Fawr

Beacons Way

4

2 Skirrid
Farm

Caer
Wood

▲
N

|_____|
300 m

P

1

1. From the car park, take the gravel track
and follow it around a sharp right bend. Continue
into woodland and follow the obvious path uphill
until you reach a wooden gate at the top of the
woodland.

2. **0.6 miles/0.9km** Continue straight ahead,
emerging onto open hillside and following the
obvious path up the main ridge of the hill to
reach the trig point at its summit.

3. **1.4 miles/2.2km** From the summit, bear left
and follow the footpath down the north-west
of the hill, turning left as you reach a path that
contours around the hill. Follow this path through
the saddle and then through woodland to reach
a path junction at the southern end of the hill.

4. **2.4 miles/3.9km** At the path junction,
continue straight ahead rather than going left
uphill. Follow the path as it curves to the left
around the end of the hill, eventually reaching
a path junction with your outward route. Turn
right here to descend back through the woods
to the car park.

Other trails nearby
The Beacons Way is a challenging, often
unmarked long-distance footpath that runs for
95 miles (153km) between Abergavenny, near to
the Skirrid, and Llangadog in Carmarthenshire.

88. Dolaucothi

Pumsaint
Llanwrda
Carmarthenshire
SA19 8US

ABOUT THIS RUN

Distance 4.5 miles (7.2km)
Ascent 902ft (275m)

Some steep ground,
   grass and woodland
   paths, gravel tracks and
   country lanes
Dogs welcome on leads
History/culture
Wildlife

Above: One of many woodland
trails at Dolaucothi.
Opposite: View down to
Dolaucothi Farm.

While they might seem like a natural part of the landscape, the undulating, wooded hills around Dolaucothi have been shaped by centuries of mining. The Romans first dug for gold here some 2,000 years ago and the mines continued working until 1938. This run follows the waymarked estate trail, signed with red arrows throughout, around Dolaucothi's varied and wildlife-rich grounds. Starting at the visitor centre, it winds its way past the caravan site and farm before climbing steadily to the trig point which, at 928ft (283m), is the highest point on the estate. Be sure to stop here to take in the views out across the Cothi Valley. From here, it descends to follow a dismantled railway path before following a trail along the banks of the River Cothi homewards. On re-reaching the farm you can either return via your outward route or loop around to the fascinating Red Kite Centre in Pumsaint, finishing along the road.

THINGS TO SEE

The gold mines

Well worth a visit while you're exploring the estate, the gold mines at Dolaucothi were first mined by the Romans in the 1st century and at their most active at around the turn of the 20th century. Perhaps inspired by the growing gold-mining industry in South Africa at the time, Edward Jones, a local lead miner, formed the South Wales Gold Mining Company, subletting the mines from the owners of the estate. The venture never made him his fortune, however, as there was too little gold to be found. Two further attempts were made in the early 1900s to extract gold from the mines but both with little success and gold mining efforts at the time ceased in 1912. Using more modern methods the Dolaucothi was again reopened in the 1930s, mining further and deeper into the rock. During 1937–8 several hundred tons of ore were being extracted each week, with 4,000 tons of ore yielding 62lb (28kg) of gold in one productive month. However, again the costs of extraction outweighed its value and the mine closed for good in October 1938.

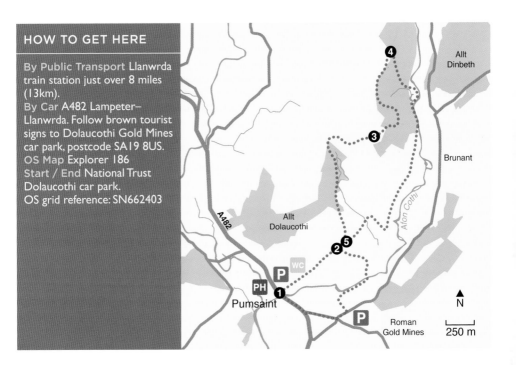

By Public Transport Llanwrda train station just over 8 miles (13km).
By Car A482 Lampeter–Llanwrda. Follow brown tourist signs to Dolaucothi Gold Mines car park, postcode SA19 8US.
OS Map Explorer 186
Start / End National Trust Dolaucothi car park.
OS grid reference: SN662403

1. From the start, cross the road and pick up the red estate trail waymarkers, following these throughout. Pass the caravan park and cross the bridge, continuing alongside the walled garden.

2. 0.6 miles/1km Bear right across the field to reach the woodland. Follow the stream-side path through the woods, eventually ascending to the trig point.

3. 1.6 miles/2.5km From the trig point descend to join the dismantled railway path, turning left onto this and following it through the woods.

4. 2.2 miles/3.5km Bear right off the railway path and descend through woodland to reach the River Cothi. Turn right and run alongside the river, with it on your left, all the way back to the Dolaucothi Farm.

5. 3.6 miles/5.8km On reaching the farm either turn left to return to the car park via your outbound route or continue straight on to reach the Red Kite Centre in Pumsaint, returning with care along the road to the main entrance to Dolaucothi.

Other trails nearby
Dolaucothi lies between the Brecon Beacons and the Cambrian Mountains, both of which have an almost limitless number of excellent places to run. The Wales Coast Path is also nearby, offering beautiful, though sometimes demanding waymarked coastal running.

89. Llŷn Peninsula

Porth y Swnt
Henfaes
Aberdaron
Pwllheli
LL53 8BE

ABOUT THIS RUN

Distance 3.6 miles (5.8km)
Ascent 640ft (195m)

Undulating coastal paths
with some steep and
stepped sections
May be muddy
Wildlife
History/culture
Dogs welcome but must
be on a lead on the
coast path

The Llŷn Peninsula stretches for 30 miles (over 48km) into the Irish Sea from north-west Wales, south-west of the Isle of Anglesey. Set apart from the Welsh mainland, and surrounded by a spectacular coastline, Llŷn has a character all of its own. This run begins in pretty Aberdaron, a former fishing village. Heading inland it follows a peaceful country lane that winds alongside a patchwork of fields and farmland, eventually following track to reach the coast path at Craig Cwlwm. From here you can see out to Bardsey Island, rich in wildlife and history. Tracing the intricate coastline back towards Aberdaron, look out for wildlife, including dolphins, porpoises and, on rare occasions, whales in the waves below. If the tide is out you can finish your run along the beach.

Opposite: Dinas Fawr.
Above: Bluebells at Plas yn Rhiw.

THINGS TO SEE

Delightful dolphins
Watching a pod of dolphins playing in the wild is a truly magical experience – and one that's a real possibility when you're exploring the spectacular coastline around the Llŷn Peninsula. The Welsh coast is home to one of only two semi-resident populations of bottlenose dolphins in the UK, while Risso's and Atlantic white-sided dolphins, porpoises – smaller relatives of the dolphin – and whales – mainly pilot and minke – can also be seen here. Some of the best places to spot these fascinating marine mammals are the Saint Tudwal's Islands, Cilan Head and off Bardsey Island.

Island life
Bardsey Island lies about 2 miles (3.2km) across Bardsey Sound at the tip of the Llŷn Peninsula. Covering an area of over 440 acres (178ha), much of which is farmland, with a mini mountain at its centre and 13th-century ruined Augustinian abbey, it's a fascinating place to visit. The island is home to a diverse range of wildlife such as grey seals, and over 300 species of birds, including choughs, puffins and Manx shearwaters. You can stay on the island, too: the Bardsey Island Trust arranges holiday lettings from April to October across a number of cottages and farmhouses.

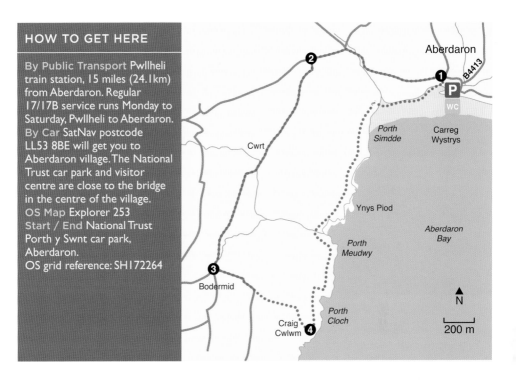

HOW TO GET HERE

By Public Transport Pwllheli train station, 15 miles (24.1km) from Aberdaron. Regular 17/17B service runs Monday to Saturday, Pwllheli to Aberdaron.
By Car SatNav postcode LL53 8BE will get you to Aberdaron village. The National Trust car park and visitor centre are close to the bridge in the centre of the village.
OS Map Explorer 253
Start / End National Trust Porth y Swnt car park, Aberdaron.
OS grid reference: SH172264

1. Turn left out of the car park onto the road and then left again uphill on a quiet lane as views open up across Aberdaron Bay.

2. **0.6 miles/1km** At a road junction with a house in the centre of it, turn left, signposted to Uwchmynydd. After a short distance take the next turning left, signposted Porth Meudwy and Tir Glyn campsite. Follow this lane, passing the National Trust Cwrt farm on your right and then a footpath to Porth Meudwy on your left. Don't take this but continue along the lane, passing Tir Glyn campsite on your left.

3. **1.6 miles/2.6km** Take the next left turn, opposite a red postbox and between a house and a barn and follow this between some houses. After the houses, the road bends to the right – take the footpath to the left just on the bend and before you reach the ruined house on your right. Follow the footpath through fields to reach the coast path.

4. **2.2 miles/3.5km** Turn left onto the coast path and follow it back to Aberdaron. At low tide you can descend to the beach just before the finish, however at high tide stick to the coast path until you can descend safely to the car park (both options are clearly signed from the route).

Other trails nearby
There's a great network of footpaths and quiet lanes crossing the Llŷn Peninsula, including the Wales Coast Path, which runs all the way around the peninsula.

90. Cemlyn

**Bryn Aber
Cemaes
Isle of Anglesey
LL67 0DY**

ABOUT THIS RUN

Distance 3.1 miles/5km
Ascent 269ft (82m)

Grassy coastal trails,
  quiet road
Coastal
History/culture
Wildlife
Dogs welcome

Situated on the wild north coast of Anglesey, Cemlyn is a unique and special place, with its elliptical shingle ridge, intricate coastline and abundance of wildlife. The dramatic views in either direction from the headland at Trwyn Cemlyn couldn't be more different: to the west stretches the Anglesey coast, dotted with islands and edged with hidden beaches, while across the crescent of Cemlyn Bay to the east, stands the now-decommissioned Wylfa nuclear power station. This exhilarating run follows the Wales Coast Path around the Cemlyn peninsula, starting at Bryn Aber on the east coast and tracing an anti-clockwise loop, finishing across farmland to reach the lagoon. The final stretch takes you across the causeway and back to Bryn Aber. The start/finish area does flood at certain times of the year, so it may be worth avoiding after heavy rainfall.

Above: Sunset at Cemlyn Bay.
Opposite: Arctic terns come to
Cemlyn Lagoon every year.

THINGS TO SEE

Welsh wildlife
Cemlyn lagoon was established in the 1930s by Captain Vivian Hewitt of nearby Bryn Aber. Hewitt built the first dam and weir at Cemlyn, replacing the natural tidal saltmarsh with the aim of creating a haven for birds. The shingle ridge that separates Cemlyn Bay from the lagoon is known as Esgair Cemlyn and is an important habitat for many species of plant such as sea kale, sea campion and yellow horned-poppy. Several unusual aquatic plant species also thrive in the lagoon, including the rare spiralled tassleweed,

while waders and wildfowl can be seen around its adjacent shorelines. Between May and July the islands within the lagoon host large nesting colonies of common, Arctic and Sandwich terns – the only nesting colony of Sandwich terns in Wales. During this time there are restrictions in place to protect the wildlife so please adhere to signs. Further afield around Cemlyn, areas of gorse and grassland provide habitat for many different butterflies and other invertebrates, or you might spot grey seals on the rocks just off the headland.

By Public Transport Holyhead
train station 16 miles (25.7km).
Then Amlwch to Holyhead
bus service, alight at Tregele,
2 miles (3.2km) from the start.
Check routes and times before
you travel.
By Car A5025 from Valley,
follow sign to Cemlyn National
Nature Reserve in Tregele
(opposite Douglas Inn).
On approach to Cemlyn NNR
take second turning to the
right then turn right again, after
farm buildings, past Bryn Aber
walled garden to the car park.
There is a 2.2m height
restriction on the car park.
Postcode LL67 0DY.
By Bicycle National Cycle
Network Route 566 passes
nearby.
OS Map Explorer 262
Start / End Bryn Aber
car park (not NT).
OS grid reference: SH329936

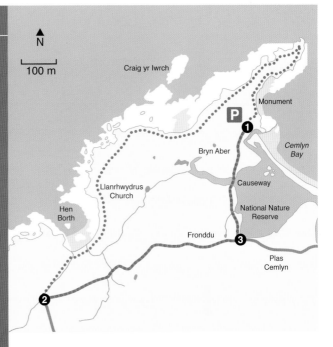

1. From the car park, head out towards the
headland, past the monument. Turn left through
the kissing gate and follow the Wales Coast Path
around the edge of the headland until you reach
the bay at Hen Borth. Turn left here, through the
kissing gate, and follow the path as far as Hen
Felin and the footbridge.

2. 1.9 miles/3km Cross the footbridge and turn
left onto a lane, following this towards the Nature
Reserve and lagoon.

3. 2.7 miles/4.3km Just after Fronddu, turn
left, rejoining the coast path and crossing the
causeway to return to the car park.

Other trails nearby
The Anglesey stretch of the Wales Coast Path
runs for 124 miles (200km) around the Isle of
Anglesey, offering intriguing and diverse running
and scenery. Holyhead Mountain, on the far
west of Anglesey, is also a fascinating place to
run (not NT).

91. Dolmelynllyn

Ganllwyd
Gwynedd
LL40 2TF

ABOUT THIS RUN

Distance 4.4 miles (7km)
Ascent 1,119ft (341m)

Some steep ground, grass
and woodland paths,
surfaced road
Waymarked trail
Dogs welcome on leads
History/culture
Wildlife

The National Trust's Dolmelynllyn estate covers an expanse of rolling hills, farmland and ancient woodland – some of which is classed as rare temperate rainforest – cut through by meandering streams, fast-flowing rivers and tumbling waterfalls. At its centre stands the grand mansion of Dolmelynllyn Hall, now a hotel. This run follows the fully waymarked estate walk, taking in trails travelled by humans for thousands of years, through a fascinating and beautiful landscape that has changed little during this time. Starting in the centre of Ganllwyd village it crosses the spectacular Rhaeadr Ddu falls, inspiration to generations of artists and writers, before heading through forest and out onto open mountainside until finally descending back to the valley to the finish.

Above: River Gamlan at Dolmelynllyn.
Opposite: Ancient woodland at Coed Ganllwyd.

THINGS TO SEE

The lakeside trail
The ornamental lake at Dolmelynllyn has recently seen the addition of a 0.6 miles (1km) circular multi-user path with viewing platforms extending out over the lake. Developed to enhance accessibility to the site, it's perfect for wheelchairs and running buggies.

Fantastic forests
Dolmelynllyn is one of western Europe's most important sites for its ancient trees, lichens, mosses, ferns and liverworts, which live in an ideal environment created by the spray from the waterfalls – a rare pocket of temperate rainforest still thriving in Britain. The surrounding forests are a great place for spotting wildlife, including deer, red squirrels, pine martens, otters and birds such as merlins, buzzards and red kites.

By Public Transport
Barmouth train station,
12 miles (19.3km). Buses
from Barmouth to Ganllwyd.
By Car Follow the A470 to
Ganllwyd village, the car park
is in the village centre. Post
code LL40 2TF.
OS Map Explorer OL18
Start / End Ganllwyd
village car park (not NT).
OS grid reference: SH727243

Ganllwyd ❶ 🅿

Rhaeadr Ddu/
Black Waterfalls

Coed Ganllwyd
(National Nature
Reserve)

A470

Afon Mawddach

Ffridd Bryn-melyn ❷

Berth
Lwyd

❸

Coed
Berth-lwyd

❹

WC 🅿

▲
N

300 m

Tyddyn-
bach

1. From the start, cross the road towards the village hall and then follow the tarmac road alongside the River Gamlan to its junction with a stone footpath, waymarked towards a wooden bridge. Cross the bridge and bear right to visit the waterfalls, then continue along the path, crossing a footbridge and bearing right to reach Forestry Commission woodland.

2. 1.1 miles/1.8km Follow waymarkers through the woods, following the path left and over a wooden footbridge onto open mountainside, heading onwards and past the disued goldmine workings.

3. 2.2 miles/3.5km Join a tarmac road and follow this until you can turn right onto a footpath into woodland, just after the house on the left. Follow the waymarkers through the woods to reach the Meirionnydd National Trust Workbase and the Tyn-y-Groes Hotel.

4. 3.5 miles/5.6km Cross the busy main road with care and take the path opposite, towards the River Mawddach and the Tyn-y-Groes bridge. Turn left and follow the tarmac road back to the main road. Cross over to the pavement and turn right, to return to the village and the car park.

Other trails nearby
Neighbouring Coed y Brenin Forest Park has an excellent network of dedicated running, walking and mountain-biking trails. There is also a 0.6 miles (1km) multi-user path around the ornamental lake at Dolmelynllyn, perfect for wheelchairs, bikes and buggies.

92. Craflwyn

Nantmor
Beddgelert
Nearest postcode
LL55 4YH

ABOUT THIS RUN

Distance 4.4 miles (7.1km)
Ascent 1,082ft/330m

Steep, uneven paths,
  riverside trails, quiet road
May be muddy
Fine weather/good visibility
  recommended
Wildlife
History/culture
Dogs welcome, keep on
  leads around livestock

Snowdonia's ruggedly beautiful Nant Gwynant valley rises to the lofty heights of Snowdon to its north while, to its south, lie the relatively peaceful Moelwynion range. The National Trust's 200-acre (81ha) Craflwyn estate lies on the banks of the Glaslyn river, which flows through Nant Gwynant, forming the twin lakes of Llyn Gwynant and Llyn Dinas before tumbling through the spectacular Aberglaslyn Pass. This run begins alongside this stretch of the river where it has carved its way through the hillside, forming a deep gorge. Passing Gelert's Grave, deeply entrenched in local legend, it winds through Beddgelert village before climbing steeply up and over the hillside and former copper mine workings of Sygun and Cwm Bychan.

Above: The River Glaslyn at Craflwyn.

THINGS TO SEE

Local legends
Beddgelert is named after the faithful and favourite hound of 13th-century prince Llywelyn the Great, and a bronze statue of the dog can be found in the village. The famous tragic tale tells of the prince and his princess setting out for a day's hunting together, leaving their baby in the care of Gelert. On returning home they were horrified to discover their baby was missing and Gelert's muzzle was covered in blood. Llywelyn immediately drew his sword and, in despair, killed his favourite hound. As Gelert fell to the ground, he let out a mighty yelp and a baby's cry was heard from a dark corner of the room. Llywelyn discovered his heir unharmed but, by its side, lay the mighty wolf Gelert had killed to save the child. Grief-stricken and filled with remorse, Llywelyn gave the faithful hound a ceremonial burial by the river and is said to have never smiled again.

HOW TO GET HERE

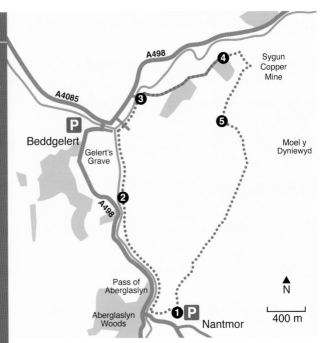

By Public Transport
Penrhyndeudraeth train station
6.5 miles (10.5km), Porthmadog
7 miles (11.3km) and Rhyd Ddu
6 miles (9.7km). Buses to
Nantmor and Beddgelert.
By Car Nearest post code
LL55 4YH (Nantmor village).
From Beddgelert follow the
A498 towards Porthmadog.
After approximately 1 mile
(1.6km) turn left over the
River Glaslyn onto the A4085
signposted Penrhyndeudraeth.
After about 0.2 miles (0.3km)
turn left up into the car park.
From Penrhyndeudraeth
follow the A4085 signposted
Beddgelert for approximately
6 miles (9.7km). After Nantmor
village turn right into the car
park. From Porthmadog follow
A487 towards Caernarfon for
approximately 6 miles (9.5km).
Turn right over the Glaslyn
River onto A4085 signposted
Penrhyndeudraeth until
reaching the car park as above.
OS Map Explorer OL17
Start / End National Trust
car park, Nantmor.
OS grid reference: SH597462

Other trails nearby
There's a wealth of fantastic
running across Snowdonia
National Park. An ascent of
Snowdon, via one of several
different, varied routes to the
top, is a must-do while you're
in the area.

1. Leave the car park and turn left for Aberglaslyn, running up
through woodland to reach the river. Turn right and follow it
upstream on the fisherman's path alongside Aberglaslyn gorge.
Take care here as the path is narrow.

2. 1 mile/1.6km Cross the railway line with care and continue
to follow the path alongside the river, bearing right at the
buildings in Beddgelert to skirt the base of the hillside but
staying close to the river.

3. 1.7 miles/2.8km Where the path joins a road at a bridge,
bear right and continue following the road past several houses
and a campsite.

4. 2.4 miles/3.8km Just before the road reaches a junction and
car park, turn right onto a footpath which zigzags up the hillside.
Stay right at the path junction, following the path steeply uphill,
which, again, zigzags up the hillside, passing the copper mines
on your left.

5. 3 miles/4.8km At the path junction (grid ref SH602481)
bear left, following the path straight ahead and joining a small
stream, following this as it descends off the hillside down Cwm
Bychan, running through woodland to return back to the car
park at Nantmor.

93. Cwm Idwal

Ogwen Cottage
Nant Ffrancon
Bethesda
LL57 3LZ

ABOUT THIS RUN

Distance 2.6 miles (4.2km)
Ascent 423ft (129m)

Rough, undulating paths
 with some steep sections.
Wildlife
History/culture
Dogs welcome on leads

Nestled in a rocky bowl at the meeting point of the great mountain ranges of the Carneddau and Glyderau, Cwm Idwal is Wales' oldest Nature Reserve, a place of peaceful llyns and rare mountain wildlife encircled by dramatic peaks and looked after by the National Trust, the Snowdonia National Park Authority and Natural Resources Wales. With over 60 miles (97km) of paths this is a popular place for walkers, fell runners and rock climbers and the National Trust's Ogwen Cottage Ranger Base and the National Park visitor centre at the heart of the valley are excellent resources where you can find out more about this fascinating place and how to explore it safely and enjoyably. This run is a great way to start, making its way up into the cwm from Ogwen and following an engaging trail around the edge of the Llyn Idwal.

Above: Cwm Idwal Valley.
Opposite: Llyn Idwal – the rough path requires good footwear.

THINGS TO SEE

Upland wildlife
There's an abundance of wildlife in and around Cwm Idwal, thriving in this harsh upland environment. Look out for hardy Welsh mountain ponies, feral goats, otters fishing in the shallows at dusk, water voles and birds such as dotterel and peregrine falcons. Rare Arctic alpine plants include the moss campion, Snowdon lily, alpine lady's mantle and purple saxifrage.

Mountain treasures
The 21,000 acres (nearly 8,500ha) of upland surrounding Cwm Idwal were acquired by the

National Trust in 1951 from the Penrhyn estate and include eight upland farms and nine peaks almost 3,000ft feet (900m) including the famous Trfyan. There are over 1,000 archaeological sites here including seven scheduled ancient monuments. In 2017 a team of Rangers working on a footpath near Llyn Ogwen discovered a sword buried in the ground. After careful cleaning and verification, experts now believe it dates back to the 6th century, around the time of King Arthur, supporting the local legend that Excalibur was cast into Llyn Ogwen.

HOW TO GET HERE

By Public Transport Snowdon Sherpa buses run from Betws-y-Coed and Bangor to Ogwen car park. Pick up available from Capel Curig and Bethesda.

By Car From Bangor travel on the A55 then turn towards Bethesda along the A5 trunk road. Continue on A5 into the Nant Ffrancon Pass. From Betws-y-Coed travel along the A5 to Capel Curig. Continue on A5 to Ogwen Lake.

OS Map Explorer OL17

Start / End Ogwen Cottage and Ranger Base (not NT).

OS grid reference: SH650603

Map labels: Rhaeadr Ogwen Waterfall ❶ · Llyn Ogwen · A5 · Pen y Benlog · Outdoor Pursuits Centre · ❹❷ · Stepping Stones · Llyn Idwal · Clogwyn y Tarw Gribin Facet · Cwm Idwal (National Nature Reserve) · Sub-Cneifion Rib · ❸ · N · 200 m

1. From the Ogwen Cottage Ranger Base, cross the bridge to the Snowdonia National Park visitor centre. Take the steps to the left of the building and continue through the mountain gate and over the oak bridge. Bear right where the path forks and follow this main path right up to the lake shore.

2. **0.6 miles/1km** Turn left and take the path along the eastern shore of Llyn Idwal, following it as it climbs gradually to reach a junction with a path on the right, with the famous Idwal Slabs, popular with rock climbers, straight ahead.

3. **1.1 miles/1.8km** Turn right onto this path, following it around the southern end of the lake, bearing right where another path joins from the left and continuing along the western shore and around the northern end of the lake.

4. **2 miles/3.2km** Cross the slate footbridge and turn left, joining your outward path and following this back down to Ogwen Cottage.

Other trails nearby

From the same starting point at the Ogwen Cottage Ranger Base, a loop around the neighbouring Llyn Ogwen also makes for an excellent run, or can be combined with the Cwm Idwal route for a longer run of about 6 miles (9.7km).

223

94. Chirk Castle

| Chirk |
| Wrexham |
| LL14 5AF |

ABOUT THIS RUN

Distance 3.8 miles (6.1km)
Ascent 715ft (218m)

Tracks, grassy trails, woodland, some steep sections
May be muddy
Family friendly
Wildlife
History/culture
Dogs welcome, keep on leads around livestock

An imposing fortress standing high on an outcrop overlooking the confluence of the rivers Dee and Ceiriog, Chirk Castle was built in the early 14th century as a statement of English intent in these historically disputed borderlands. The 480-acre (194ha) estate surrounding the castle is fascinating to explore and includes a well-preserved section of Offa's Dyke, ancient woodland and a great network of gently undulating trails. Set within an Area of Outstanding Natural Beauty, the estate is rich in wildlife and a designated Site of Special Scientific Interest for its important habitat for a variety of insects, bats, fungi and wild flora. This run takes in a large loop around the castle, starting across the sloping flanks of the outcrop and heading through deer park and leafy woodland to the east, and is followed by an enjoyable section of the Offa's Dyke Path to the west.

Above: Trail through the estate at Chirk Castle.
Opposite: Chirk Castle.

THINGS TO SEE

The Castle
Over 700 years ago, Chirk Castle's design was not as a family home but as a military fortress for defence against Welsh invasion, its position carefully chosen to maximise its strategic advantages. The round 'drum' towers allowed archers a wide firing field and created a 'killing zone' where the fields of fire overlapped, while the towers themselves, with their 16ft (5m) thick walls, were deliberately designed to splay outwards, making it difficult for the enemy to get its battering rams close to the building. Over the

400 years from 1595, however, the castle was transformed into a luxurious family home for the Myddelton family, with many of its collections on show today. For the first half of the 20th century the castle was leased by Thomas Evelyn Scott-Ellis, 8th Baron Howard de Walden, an English peer, landowner, writer and powerboat racer. A society man and patron of the arts, he spent lavishly on the castle so that he and his wife could host extravagant house parties – the 1920s Bow Room being a great example.

HOW TO GET HERE

By Public Transport Chirk train station, 1.5 miles (2.5km) from the castle, is on the Shrewsbury to Chester line.
By Car Chirk Castle is signposted from the A5 and A483. From the A5 the entrance to the estate is 2 miles (3.2km) west of Chirk. When you arrive by car at the white iron Davies Gates please continue to your right. The entrance to the estate is 1.4 miles (2.3km) further on.
OS Map Explorer 240 and 256
Start / End National Trust Chirk Castle car park.
OS grid reference: SJ267382

Other trails nearby

Offa's Dyke Path runs through the estate, while the Llangollen Canal is about 1 mile (1.6km) away.

1. Leave the car park heading in the direction of the castle, passing to the left of the Home Farm buildings and then bearing left, following the main surfaced path around to the left. At the grass triangle, continue straight ahead, following a footpath across parkland with an area of woodland to your right.

2. 0.5 miles/0.8km Bear right, following the main path into some woodland. Continue until you reach the far edge of the woods, then turn right to join a surfaced path. Turn right onto this and follow it back towards the castle, running through woodland with the castle on your right to return to Home Farm.

3. 1.8 miles/2.9km To start the western lap, turn left and follow the footpath until you reach the main road. Turn right at the road and join the Offa's Dyke Path, continuing along this as it curves generally to the right, crossing the estate to reach buildings and a road.

4. 3.3 miles/5.3km Turn right onto the road and then immediately right again, leaving the Offa's Dyke Path and joining a footpath running straight across parkland and back to Home Farm.

95. Erddig

Wrexham
LL13 0YT

ABOUT THIS RUN

Distance 2.1 miles (3.4km)
Ascent 115ft (35m)

Grassy paths and
   woodland trails
May be muddy
Wildlife
History/culture
Dogs welcome in
   some areas

The grand 18th-century country mansion of Erddig Hall stands on a dramatic escarpment overlooking the wide meanders of the River Clywedog. A peaceful retreat, the house is surrounded by 1,200 acres (486ha) of landscaped parkland, designed by William Emes to celebrate the beauty and tranquillity of the place. This shorter run is perfect for those new to running, exploring the glorious open parkland and Forest Wood to the south of the estate, running on springy grass and winding trails through the trees.

Above: The parkland at Erddig.
Opposite: Exploring the estate at Erddig.

THINGS TO SEE

Exploring the estate

In 1779, Philip Yorke I, owner of the estate at the time, and a passionate advocate of the power of the great outdoors to improve health and well-being, put up a notice on the gates at Erddig. It read: 'Mr Yorke having at great Expense, and at the labour of many Years, finished the Ground and Wood Walks about Erthig, desires to acquaint his Neighbours, that they are extremely welcome to walk in the same for their Health and Amusement.' The estate is still having its uplifting effect upon visitors today and, as well as enjoying a superb run around the grounds, there's plenty for everyone to enjoy, including a rich and fascinating history stretching back some 700 years. Incorporated into its designer, William Emes', vision of the landscape are several truly intriguing features. These include Wat's Dyke, an 8th-century defensive earthwork that stretches 40 miles (64.4km), crossing the estate, and an 11th-century motte-and-bailey castle. Built by the Normans as a defensive fortress, this would once have dominated the skyline, making the most of the natural topography and the pre-existing earthworks. Today, however, it remains as a fascinating sequence of raised earthen mounds, hidden within the trees.

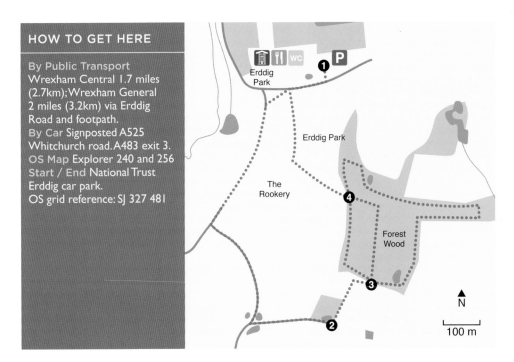

Erddig
Park

Erddig Park

The
Rookery

Forest
Wood

N

100 m

1. Leave the car park and turn right onto the main path. Follow this for a short distance to where it divides into three, with the right-hand path leading towards the house. Take the middle path, also the Wat's Dyke Way, heading out into the parkland. Follow this surfaced path with trees on your right until you reach a house on your right. Turn left here, leaving the Wat's Dyke Path and heading across the grass on a footpath, following the line of trees until you reach a set of three ponds. Turn left here to reach Sontley Lodge Farm.

2. 0.7 miles/1.1km Turn left at the farm and follow the surfaced path straight ahead, around the right-hand bend and then left into Forest Wood. Turn left and follow the path around the western edge of the woods, to reach the point at which you entered the woods.

3. 1.1 miles/1.8km Turn left and follow the path around the eastern edge of Forest Wood, emerging onto a surfaced path that bisects the wood. Finally, run the path that loops around the northern section of the wood, returning again to the main path.

4. 1.7 miles/2.8km Turn right onto the main path and follow this across the park to rejoin your outward route back to the car park.

Other trails nearby

Wat's Dyke runs through the northern Welsh Marches, generally parallel to Offa's Dyke. The Wat's Dyke Way runs for 61 miles (98km) through Overton, Wrexham, Caergwrle, New Brighton and Rhosesmor.

96. Castle Ward

Castle Ward
Strangford
Downpatrick
County Down
BT30 7LS

ABOUT THIS RUN

Distance **Up to 8 miles (12.9km); can be shortened at several places en route**
Ascent **669ft (204m)**

Surfaced multi-user paths,
  some narrow and winding
Waymarked
Wildlife
Family friendly
History/culture
Dogs welcome

With its eccentric 18th-century mansion, a mixture of Gothic and classical architecture, and rolling parkland overlooking the peaceful expanse of Strangford Lough, Castle Ward is a must-visit for nature lovers and adventure seekers alike. This run follows the well-waymarked Boundary Trail, taking in everything this fascinating property has to offer, including shoreline, woodland, open grassland – spectacular with wildflowers in summer – and parkland, with plenty of places to stop to catch your breath and take in the views. There are also several opportunities to shorten the route if required. As the trail is multi-use, be aware of cyclists, horse riders and walkers. Cattle may also be grazing in some areas.

Above: Exploring the trails at Castle Ward.
Opposite: Family fun at Castle Ward.

THINGS TO SEE

Strangford Lough
Strangford Lough is the largest sea lough in the British Isles, a unique and beautiful place that's internationally important for nature conservation. It stretches from Angus Rock, where it joins the Irish Sea, to the vast sand flats at its northern end, some 20 miles (32.2km) away, and is dotted with around 100 islands. The lough is one of only three designated Marine Nature Reserves in the United Kingdom, with a complex, balanced and tide-dependent range of species and habitats. A

staggering 2,000 species of marine wildlife are found in or around the Lough, of which 28 are not recorded anywhere else in Northern Ireland. It's a great place to spot birds, too: look out for curlew, grey heron, turnstone, guillemot, redshank and even little egrets.

There are many ways to explore Strangford Lough, from running the trail along the shore and through the sheltered woodlands to heading out in a canoe to discover it from a completely new perspective.

HOW TO GET HERE

By Public Transport Ferry from Portaferry. Ulsterbus 16E, Downpatrick to Strangford.
By Car 8 miles (12.9km) north-east of Downpatrick; 1.5 miles (2.4km) from Strangford on A25.
OS Map NI Discoverer Map 21
Start / End Shore car park.
OSNI grid reference: NW677031

Audley's Castle

Harry's Island

Castle Ward Forest Park

Castle Ward House

Tullyratt

A25

N

400 m

1. This run follows the red 'Boundary Trail' waymarkers throughout. From the start, follow the waymarkers along the lough shore, going around Audley's Castle.

2. **2 miles/3.2km** Cross the Audleystown Road onto the farm trail. Follow the trail through mature woodland to West Park behind the old walled garden.

3. **3.1 miles/5km** Turn right towards the boundary wall before contouring through the farmland to reach Mallard Plantation, a mature coniferous woodland. Up to this point, this trail is multi-use so expect horses, bikes and a range of other users.

4. **4.3 miles/7km** The trail branches left and becomes a narrow single track for cyclists and walkers only. Follow the trail to Base Camp, soon crossing a bridge and continuing through beautiful landscape.

5. **5 miles/8km** Crossing the road at the main entrance to the property, continue through the historic grounds of Windmill Plantation and cross Church Walk with a view of Castle Ward house to the left.

6. **6.8 miles/11km** Continue across Deer Park to Strangford Avenue to return to the Shore car park.

Other trails nearby

There's a great choice of different waymarked trails to follow around Castle Ward and Strangford Lough, including the 1.8-mile (2.9km) Castle Trail, the 1.2-mile (1.9km) Shore Trail and the 2.5-mile (4km) Farm Trail. Pick up a leaflet of all the trails at the visitor centre.

97. Divis & the Black Mountain Ridge Trail

Divis Road
Hannahstown
Belfast
BT17 0NG

ABOUT THIS RUN

Distance 4.2 miles (6.7km)
Ascent 902ft (275m)

Good trails, some steep
and rough ground
Waymarked trail
Urban escape
Dogs welcome on leads
History/culture
Wildlife

Divis is a large area of mountain and moorland set within the Belfast Hills in Northern Ireland's County Antrim. The hills form a scenic backdrop to Belfast city and offer a peaceful and inviting escape with their varied landscape and abundance of wildlife. The terrain is interesting and diverse, with trails that wind across moor and heathland, over summits and along stone tracks and boardwalks.

The Ridge Trail begins with a tough but rewarding climb to the trig-point-topped summit of Black Mountain, from where there are outstanding panoramic views across Belfast and further afield, including the Antrim Plateau to the north, Scotland to the east and the Mourne Mountains to the south. From here, an exhilarating ridgeline run and an enjoyable descent bring you to the Divis Coffee Barn, a perfect spot for a post-run refuel.

Above: Divis and the Black Mountain.
Opposite: Exploring Divis and the Black Mountain.

THINGS TO SEE

Purple hills
Visit in autumn and Divis is ablaze with purple as the devil's-bit scabious, a member of the honeysuckle family, comes into bloom. The blue-violet and occasionally pink flowers with their curious antlers carpet the hillsides from late summer through to October.

The mountains are a mosaic of grassland heath and sphagnum bog and are home to a range of wildlife. Look out for Irish hare, stonechats, skylarks, snipe, ravens and even peregrine falcons, searching for prey from the air.

HOW TO GET HERE

N

300 m

Black Mountain Trigonometry Point

Divis Transmitter Mast

The Barn and ranger office ❺

❶

P **WC**

Collin River Bridge

R. Collin

Black Mountain

❷

❸

Upper Springfield Ward

❹

Glencolin Ward

B38

B38

1. Follow the trail from The Barn towards the Divis transmitter masts, bearing right onto a section of wooden boardwalk, shortly before reaching the masts.

2. 1.5 miles/2.4km At the end of the boardwalk, turn right onto a gravel path towards the summit of Black Mountain, passing the Bobby Stone, to reach the trig-point-topped summit at 1,275ft (389m).

3. Continue to follow the gravel path as it winds its way along the ridge towards Black Hill crossing the first stile.

4. 2 miles/3.2km Follow the path as it leaves the ridge before reaching Black Hill and continues to weave its way back towards The Barn, crossing another stile and the Collin River

5. 3 miles/4.8km Turn left when you reach the access road to return to The Barn.

Other trails nearby
There's an excellent network of walking and running trails right across the Belfast Hill. A leaflet of marked trails is available from belfasthills.org.

98. St Abb's Head

Northfield
Eyemouth
TD14 5QF

ABOUT THIS RUN

Distance **3.3 miles (5.3km)**
Ascent **679ft (207m)**

Surfaced road and grassy
paths, take care near
cliff edges
May be muddy
Wildlife
Dogs welcome on leads

Lying on the north-east coast of Berwickshire, in the southern Scottish Borders, the dramatic and windswept coastal headland of St Abb's Head is renowned for its vast seabird colonies. Looked after by the National Trust for Scotland, the area has been a designated National Nature Reserve since 1984. This run takes you straight to the north of the headland and around Mire Loch, passing the remains of St Abb's Nunnery, Kirk Hill and St Abb's Lighthouse. The return stretch follows the coastline, with spectacular views and plenty of birdlife to watch. Combining a wild and remote feel with straightforward route-finding and a tearoom at the finish, this is a great stop-off en route to the Scottish Highlands.

THINGS TO SEE

St Abb's wildlife
From the swans, damselflies, dragonflies, eels, perch and sticklebacks on the loch to thousands of nesting seabirds on the rocky outcrops, St Abb's is a special place for wildlife. Look for guillemots, razorbills, puffins, kittiwakes, fulmars, shags and herring gulls gathering on the rocks and soaring over the waves.

The lighthouse
The 300ft (91m) cliff at St Abb's Head is often obscured by fog and, following the sinking of the paddle steamer Martello on Carr Rock in 1857, the current lighthouse was designed and built by brothers David and Thomas Stevenson in 1862. At the time it had an oil burning light, converted

to incandescent in 1906 and, finally, to electric operation in 1966.

Kirk Hill
A short distance south-east of the lighthouse is Kirk Hill, on which stand the remains of the 7th-century monastery settlement of Saint Æbbe, established by the abbess within the remains of a 6th-century fort known as Urbs Coludi (Colud's Fort). Both nuns and monks lived at the monastery in basic beehive huts made from mud and branches. The settlement would have been protected by a 10ft high (3m) turf rampart on the landward side, the remains of which can be seen as a low ridge around the rim of the hill.

By Public Transport Nearest train station Berwick-upon-Tweed, 13 miles (21km), then bus service 235 to St Abb's. By Car A1107 to Coldingham then B6438 towards St Abb's. Car park and visitor centre is signed on the left on the B6438.
OS Map Explorer 346
Start / End National Trust for Scotland St Abb's Head car park.
OS grid reference: NT913674

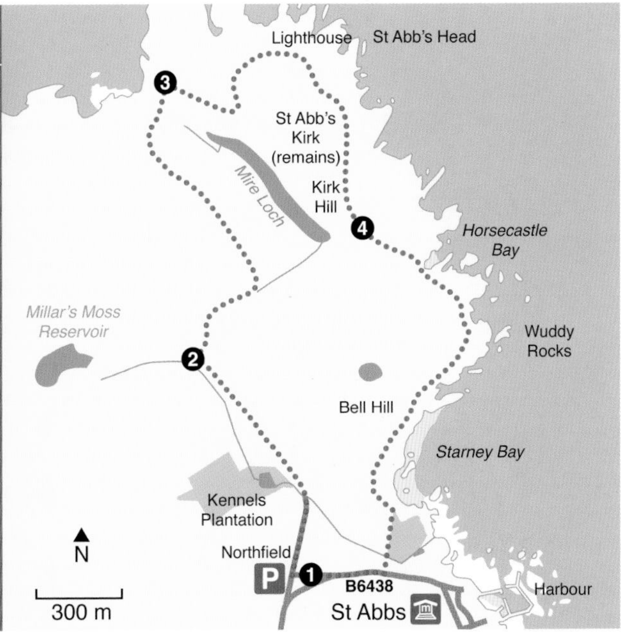

Lighthouse St Abb's Head
St Abb's Kirk (remains)
Mire Loch
Kirk Hill
Horsecastle Bay
Millar's Moss Reservoir
Wuddy Rocks
Bell Hill
Starney Bay
Kennels Plantation
Northfield
N
300 m
B6438
St Abbs
Harbour

1. Turn right out of the car park and follow the lane north, passing the visitor centre on your right.

2. **0.6 miles/1km** Stay right where two tracks split off from the lane, following the lane towards Mire Loch. Follow the lane around to the left and run along parallel to the loch, with it on your right, until you reach the coast path.

3. **1.4 miles/2.2km** Turn right onto the Berwickshire Coastal Path and follow it around the headland, with the sea on your left, passing the lighthouse. Continue following the coastal path south, passing Mire Loch, this time on your right.

4. **2.2 miles/3.5km** At the end of Mire Loch, stay on the coastal path, continuing along the coast until you reach the B6438. Turn right just before the road and follow the footpath all the way back to the car park.

Other trails nearby
The Berwickshire Coastal Path runs for 30 miles (48km) from Berwick-upon-Tweed in the south across the Anglo-Scottish border to Cockburnspath in the north.

Opposite: Thrift speckles the headland at St Abb's Head.

99. Glencoe

Glencoe visitor centre
Glencoe
Argyll
PH49 4HX

ABOUT THIS RUN

Distance 1 mile/1.6km
Ascent 154ft (47m)

Undulating unsurfaced trail
Waymarked
Wildlife
History/culture
Dogs welcome on leads
Family friendly

Nothing quite prepares you for your first glimpse of Glencoe. Every time you visit, in fact, it is higher, wilder and more impressive than you remembered. One of Scotland's most famous glens, the dramatic landscape was formed first by violent volcanic eruptions and then by the movement of massive glaciers. Its human history is no less turbulent. Inverigan, shortly after the halfway point on this run, was the site of the tragic Massacre of Glencoe in 1692.

This route is short but scenic, taking you through beautiful, wildlife-rich birch woods and through Glencoe's magnificent mountain landscape, starting and finishing at the National Trust for Scotland's Glencoe visitor centre. There's an option to extend the run to Glencoe village, should you wish, adding around an extra 2 miles (3.2km).

THINGS TO SEE

Glencoe legends

The legendary Celtic hero Fingal is said to have lived in Glencoe. Fingal was the leader of the Feinn, a band of fierce warriors, and his name lives on in several place names around the glen, such as Dun Fionn, 'the hill of Fingal' on the north, and Sgorr nam Fiannaidh, 'rock of the Feinn'. Fingal's son was the poet, Ossian, sometimes known as Fionn mac Cumhail and later anglicised as Finn McCool. The name 'coe' may refer to the river Cona, Ossian's legendary birthplace.

Glencoe wildlife

With its unique combination of rare geology and range of habitats, Glencoe is a designated National Nature Reserve. Local Rangers work hard to ensure visitors can enjoy the dramatic landscape while allowing wildlife to flourish. High in the mountains are rare alpine flowers, mosses, lichens, ptarmigans and mountain hares, while the glen is home to sheep, wild goats and red deer. Look out for red squirrels and pine martens in the forest and many different birds from rock-hopping dippers to golden eagles, soaring regally overhead.

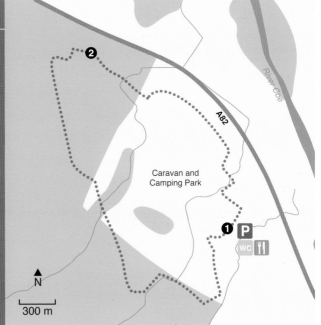

HOW TO GET HERE

By Public Transport Regular City Link and Stagecoach buses connect local towns and cities to Glencoe.
By Car On A82, I mile (1.6km) from Glencoe village.
OS Map Explorer 384
Start / End Glencoe visitor centre.
OS grid reference: NN112575

Caravan and Camping Park

N

300 m

1. From the car park head towards the visitor centre – either go through the building or turn right and follow the path around, picking up the blue Woodland Walk waymarkers. The trail takes you through an area of conifer forest, which is gradually being replaced with native trees.

2. **0.6 miles/1km** The trail reaches Inverigan, where there's a ruined house. Either follow blue waymarkers from here back to the visitor centre or turn left onto the path to Glencoe village, I mile (1.6km) away – please take care crossing the A82 if you choose this route.

Other trails nearby
The Glencoe Lochan Trails are gentle, waymarked trails around the peaceful shores of the lochan (small loch). Another route ideal for beginners, although not National Trust for Scotland property, this is an enjoyable run through ornamental woodland set within the wild and dramatic setting of the glen.

Opposite: Glencoe.
Right: Running in Glencoe.

235

100. Balmacara estate

The Square
Balmacara
Kyle
IV40 8DP

ABOUT THIS RUN

Distance 3.4 miles (5.5km)
Ascent 977ft (298m)

Surfaced road and
  gravel trails
Waymarked
Wildlife
Dogs welcome on leads

Covering the rocky moors and wooded hills overlooking the Kyle of Lochalsh towards Skye, Balmacara is a traditional crofting estate. Rich in wildlife and history yet peaceful and relatively undiscovered, ease of access and a well-maintained 17-mile (27.3km) network of trails makes running a perfect way to explore. This run starts in pretty Balmacara Square with its friendly café and gallery and informative visitor centre. Following scenic, winding trails there's a good climb to reach the forested foothills of Sgurr Mor, from where there are spectacular views out across Loch Alsh to Skye and the narrows of Kyle Rhea. Well-signed forestry tracks lead you to the quiet lane just outside Reraig, from where it's generally downhill, accompanied by beautiful views, all the way to the finish.

Above: Looking across Loch Alsh towards Skye. Opposite: Trails through the Balmacara estate.

THINGS TO SEE

The estate

The Balmacara estate is a great example of a traditional Highland crofting: small-scale, low-intensity agriculture that benefits communities and the environment. The moors, woods and crofting settlements, interspersed with lochs and edged by an intricate coastline, provide a diverse range of habitat for a rich variety of native flora and fauna. As you run through ancient, lichen-clad oak woods and dense pine forests, look for pine marten and red squirrels, while otters can often be spotted fishing at the water's edge. The estate has been lived and worked on for millennia and is dotted with fascinating archaeological sites and historically significant buildings, charting the passage of time from early settlers to modern-day inhabitants. The beaches at Balmacara Bay and Reraig are also fascinating to explore, covered in shells and a great place to watch seabirds, spot seals and perhaps even see otters, whales and dolphins.

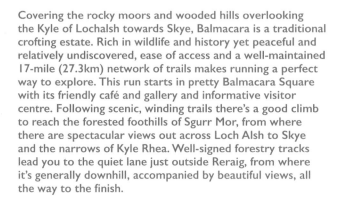

HOW TO GET HERE

By Public Transport Inverness train station 76 miles (122km), then bus service 917 to Portree stops at Balmacara.
By Car Balmacara Square is 3 miles (4.8km) east of Kyle of Lochalsh, off the A87.
OS Map Explorer 428
Start / End Balmacara Square car park.
OS grid reference: NG806284

Coille Mor

N

300 m

Balmacara

① P

Sgùrr Mòr

Waterfall

②

Memorial   Caravan and Camping Park

A87

Loch Alsh

1. Turn right out of the car park and follow the lane south towards Reraig. After a short distance turn left, following a 'forest walks' signpost into a field and alongside a stream. Follow the path through a gate and uphill until you reach a wide forestry track. Turn left onto this and then take the next right at the blue and red marker, following the track through pinewoods, eventually descending past a waterfall to reach a road.

2. **1.4 miles/2.3km** Turn right and follow the road past the houses, staying straight ahead on the path where the road bears right. Follow this path over the hill, descending to reach a road. Turn right onto the road to return to Balmacara car park.

Other trails nearby

There's a wealth of excellent trails around the Balmacara estate, while Skye is just across the water and is home to outstanding running from coastal trails to the grand challenge of the Cuillin Ridge.

Index

Acknowledgements

Our heartfelt thanks to the incredible teams of publishers and editors we've had the privilege to work with on this book: Katie Bond, Amy Feldman and Emily Roe at the National Trust and Peter Taylor and Kristy Richardson at Pavilion. Thank you to Mel Handford, Mimi Rousell, Rob Joules, Pat Kinsella, Richard Snow, Felicity Hindle and the rangers, staff, photographers and volunteers at the National Trust and National Trust for Scotland who have given generously of their time and expertise. To our wonderful and supportive friends and family: Lucy, Sam and Osker, Renee McGregor, Eryl and Russell, Chris and Clare, Geoff and Imogen, Sarah Churchill, Ros, Tony and Amy; and, always, to E & H.

Picture credits